SEE WILLY SEE
by Faith A. Colburn

Prairie Wind Press

Copyright© 2019 Faith A. Colburn
All Rights Reserved
ISBN 13: 978-0-9972677-4-7
ISBN 10: 0-9972677-4-7
Library of Congress Control Number 2019913739
PRAIRIE WIND PRESS, North Platte, Nebraska

Dedication

To my father who died during my sixteenth year when I hadn't realized fathers had lives before becoming fathers.

Acknowledgements

Many thanks to my friend Susan Grady Bristol for a great beta read and to Barbara Salvatore for her suggestions on how to better portray my Native American characters. Thanks too, to my cover designer, Brittany Roos, I simply didn't have the imagination to bring all the elements together.

Foreword

Each of my three related books started with some facts about my parents. My father served in an Army regiment nicknamed the Bushmasters. They were the 158th Infantry Regiment, of which the Arizona National Guard constituted the core.

I spent many hours getting to know the regiment. At first, I just wanted to learn about my dad, but as I got familiar with the unit, I realized I wanted to write more about those guys. The Arizona Guard consisted of Native Americans, about twenty-two separate nations, and Hispanics, with a few cowboys thrown in. They suffered unwavering discrimination. Those became my guys, and I wanted to keep them alive almost as much as Dad did.

My father and I never really had an adult-to-adult conversation, but I overheard some things, and I used those facts, but mostly regimental histories and morning reports. I invented a ghost platoon in Second Battalion, George Company. I made my unit follow along with the real George Company, but I gave them their own little quirks and engaged them in a few insubordinate activities.

Introduction

Like all families, mine had issues, many as a result of surviving tough economic times and then making it through a world war. I wanted to explore how families can survive such disruptions with resilience and grace. I believe there are people who have an instinct for thriving. I've met a few. But how about the rest of us?

I'm optimist enough (some would say crazy enough) to think that we can learn a lot through stories. Maybe it's the only way in the end. I tried to speculate on how my family could have made their lives better. My way of exploring involves stories.

I have one published work along this vein. It's called *The Reluctant Canary Sings* and the five facts I know about my mother, before me, serve as a basis for a story about one family nearly crushed by the Great Depression. This is the second book, not in a series, but the second of three related novels. It's about a close, well-functioning family that stays in touch even though separated by thousands of miles. They would have every expectation of thriving—so I put even more pressure on them.

The third book, drafted and ready for rewriting and revising, puts the two together to see how they can make a rich life out of what's left. We'll see how that works out and whether I can talk coherently about families, through stories. See what you think.

Table of Contents

Dedication i

Acknowledgements ii

Foreword iii

Introduction iv

Table of Contents v

Epigram 1

PART ONE: WILLOW GROVE, NEBRASKA 3

    June 15, 1940 – Willow Grove, Nebraska 3

    July 8, 1940 – Willow Grove 15

    October 1, 1940 – Willow Grove, Nebraska 26

    November 18, 1940 –Willow Grove 37

    November 19, 1940 – Willow Grove 44

    November 20, 1940 – Willow Grove 56

    November 23, 1940 – Willow Grove 64

    December 1940 – Willow Grove, Nebraska 73

PART TWO: PANAMA CANAL ZONE 77

    June 14, 1941 — Fort Clayton, Panama Canal Zone 77

    August 31, 1941 – Fort Clayton, Panama Canal Zone 85

    December 7, 1941 – Fort Clayton, Panama Canal Zone 92

    January 15, 1942 – Camp Paraiso, Panama Canal Zone .. 102

    April 5, 1941 – Camp Paraiso, Panama 108

    May 12, 1942 – Camp Paraiso, Panama 115

    August 7, 1942 – Camp Paraiso, Panama 129

    November 24, 1942 – Panama City, Panama 137

    November 27, 1942 – Camp Paraiso, Panama 153

PART THREE: SOUTHWEST PACIFIC 161

    January 6, 1943 – Aboard Ship 161

    January 30, 1943, — Brisbane, Australia 184

PART FOUR: COMBAT 187
    March 17, 1943 —Port Moresby, Papua New Guinea 187
    December 20, 1943 --Arawe, New Britain 194
        December 21, 1943 199
        December 22, 1943 201
        December 23, 1943 204
        December 24, 1943 208
        December 25, 1943 209
        December 26, 1943 211
        December 28, 1943 212
        December 29, 1943 213
        December 30-31, 1943 215
        January 1, 1944 216
        January 10, 1944 217
        January 17, 1944 220
        January 18-March 15, 1944 222
    March 15, 1944 —Finschafen, Papua, New Guinea 225
    May 21, 1944 - Arare, Dutch New Guinea 229
        May 23-24, 1944 -- Arare, Dutch New Guinea 230
        May 25, 1944 -- Tirfoam River, Dutch New Guinea 234
        May 26, 1944 - East of Snaky River, Dutch New Guinea
        245
        May 27, 1944 - West of Snaky River, Dutch New Guinea
        250
        May 28, 1944 -- Hill 225, Dutch New Guinea 252
        May 29, 1944 -- Snaky River, Dutch New Guinea 264
        May 30, 1944 —West of Tor River, Dutch New Guinea 266
        May 31, 1944 –Arare, Dutch New Guinea 267
        June 1, 1944 – Tor to Tirfoam River, Dutch New Guinea
        281

June 22, 1944, Finschafen, Papua, New Guinea 288
July 2, 1944 - Noemfoor Island, Dutch New Guinea 291
   August 10, 1944 — Noemfoor Island, New Guinea 300
   August 15, 1944 - Noemfoor Island, New Guinea 302
PART FIVE: THE ROAD HOME 309
   August 16, 1944 – Noemfoor to Port Moresby, New Guinea 309
   September 30, 1944 -- Australia 311
   October 15, 1944 —Aboard Ship, Southwest Pacific 312
   October 30, 1944 – San Francisco Bay, California 320
Reader's Guide 323
Author Bio 325
Other Works by this Author 326
Sample Chapter: Gravy 328
   March 31, 1945 — Colorado Springs, Colorado 328

SEE WILLY SEE

Epigram

"I was a hobo. They called me C. Willy C."

"See What?"

"My initials, Connor William Conroy." He frowned, thinking. But then, I guess I saw a lot of country."

SEE WILLY SEE

SEE WILLY SEE

PART ONE: WILLOW GROVE, NEBRASKA

June 15, 1940 – Willow Grove, Nebraska

Connor couldn't stop worrying about Nora. If someone needed help, his sister would help. That could cost her life and it would be his fault. As he worked in hard sun chopping weeds from ditches and fencerows, machete flashing, shirt soaked with sweat, he thought about his sister over there in Paris with the Nazis poised on the French border. Wheat next to the tangled fence row where he worked made a dry, rustling noise in a breeze that barely stirred its stiff beards. A lone mosquito whined around his head. He looked down the hill toward the pond, dark and muddy with not a ripple on its surface. He'd give anything to get his sister into the silly little rowboat their dad had made for them when they were kids.

Only eighteen months apart and just the two of them, Connor and Nora had spent their childhood exploring the farm together. Their dad farmed a half-section, 320 acres. They had sun-scalded short-grass pastures to roam, picking yellow coneflowers, daisy fleabane, and round, pink balls of common milkweed. They chased butterflies, admirals, monarchs, tiger swallowtails. They climbed trees and looked into birds' nests, turned over clods and watched fleeing ants. That had changed with the dust storms and Connor's high school graduation, when he headed for California seeking a job. With over twelve million people in the United States unemployed, he'd managed to get a few jobs picking fruit. When the crop harvest had run out, he'd got on with the Civilian Conservation Corps. After his two years in the Corps, he'd become a hobo, riding the rails and living on the bounty of the national park system.

SEE WILLY SEE

While he'd knocked around the country from park to park, living on what he could catch, trap, or pick, the Nazis had taken over Germany and, by the time he'd returned to the farm, they'd moved to take the rest of Europe—and his sister had decided to work right in the middle of it. Worse yet, Connor had goaded her into it. It drove him crazy that he remained safe at home while she worked in a war zone. He whacked at a tough musk thistle releasing a sharp, acid odor from the severed stalk.

Still, he'd already lost his chance to go to college. He'd given up five years hopping trains, taking handouts, working the occasional odd job, and living on the land. Didn't he deserve a chance to build his future? Nora was doing what she wanted to do, anyway.

He took a savage swipe at a cocklebur. Whacking and slashing at firebush, sunflowers, burs, and hemp, he worked his way across the ridge of the hill, ignoring the dust he raised, inhaling its dry, earthy smell. The country hadn't quite recovered from the drought.

He could enlist, but there wasn't any point. America remained neutral. Maybe he could join the Canadian Army. That might get him close enough to save his sister—but he knew darned well she wouldn't leave until they closed the consulate.
I want her safe, but don't I deserve to have a life and a home?

Connor's parents, Claire and Henry, knew only what they heard on the wireless and what Nora wrote in her letters. But Connor had read the ones she wrote to their former neighbor Pauline—Nora's best friend and Connor's sweetheart. Her latest had him panicked.

> Dear Pauline (and Connor),
>
> Bright, clear skies and gorgeous spring in Paris—but the trickle of refugees I told you about has become a torrent. Every day, we see Belgians and Dutch and people from Luxemburg. Thousands of them come

into the city and fill every train car available, happy to stand if they can escape. Cars jam the streets, slowed by farm families with wagons, maybe a cow tied on behind, and some chickens in crates on top.

Remember the Mormons we read about in history? I think I know what that looked like. I see carts piled with mattresses and furniture, maybe a couple of buckets tied on the sides, a man between the shafts, and the whole family pushing.

Parisians show enormous sympathy for the poor souls, helping any way they can—a little money, some provisions, water, or advice on routes. Then they go back to their day-to-day routines and talk about how glad they are that they're safe. They're still sitting in the cafés, sipping espresso and watching the human flood. When they talk about the war at all, they say the French Army will hold the Germans at the Maginot Line. But I look at the map. The Germans are in Belgium. Why wouldn't they go around the Maginot Line and come in from the north? I have to wonder, too, if these people have ever heard of the Luftwaffe.

Meanwhile, just to make this even more surreal, while the people enjoy their "safe" city, the newspapers go on and on about rapes and atrocities committed by the Germans during World War I. The contradictions take my breath away.

Well, I've got to get some sleep. We're overwhelmed, preparing exit visas and letters of transit, not to mention all the dispatches and the actual negotiations with French authorities who seem to be absent without leave.

Nora

Connor agreed with his sister. The Germans would definitely go around the Maginot Line and sweep in behind.

He had worried his way through Nora's excited dispatches about seeing the Eiffel Tower, walking the Champs Elysée, and learning to read the newspapers as she improved her high school French.

He couldn't share her enthusiasm when she'd received a promotion. He wanted her somewhere else—somewhere safe. He'd only mentioned the Foreign Service because it was the first thing off the tip of his tongue. He hadn't meant it as a suggestion—but his sister had picked it up and run with it. How could he have known when he'd goaded her into going to school that she'd end up in a war?

He knew the U.S. would get in it before long. He'd said so the night before at dinner. His mom had done that pushing thing with her hands that she did when she didn't want to talk about something. He'd turned to his dad.

"Look Pop, Roosevelt's declared a national emergency. The car companies are making tanks; Congress approved munitions sales to the Allies and we're shipping tons of stuff to England."

Henry took a scoop of mashed potatoes and ladled gravy onto them. "I know son, but I hope we can send enough support to the British and French so they can stop it there."

"I doubt it."

"Well, there's no draft yet, so I think Roosevelt's hopeful."

"It's just a matter of time, Pop. I know I'll get dragged into it eventually. Maybe if I take the initiative now, I can be out before it all goes to hell. Maybe if I get over there, I can talk some sense into Nora."

His mother gave him a sharp look. "Isn't it bad enough Nora's over there getting bombed? You want to get into it too?"

"I don't necessarily want to, but maybe I can get in and get out."

His mother's hands pushed.

Nora had written reassuring letters to the family about the safe bomb shelter under the consulate. They'd received one that morning, full of Nora's busyness and all the papers she had to type and how they had to go to the shelters sometimes at night for an hour or two—a minor annoyance, she'd written. Good thing she's reassured their mom, because the family had begun hearing on the radio that the Germans were bombing Paris. Connor wondered how reassured his parents were. He hoped Pauline would have another letter when he picked her up for their date that night.

But first he had a fencerow to clear. In the drainage ditch still worrying about Nora, he swiped at a clump of blooming hemlock, releasing a cloud of pollen that made him sneeze.

"Aw Hell," he said.

He finished the fencerow and returned to the farmyard where he helped his father with chores, pumped a kettle of water at the pitcher pump, set it on the stove to heat, and ate supper with his parents. By the time the dishes were done, Connor's water had boiled, so he dragged in the copper washtub and bathed. Cleaned up and dressed, he headed for Hastings and a Saturday dance with Pauline. When he knocked, she waited for him with a letter in her hand.

"Come in and sit. I'll get us some lemonade."

He took the letter and did as she told him, beginning to read and feeling his way back into an overstuffed chair.

SEE WILLY SEE

Dear Pauline,

The Germans are coming, and the Parisians seem utterly shocked! The authorities have burned petroleum reserves outside the city, so the air is full of soot. It stinks! You know how you spilled oil on the car engine that time? Ten times worse. My eyes water all the time. It gets on everything. I have to wash my hair every night and it's greasy by noon. It settles on every document I type so there are fingerprints and smudges on them. There's just nothing I can do about it.

We have a good bunker under the consulate, but those huge blasts roar and thump overhead, shaking dirt and bits of concrete from the ceiling. The car factory took the first hit. Almost 300 people died that first night, most of them civilians. I'm sure Mom and Pop have heard about the bombing, so I'll try to call them and tell them I'm okay. Mom'll worry anyway but it's the best I can do. The authorities have restricted phone service, so I hope I can get through. (She hadn't yet.)

I'm simply amazed at how Paris has turned on the refugees in only a few days. Rumors fly now that they're some kind of German spy network. So, the Parisians refuse them any help at all.

It's the kids, Pauline. In that stream of refugees, I see little children who have gotten separated from their parents. In Paris, even though the bombing has gone on for only three days, we already have orphans—kids whose parents died in collapsed houses or in the streets—wandering around, bloody and confused. I wasn't supposed to, but one morning before dawn, I went into one of the bombed-out areas. I saw a little guy, he couldn't have been more than two or three, tearing along the side of the street, through the rubble. You know how babies like that

SEE WILLY SEE

run? I started to grab him, but one of the gendarmes managed to catch him first and take him somewhere. I don't know where. Nothing I could have done for him, I guess.

Now, in addition to Belgians and Dutch, we have people coming from northern France. Parisians too, are starting to leave—the ones who have money. The poor sots who have to work for a living continue to go to the factories because they're dependent on their paychecks. The French authorities can't seem to figure out what to do or how to defend the city. It's chaos here and nobody seems to know what to do about it.

Nora

Connor looked up, the letter trembling in his hand. "I got her into this, you know."

Pauline took the paper and laid it on an end table, sat across from him, and took his hands.

"How do you figure? To me, she looked pretty excited to go. So how are you responsible?"

Head in his hands, he started talking, remembering the evening and filling in the details for Pauline.

I'd just retired from being a hobo and come back to the farm, you know, settled into the routine. I helped Pop get ready for winter, making repairs on sheds and equipment and stuff. During the long nights, we all talked about where I'd been and about riding the rails and people I'd met.

"One night we sat alone by the heater stove, looking at my pictures. Nora sighed one of her great big sighs and told me she envied me because I'd got to go all the places in the pictures and meet all kinds of new people. I could almost see her lower lip coming out. She reminded me that she'd barely left the farm in all that time."

"So?"

"So, I asked her what she planned to do about it, and we had an argument. I kept goading her and she kept telling me there was nothing she could do. I finally got out of her that she wanted to travel, and we talked about jobs—what kind of jobs would get her off the farm.

"Well, she said she could be a secretary, or a store clerk, or a nurse, but she didn't want to be a nurse. Anyway, she said all those jobs are boring. I asked her if anything could make them less boring.

"She yelled at me, 'I don't know!' and I yelled back, 'Well, think!' and that's when Mom came bustling in from the kitchen wanting to know what we were hollering about.

"We told her it was nothing and kept looking at pictures."

"I still don't see how that makes you responsible."

"Pop came back into the house from checking all the doors were latched, you know, to keep the wind from catching them. Then we set a couple of kerosene lanterns on the table and settled down with our books, occasionally reading a particularly interesting passage aloud. After an hour or so, Mom went to the kitchen to make popcorn. Pop headed for the cellar with a lantern to retrieve some apples. Nora looked up from her novel.

"'If I could do it in Istanbul,' she says.

"I asked what she wanted to do in Istanbul, and she'd already decided she wanted to be a secretary in Istanbul, or Paris, or New York City, or Hong Kong—any of those cities you hear about on the news.

"The next step, of course, was how she'd get a job in any of those places. She didn't know how she'd do that either. I got frustrated with her then and asked if she wanted to flounder in ignorance all her life."

"That was nasty, Connor."

"I know, I know. We had a few more words before Pop came back with the apples, wondering what we were glaring about. Mom set the popcorn on the table as Nora grabbed an apple. She crunched off a big bite, glared at me, then looked back at her book. I stared at her, munching a handful of popcorn as she tried to chew her apple. When she peeked up at me, I grinned. 'Nora wants to go to secretarial school.' I said.

"See? I am responsible."

"I don't see that at all. Anyway, how did she go from being bored to Paris?"

"Well, I'd brought up secretarial school. Pop looked from one of us to the other, just chewing a handful of popcorn with that thoughtful look he gets. He glanced at Mom. She widened her eyes and shrugged. You know how she does. Pop swallowed. 'I wonder how we'll manage that.'"

"You know Nora. 'Well, we don't,' she mumbled, and I grinned at her. She'd taken a really big bite of that apple and could barely chew. She kept glaring at me, trying to keep from drooling."

"She kept arguing, like she does even when she's getting what she wants. She said she didn't have any money for school. If I couldn't go, then she couldn't. That's when I put my big foot in it. See, CCC had sent most of my money home and I'd had no expenses when I worked in the Grand Canyon. I'd sent most of that money home, too. I told her I had a grub stake. I'd help her out.

"She argued some more, so I said she'd have to pay me back with interest, when she got a fancy job with the Foreign Service. See, Pauline, not only did I goad her into going back to school and provide a way for her to do it, I'm the one who suggested the Foreign Service. I said the first thing that came into my mind."

"Oh, so what, Connor? She could have got a regular job. I offered to get her on here at Dutton Lainson."

"Really?"

"Yes, I did. But she had bigger fish to fry."

"Boy, that's the truth! When I said Foreign Service, she got that dreamy look she gets sometimes. You've seen it."

"Yeah, I've seen it and once she gets it there's no point in discussing reality."

"She does get focused. Anyway, Pop wanted to know what the heck we were talking about, especially what the Foreign Service had to do with anything. I told him that Nora wanted to see the world."

"Mom stared at her, 'Nora?'"

"'Well yes,' said Nora, 'I do. I love you and I love this place, but I want to know what's going on in the world. I'm sorry Mom, Pop, but I don't want to be a farmer's wife.'"

Connor looked up at Pauline. "We all crunched and munched for a while. You know Pop usually takes a while before he speaks.

"Finally, he asked why Nora hadn't said what she wanted, and Nora said she didn't want to hurt anybody's feelings."

"That sounds like Nora."

"Mom wanted to know why Nora thought she'd be hurt and that's when Nora admitted she didn't want to be like Mom and Pop."

"Well, Mom never hesitated for a second. 'But you are like me and your father. You love your family and you cherish the land. Did you think we had no curiosity about the rest of the world?' Nora and I just stared at them. We'd never thought of them that way. 'But you seem so contented here,' Nora said finally. 'Yes, and I suspect you'll find that kind of contentment some time. But the time for contentment is rarely when you're young,'

"Pop, of course, got right back to the issue at hand. He suggested we go to town and hunt up the typing teacher; see if he could help us find a school. Said Nora would probably have to work part time.

"So that's what we did. I took Nora into town the next day to see the typing teacher, and Everett at the Post Office, too. He told us what he knew about getting federal jobs—Civil Service exams, for example. And now Nora's in France."

When he finished, Connor looked up at Pauline. "So, it's my fault she's over there with bombs falling on her."

"Connor, that's just plain nonsense. Nora's doing what she's always wanted to do. You know, she actually wanted to skip that last year of school and go with you and Ralph."

"She never asked."

"Would you have let her?"

"No."

"Then, she talked about hopping a freight and joining you in California after she graduated."

He frowned, "You're kidding."

SEE WILLY SEE

"You think so?"

"I guess not. So, what stopped her?"

"Your dad promised her a new dress if she harrowed that field out south of the house—he was still trying to grow a crop that spring. And then she got a job at the poor farm and there she was helping people. And now she's helping people in Paris. What could be more Nora than that?"

"But she'll take risks—and get hurt."

"I admire her for that."

"Me too, Pauline, but I'm scared to death for her."

"Well, my dear," she said, taking his hands and pulling him to his feet, "Nothing we can do about it, so let's go dancing."

He rose and followed her out the door, still thinking about how Nora had lost those same five years he'd complained about—working like a dog and hardly ever leaving the farm. At least he'd seen some really magnificent country.

He settled Pauline in the car and walked around. He started the car and headed for the dancehall.

SEE WILLY SEE

July 8, 1940 – Willow Grove

Connor sat on the front step, scratching the family stock dog and looking over the hill. About halfway down, yellow wheat rustled in the wind. They would cut it in a day or two. In the bottom, cattle grazed warm-season grass between raw gullies cut by rainfall. To his right, wind stirred little dust devils into ghostly spirals on the road at the edge of the property.

"You miss Nora too, don't ya old girl?"

Freckles looked at him and wagged.

He found the favorite spot behind her ears. "We all do, an' we're all scared for her."

Connor thought about the letter Pauline had shown him on Saturday night, sharing it like she always did. He'd read it over and over. He almost had it memorized.

> Dear Pauline (and Connor),
>
> This will probably be the last uncensored letter I'm able to get out of the city. We're sending a packet of dispatches even as Nazi tanks roll into Paris.
>
> Yes. We are still in Paris. The Germans have the city surrounded and French officials have mostly fled.
>
> Somebody gave the order that Paris is an open city. That means nobody will defend it. People just picked up and left. Thousands of them got on trains—when they had the money and there were seats.

> Thousands of them drove—if they had cars and could get petrol. Thousands more walked or pushed bikes with some clothing or food or water on them. Many of them pushed pitiful little handcarts. In just a couple of days, the streets were deserted. About the only people left are old people and people too poor to go anywhere.
>
> The troops—the few troops that managed to gather themselves in any kind of order—couldn't get through the jam of cars, trucks, and people, so they're milling around like everybody else. I've heard they're making only about a kilometer an hour.
>
> Now the Germans have arrived, the bombing has stopped. That's good, but I've been hearing that they're bombing and strafing the columns of refugees fleeing south and west.

Henry came out, wedging the door against his son's back, and joined him on the step. "What're you thinking about?"

"Aw, about Nora and how we didn't have any idea what she'd do when I goaded her into taking that secretarial course." He looked out over the lip of the hill. "It was me got her interested in the Foreign Service."

"Look, son, you can't blame yourself for that. She's doing what she wanted to do."

"Well, yeah, but they've occupied Paris, Pop."

"I know. That's not your fault either."

They scratched the dog while more bits of the letter scrolled through Connor's mind.

> We issued exit visas to a family of Jews who had made their way, somehow, from Germany, and the

SEE WILLY SEE

Nazis were right on their heels, screaming in our faces, demanding lists of all the visas we've issued.

"Well," said Henry, "I gotta get ready to go do our tradin'. You comin'?"

"Nah. I think I'll just stay here with Freckles and chew my cud."

"Suit yourself, son. You've got a lot to chew on."

Henry got up and stepped back into the house while Connor circled around his crowded brain. Trouble in Europe had begun almost as soon as Nora had started school. The Nazis took Czechoslovakia while she studied. In March, Nationalists, supported by the Nazis, defeated the Republicans in Spain. Italy aligned with Hitler in May.

Connor began timing Nora's studies with Nazi conquests. At the end of summer, Nora came home for a break before taking her final tests. Connor sat with her and their parents in the evenings, listening to news about the Nazi alliance with the Soviets and a mutual assistance pact between Britain and Poland. The last days of August and the first of September, countries fell quickly. By the time Connor took Nora to the depot for final testing, Germany and Russia had divided up the spoils in Poland and Britain had declared war.

When she returned with her certificate, she applied for work with the Foreign Service. Connor tried to persuade her to look somewhere else, but she'd decided Foreign Service was her calling.

Nora followed her brother around while she waited for her Civil Service exams in Omaha. During a lull while the Europeans geared up, she and Connor tried to believe that Europe had sorted itself out and things would stabilize. Connor again took her to the train November 30. In her absence the family heard about the Soviet invasion of Finland.

Finally, on a Saturday, Connor drove into town again to pick her up at the depot.

"How'd it go?"

"Awful. When I got back to my room that first night, I just went to bed I was so exhausted. Then Thursday they gave us oral exams. They asked the darnedest questions. It's a good thing I listen to the news with you and Pop."

"How'd you do?"

Nora remained silent until Connor feared (or hoped) that she hadn't passed.

"I qualified!" she squealed. "Now I have to find out what postings are open. I think there's something at the consulate in Paris."

"Paris! Are you crazy? The Germans will be in Paris in a year—probably less."

"We'll really have work to do, won't we?"

"Yeah. Work to get the hell out of there!"

"Connor, you were the one who suggested the Foreign Service."

"I didn't expect you to sign up for a war zone!"

"It's not a war zone."

"Yet."

"That's where I think I can do the most good, and if I can get it, I'm taking it."

Nora put her hat in the ring and, in less than a month, Connor sat on her bed, watching her pack for winter in Paris. The whole family escorted her to the station when she left for Washington

SEE WILLY SEE

on the Burlington Northern and Santa Fe, right after New Year's.

Her first letter—a note really—described stepping off the train in Union Station.

> Hi Family,
>
> I stood on the platform for a few minutes to get my bearings and people just ran past me—it seemed like there were hundreds of them. I got my wits about me and walked inside. It's a magnificent building, the ceiling must be four stories high with sound echoing all over and a mob of people running everywhere like ants.
>
> Boy, was I thrilled when I found my way to a taxi stand! I got to my hotel and found out that they had to double us up—too many people in town and not enough rooms. I'm rooming with a nice Southern girl with a cute accent, and a pile of frilly clothes. I love them.
>
> They pick us up at the hotel every morning and bring us back every night. This place just hums—cars and trucks scatter everywhere, splashing mud and dirty water. People talk a mile a minute.
>
> I'll be on a boat to London in a week. Going by way of New York City! They said we'll visit Wall Street and the Empire State Building, and the world's fair! I'll tell you all about it.
>
> Then on to Paris. Can't wait!
>
> Nora

Almost a month later, she dropped a postcard from London.

SEE WILLY SEE

Dear Family,

London looks a lot like Washington with people storming around shouldering everyone and everything out of the way. They're already rationing food here—butter, bacon and sugar. They seem to be keeping a stiff upper lip as they say, but everybody's scared. Germany's sweeping across Europe so fast that London feels like it's right in the crosshairs.

Nora

"Where do the Nazis have to go, before they get to London?" Claire held the letter in trembling hands.

Connor knew she could answer her own question. "France." He stood for a long moment, watching his mother trying to squash her fear.

"She'll be all right," Henry said. "We raised us a resourceful girl."

And then that girl got to Paris.

Dear Family,

I'm here! I can see the Eiffel Tower from the café where I stop for dinner—that's supper to you. I've seen sunshine for the first time since I left Nebraska. It's clear and cold. They have braziers—these kind of metal pots filled with live coals—so you can eat outside. It doesn't get very cold here. It rarely freezes, but it feels cold when the wind blows off the Seine. I'm thrilled I have my good winter coat and those gloves you knitted for me, Mom.

People sit around the cafés here in the evening, reading and talking. There's a lot of talk about the war and how soon the Germans will attack France.

Some of the older men, soldiers from the last war, I think, seem to believe the French can hold them off, but not everybody. The authorities say nothing.

I'm getting overwhelmed already, by people trying to get out of Europe. We have hundreds of applications for travel to the U.S. every day. People line up outside the embassy and stand, heads down, feet shuffling, rain or shine, in endless patient lines. I sometimes wonder if they don't spend the night there waiting for some reason to hope.

I've got to go now. There's just so much to do, I'm working most nights until late.

Nora

Her letters to her parents had delicately ignored the air raid warnings but she'd not been so delicate in her letters to Pauline—letters she'd known Pauline would share with Connor.

Back in Nebraska, Connor waited for the inevitable, helping his dad with winter chores and maintenance. At noon on March 16, when he and Henry came in for dinner, he washed up and Henry flipped on the radio. Connor listened to the drone of commodities markets: 'barrows and gilts $23.10 hundred weight; pork bellies $20.' After a brief break, the radio switched to weather: 'Highs today in the high seventies, ten percent chance of rain overnight.' Henry joined his son soaping his face and neck. With their hands immersed in cool water, they learned the Germans had bombed Britain.

"You know I'm on the draft board?" Henry said.

"Yeah, I know."

"You don't have to go. You're necessary farm labor."

"How would that look? You made it through the drought without me."

SEE WILLY SEE

"I don't care how it looks. You're my son." He gave Connor a look. "We got through the thirties because there wasn't anything to do."

"Well, we'll see what happens. We don't even have a draft—yet."

They were planting corn when Germany invaded Denmark—and Norway. They were in the fields with machetes chopping sunflowers and cockleburs when the Nazis invaded Belgium, Luxembourg and the Netherlands—and then the north of France, just like Nora had predicted.

Nora called at 10:45 that evening. Connor picked up the 'phone.

"I just wanted you to know we're all right here. We have air raid warnings, but we're in a safe shelter."

"When are they getting you out of there?"

"The U.S. is neutral, Connor. We don't have anything to worry about. We're trying to get as many Jews out of the country as we can. But Britain won't take them, and Congress is dragging its feet. I'm just overwhelmed with typing and filing forms."

"You stay out of trouble and go to the shelters if there's even a hint of an aircraft. Don't mess around."

"Okay, Connor. They're gonna cut me off in a minute. Could I talk to Mom and Pop?"

He could hear Nora's reassuring voice as she talked with their parents. When she hung up the family stood staring at each other. Abruptly, Claire sat, wringing her hands.

"How long will she be safe there?"

"I don't know," Henry said, "surely they'll get them out soon."

Connor kept his thoughts to himself. From what she said, it didn't sound like they were getting ready to make any moves.

"She just had to see the world," Claire said.

"She'll be all right, Mom. No one's really safe anyway, as long as Hitler's allowed to run roughshod."

"They'll be cranking up the draft pretty soon," Henry said.

Claire shuddered.

"It hasn't happened yet," Connor said, "so let's get everything done that we can, just in case."

It only took five days for Holland to surrender. As Belgium surrendered, the Allies evacuated shattered troops from Dunkirk in a citizen rescue that stunned the world. The winter wheat swished Connor's knees when Germany bombed Paris. He smelled alfalfa blooming when Norway fell.

On June 27, they got another call from Nora. Connor and Claire held the receiver so both could hear while Henry paced.

"I don't know how long I can stay on the line. It's been cutting out all day," she said. "Paris has fallen and we're getting ready to move, so you might not hear from me for a while."

"Are you all right?" Connor interrupted.

"Yes. The Germans have been on their best behavior for some reason. Can't say I trust them. They've set up headquarters here. Hitler came a few days ago. That got everybody excited." The line cut out. ". . .and we're going on south to . . ." The line crackled and died.

"Oh no!" Claire cried as Connor hung up the dead receiver.

"What did she say?"

"Said the embassy's getting ready to move."

"Why'd they wait so long?" Henry embraced his wife, looking over her head at Connor who stopped his own pacing and stared at his parents.

"C'mon Mom, Nora's strong and smart. She'll be all right if anybody is. And remember she said the Germans were behaving. We'll just have to wait and see what happens."

"I don't think I can." Claire collapsed in a dining chair, making it groan.

Henry's face softened. "Sure, you can. Look at all you've survived already."

As they filled the loft with cured hay, they learned that the embassy had indeed moved—south to join the Pétain government in unoccupied Vichy, France, not to Britain like they'd hoped.

Connor felt his life had become surreal as the family went about its normal tasks. July 12, they gathered with the neighbors to harvest wheat, day by day, farm by farm, field by field, like they usually did, while the war spread on the other side of the world where his sister continued to risk her life. Nora called once more to reassure her family that she arrived safe in Vichy and the embassy continued doing its work. Neither Pauline nor the family had had a letter since then, but Connor knew his sister would keep trying to rescue people, occupation or not.

Connor learned German U-boats were trying to cut off Allied war supplies by sinking merchant ships. He wondered when it would be American ships. What if Nora were on a ship being evacuated?

"We should be in this," he would mutter under his breath as he scooped grain, even though he had no desire to go to war. He only wanted his sister out of it.

In the middle of wheat harvest, the Battle of Britain began. While Germany's Luftwaffe pounded England, the Soviets conquered Lithuania, Latvia, and Estonia. While Connor and Henry cut hay the second time, the war spread to East Africa where Italy occupied British Somaliland.

In September, President Roosevelt signed a draft bill and Connor realized he'd soon get caught up in another war that spread around the world like a cancer—just like his Uncle Earl had got caught more than twenty years earlier. He tried, day-after-day, to get his family ready for his absence—maybe for a long time.

He still felt he deserved to get started with his delayed life. He wanted a family, a home, and all the things he'd missed as he wandered around the mountain states. He could admit that he hadn't suffered much, but he certainly hadn't made any money or started a family or, he reminded himself, lost a farm.

He could take that necessary-farm-labor deferment his dad offered, but he doubted that it would last if the country went to war—and then he'd be in the middle of the worst of it. Or he could enlist right away and maybe get his service over before the U.S. got into the fight.

He still toyed with the idea of joining the Canadians. That would probably get him into Britain and from there maybe he could get to his sister and get her the hell out of France.

If he didn't decide soon, the government would probably decide for him.

SEE WILLY SEE

October 1, 1940 – Willow Grove, Nebraska

"Connor," his mother said, "You'll be expected to kill people!"

Connor knew that, but Congress had passed the draft bill. He looked steadily at his parents while he went over his reasoning again.

How can I stay at home when my sister could die? My friends are already signing up. That's why I brought it up now, but I almost wish Mom and Pop would talk me out of it.

He remained silent for a long moment head bowed. The dark corners of the kerosene-lit room seemed to expand, the edges of the buffet and kerosene heater soft in the dim light. He swallowed hard a couple of times his mouth dry. His mother sure knew how to make him stop and think, but wasn't that what he wanted?

"I know, Mom," he said at last, "but the Germans have taken over Europe. They've been bombing the hell out of Britain for weeks now. When, not if, they take over Vichy, Nora will have nowhere safe to go. How will she get away? We have to stop them."

Connor had interrupted a quiet evening with his parents. Henry'd been sitting at the table in companionable silence with his wife and son. The lantern cast a warm halo around the threesome. Henry read one of his farm journals and Claire had settled in with a Zane Grey novel. Connor had just reread the latest letter they'd received from Nora. It didn't say anything, like she'd warned back in July. The letter had phrases, whole sentences, blocked out in impenetrable black ink.

SEE WILLY SEE

"The weather's been beastly, cloudy and cold all the time. We're doing a lot of paperwork," she wrote. "We're perfectly safe. The French officials cooperate with the Nazis and . . ." Then a hole—a nice, neat, rectangular hole ended the sentence. He wondered if they couldn't have just crossed out the rest of the sentence. The hole made the missing words even more ominous.

He could read anything into that. The fact she used the word Nazis rather than Germans sent a shot of adrenalin up his spine. He'd heard that people disappeared in Nazi-occupied zones. He tried to image what he would do if Nora disappeared. How would he know? How long would it take the Foreign Service to tell her family?

Would the Germans take her wherever they took the others? But where? His imagination stopped at the edge of a void. He knew from her letters to Pauline that Nora helped people who would otherwise disappear. She would keep doing that, even if it cost her life.

He shook his head, set the letter aside, and cleared his throat. "Pop, I think I'm gonna enlist."

His dad looked up without speaking and his mom's face blanched, an even whiter spot in the dim room.

"Connor, you can't," Claire said. "Your dad needs you. You're just getting started after all that time you lost wandering around looking for work."

"I know, Mom, but they're already drafting people. Dad's on the draft board, you know. I don't want him to have to make that decision. Anyway, maybe by the time we get into it, my year will be up."

"Not likely," Henry said.

"Yeah, maybe not."

"You know Pauline won't wait for you," Claire said.

Connor's high school debate training took over and he found himself arguing a case he really didn't want to win. "Maybe if everybody has to go, Pauline'll change her mind."

"I wouldn't count on it, son," his father said. "We all know Pauline. When she sets her mind to something, she hangs on like a snapping turtle."

"She's just scared because of her Uncle Harry."

"Don't dismiss Harry, Connor," Henry said. "What happened to him in the Great War happened to a lot of men He's just another wreck. And remember my brother Earl, still under the sod over there."

"Well, I know, but a lot of guys didn't even get into battle."

"Once you sign up, you don't decide that."

"Dad, if this gets as bad as I think it will, you can't keep me out of it. If I get in ahead of time, maybe I'll get out sooner."

"Maybe. I don't know how that'll work. I think the rules'll change if we get into it."

"Your dad will have to give up some of the land if you're not here to help. He can't take care of everything without you. He's worn out from the dust storms. And you'll be that much farther behind. You might never catch up."

"Mom, everybody's giving up stuff. Sometimes I think I'll never have a home and family of my own, but if we don't win the war, it may not matter. Hitler is dangerous and we gotta stop him."

"I'm against this, Connor. I'm already worrying myself sick about Nora. I can't lose both of you."

"I could end up in France. Maybe I could look out for her."

"I wouldn't count on that, Connor," Henry said.

"Maybe not, Pop, but maybe if I get over there, I can find a way."

His mother closed her book with a snap. "The whole German army is in France, and you want to go there?"

"I don't necessarily want to go, but I think the only choice I have is when, and if I can help Nora . . ."

"She's in the American Embassy, Connor, and I have to believe they'll close the embassy and send everybody home. She said they're moving."

"She got cut off. She didn't say where, except she said they're going south. South is not home."

"Surely they're coming home, maybe by a safer route." She paused and Connor knew he'd challenged a formidable debater. She'd also debated in high school.

"By the time you get there, she'll be here." His mother paused and gave him one of her looks. "You're a necessary farm worker."

"You and Pop got along without me for five years. I know it'll be hard, but I have to go. You can sell my cows if you have to and I'll just start over again. Done it once already."

Claire rested her elbow on the table, forehead in hand. She shook her head. "You've only been home a year. You've barely got a start."

"Better than being all set up and having to sell out."

"Connor, soldiers have to eat. The reason they have a deferment for necessary farm labor is because we need to produce enough food to take care of them. You can do your part that way."

SEE WILLY SEE

He didn't dare let his mother see him grin, but he appreciated her impeccable logic. He looked at his toes to hide the rise in the corners of his mouth.

Maybe she's right. Maybe I should stay and help feed the troops. I keep hearing when we get into it, we'll be done in a year. He sighed. *I can't be that optimistic, given the way the Germans have swept Europe. And everybody seems to forget the Japanese. If they get into it, we'll be at war on two fronts.*
He realized his mother hadn't finished.

"And you can have your family and build up your farm business at the same time."

That sounded really good to Connor. He'd said the same things to himself during the months since Nora had left for Europe. But he could feel her pain, seeing people treated like cattle or worse. He knew her determination to take care of them. How could he hold back?

"Mom, I'm ashamed that Nora has been in France doing her best to keep people alive and I've done nothing."

Claire's book dropped to the floor. Her eyes widened and Connor could see her giving up. He wasn't sure he wanted her to. She had one more salvo to fire.

"If you're sure, I want you to see Harry before you sign up."

"That's a good idea, Connor," said his father. "Before you do anything, you ought to know as much as you can about what you're getting into."

"All right, but even if he scares me to death, I think I'm gonna have to go sometime." He paused as his parents stared. "Let's not talk about it anymore tonight. I'll go see Harry and take it from there."

He stood and left the room on shaky knees.

SEE WILLY SEE

He stepped outside into a night lit only by stars. Once his eyes adjusted, he walked in the star shadow of the garage as he headed out the driveway to the county road. He followed the section line over the hills to the west. Eventually, his long-legged stride slowed to a stroll as he passed Ollie Parson's old place. He turned south, still following the section line, where he passed the Jondle Killough place. Along the pasture fence he noticed a grasshopper pinned to a barb on the wire, the work of a butcher bird. He noted animal tracks in the dust—raccoons at the bottom of the hill where the pond went under the bridge, rabbits, and a scattering of birds mixed in everywhere. At the end of an hour, he'd followed roads around the south section—the one he'd hoped to own someday.

Once he'd encircled the entire square and returned to his start, he entered the house and found the front room deserted. His parents had apparently gone to bed. He followed their example.

Two days later, as he drove to Harry's little two-room house in Cowles, Connor considered what he knew about the man. Harry rarely left his house, except to go into town once a month to buy staples. His hair always appeared greasy, and a dirty beard straggled across his chest. Even his beetling eyebrows had turned gray. He knew Harry had served in the Army during World War I in a battle for a place called Argonne Woods in France.

After he knocked, Connor stood listening to muttering and thuds he couldn't place until he heard Harry's muffled, "Come in."

Connor found the older man perched on a straight-backed chair next to a hot pot-bellied stove. The room stifled him with the smell of tobacco. He couldn't imagine a stench that strong unless Harry had been spitting on the stove. Connor didn't know how he'd stay in the room long enough to have a conversation, but he plowed ahead anyway.

"Hello, Harry," Connor said, dragging a chair over from the table and sitting. He took a shallow breath and began. "Harry, Pauline tells me you fought in World War I."

Connor could barely discern Harry's nod. He looked at the gray man who breathed but lacked any spark. If anything could persuade Connor to stay in Nebraska, Harry would do it. He plunged ahead.

"Harry, you've heard about Hitler and what he's doing in Europe?"

Connor paused but got no reaction from the other man. He took a deep breath. "I'm thinking of signing up."

Harry drug his gaze from the floor and regarded Connor without a word.

"I don't want to intrude, and I understand if you don't want to talk to me. I just wondered if you could tell me something about what it's like; what I'll have to face."

Harry just looked at him through faded, expressionless blue eyes.

"Well, I guess I've intruded," Connor said, standing.

Harry grabbed his wrist. "Sit."

Connor sat in a chair identical to Harry's. He'd noticed it matched two others lined up around a table that appeared unused. He glanced around the dimly lit room shielded from daylight by tightly drawn curtains. The sparsely furnished house held only the stove, a table and two chairs and a counter-top with a pitcher pump and a cupboard on the far side. He could see a bed through the open door of another room.

Harry interrupted his inventory. "What do you think I can tell you?"

SEE WILLY SEE

Connor flinched at the steel in the man's unblinking eyes. "Just what was it like?"

"Well," Harry said, his voice flat. He stopped. The fire in his eyes flickered out as if that little bit of spirit had died. "They said it was only a week. Seven days they said."

He paused, continuing to stare at the stove. "I was in the 308th Infantry Regiment, Company C. Replaced some guy got wounded the first day in France. Didn't have no idea what would happen. We was gonna win the war for the Allies."

Harry just sat there—uncanny how still he sat. He didn't even blink. He glanced at Connor out the corner of his eye.

"Why 'n hell you want to go over there anyway?"

"My sister's in France. In Paris. Hitler's bombing Paris."

"You can't help her. Just get yourself killed too." Harry paused a long time. Connor wondered if Harry'd forgotten him. "What 'n hell's she doin' there?"

"She's at the American Embassy. I kind of got her into it."

"Tryin' to make peace with them Germans?"

"I guess so."

Harry grunted and reverted to silence. Connor began to stand.

Harry came back to life, raising his head abruptly. "What was it like?"

Connor returned to his seat.

"It was Hell, son, like burning up. Guns roared. Men screamed. Shells whistled, blasted. Noise so loud it hurt. Felt like it would squash the life out of you carryin' all that weight. You can't move. And you can't breathe."

He resumed his staring, like he gathered up something from inside himself.

"And then a piece of Phil fell on me. Blood splattered all over my face. His belly ripped open. Him holding himself together. His belly, all twisted with guts coming out. Didn't know what to do. Screamed for stretcher bearers."

He stopped, staring at the stove.

Connor had a vivid imagination. His hair stood up on the back of his neck as if a warm, wet piece of meat rested there. He stared at Harry's face, aghast at the lack of emotion. He felt his chest tighten when he realized that tears were streaming off that emotionless face into the beard.

Connor didn't know what to do. He'd never seen a grown man cry. Not like that. He stood and put his hand on Harry's shoulder.

"It'll be all right," he said.

Harry shrugged him off. "No. It won't. It won't never be all right. Phil's dead an' Otto's dead an' Artie's dead an' I don't know what happened to Charlie."

He ticked them off on his fingers, still staring at the stove, his voice a monotone. ". . . an' Scotty's dead an' . . ."

Connor sat again, looking into Harry's face, but the man's eyes had gone somewhere he couldn't reach. He got up and left, gently closing the door behind him. He almost ran to his car, still hearing that spectral voice as it counted cadence for the dead and disappeared, until he slammed the car door. He struggled to drive normally when he wanted to spin his wheels and throw up a dust cloud getting out of the barnyard.

The sun sank directly ahead of him. He could barely see the road. Squinting at the ditch on his right, he managed to stay on the gravel until he reached home. From the porch, he smelled a roast cooking. He slipped around to the back door and went up the stairs to his bedroom, where he flopped on the bed, trying to calm his breathing.

He said nothing at supper, keeping his eyes on his plate, shoving food from one side to the other.

"Well?" Claire passed the green beans around. "Did you talk to Harry?"

"Yes." He laid his fork down on the edge of his plate.

"How was he?"

"I'm afraid I woke his sleeping demons up." He flinched as he thought of the storm that must lie under that emotionless demeanor.

"I don't think they sleep very sound." Claire took some beans and set the bowl in the middle of the table.

"No. He's not good."

"He'll probably never be all right."

"Probably not."

He picked up his knife.

"Is that what you want for yourself?"

He looked up at his mother, feeling unsettled. 'Course not. He's just pitiful."

"I don't think he wants pity," Henry said. "I think that's why he stays in that little house so much."

SEE WILLY SEE

"Maybe so. He just sat and called out the names of all the men they lost. He still called them out when I got to the car." He shuddered. Logic couldn't quiet the emotional storm Harry had started.

"So, you've changed your mind?" He heard hope in his mother's voice.

He couldn't speak. Despite his misgivings, war still loomed as large as before. He sighed. "I still don't think I can stay out of it, Mom. If we all say we don't want to be like Harry, Hitler will take over the whole world."

What in Hell's the matter with me? I keep arguing the wrong side.

"Just don't go, Connor." She made that familiar pushing gesture with her hands.

"Mom, our people didn't hide at home when the Revolutionary Army sent the Brits back to England or when the Union fought the Rebs to a stand-still. Our people were there. The only way to keep this country is to fight for it."

Where the hell did that come from? He got up and left, hearing his father's voice as he strode across the room. He remained in the doorway to hear.

"We were lucky, Claire. We came between wars."

"Not if we have to sit here and wait to hear that our children are dead," Claire said. "I don't call that lucky."

"I guess I don't either," Henry said. "I guess I don't either."

Connor shut the door trying to figure out when he'd turned into such a damn patriot. Why him? Hadn't he lost enough already?

SEE WILLY SEE

November 18, 1940 – Willow Grove

Connor and Henry worked together to repair a big hole Connor's fence-crawling cow had made running off into the neighbor's alfalfa patch. The weather hadn't turned cold yet and despite the annoying cow, Connor enjoyed working with his dad. He loved grass wind, especially in a late fall when it carried the warm, dusty scent of baking soil. Splashes of purple ironweed and white snow-on-the-mountain scattered through the draws. He could have done the work himself while his dad worked on the equipment, but he appreciated his father's company after the years away.

Henry grabbed the wire stretcher out of his fencing bucket. "Where'd you say you got that cow?"

"Just this side of hell, I think." Connor fished out the fencing pliers from a supply of staples, a little coil of barbed wire, and two pair of leather gloves. He handed one pair to Henry.

"I hope she has a calf in her," Henry said around a mouth full of fencing staples. "But I won't be sorry to see her go, if not."

Connor hooked a staple with the pliers and pulled it out into his open palm. "Maybe we should eat her. We could help Mom cut her up and can her."

"Some of your mom's beef pot pie would taste good when the snow flies, but let's give her a chance." Henry walked a few yards down the line to the break in the wires. Connor watched him attach the stretcher to broken ends of the bottom wire. He was pulling stapes from another post when Henry said something more.

"I couldn't hear you Pop."

SEE WILLY SEE

Henry raised his voice over the swish of breeze in the grass. "I sure wish we'd been able to get you into college."

"I know, Pop, what made you think of that now?"

Henry ratcheted the wires tight. "Here. Bring me that roll of wire." He spliced wire into the break and looked up at Connor. "I think about it all the time, especially since you decided to enlist."

A little shiver ran down Connor's spine at mention of enlistment. He shrugged. "It's not so bad—coulda been worse. And a college degree wouldn't keep me out of the Army."

"You coulda been an officer."

"They get killed too."

Henry released the fence stretcher and began putting a patch into the next strand while Connor removed staples from two more strands of wire and moved on to the next post. As he tapped the staples' legs together on top of the post, he remembered his high hopes six years earlier.

He'd been just seventeen on May 6, 1933, when he walked across the stage at Willow Grove High School, shook hands with the superintendent, took his diploma, flipped his tassel, and stepped down onto the floor of the gymnasium, grinning. What a great day, he'd thought. He'd spent the afternoon driving around the country with his friend Ralph, whooping and hollering, dust boiling up behind his little jalopy.

Connor'd already known what he wanted to do. He would study horticulture. Two things about horticulture excited him—Bessey Forest, the largest man-planted forest in the world, up north in the Sandhills. He'd hiked the forest and climbed the fire tower—took a cool-off break in the Dismal River.

Nectarines were his other inspiration.

SEE WILLY SEE

"See," he explained to Ralph, "that year in California—you know when we helped Uncle Lawrence move—I ate my first nectarine."

He'd eaten nectarines until he'd made himself sick. His uncle's new neighbor told him they were a cross between a peach and a plum and that Luther Burbank had developed them.

Connor wanted to be like Luther Burbank or Charles Bessey. He dreamed of doing something new with plants. He'd never been much of a stockman, both of his parents would attest to that, but he loved working with plants.

"They don't kick you and step on your feet and run over you," he said. "Or try to eat you like that crazy old sow that tried to take a chunk out of my leg. Good thing I had on my canvas coveralls that day."

On Monday after graduation, though, the first of the local banks, the Settler's Bank of Blacksville, closed forever. His father had been through bank closings. He'd cautioned Connor never to borrow money. He might lose cash in a bank closing, but if nothing's mortgaged, he wouldn't lose the ability to make more. Losing money hurt, though, and Henry had some new wrinkles in his forehead.

"Don't worry Connor," he'd said, "that was the smallest account and there'll be money for college in fall. That's why I had money in three banks."

On May 20, the bank in Mortonsburg closed and the lines in his father's forehead deepened. "If we get a really good crop this year, we'll be all right. This dry spell can't last forever."

Every day, Connor looked up at bald, blue skies filled with light and heat. The drought held, so did the wind. Hardly a breeze stirred that spring. He joked that he could drive the team and wagon into the cracks in the yard. Instead of going to sleep to the sound of a breeze humming in the screens, and lightly moving air cooling his bedroom, Connor tossed and turned, sweating into the sheets. During the day, the sun beat down without respite as he helped his dad with the farm work.

In July, the neighborhood formed its usual harvest crew to cut wheat. Connor enjoyed working with the neighbors, going from farm to farm, working in the hot sun, eating pork roasts with carrots and potatoes or fried chicken, mashed potatoes, and white, chicken gravy, plus his favorite, lemon meringue pie. They'd all nap under shady trees in the yard before going back and working some more.

"Knee High by the Fourth of July" did not apply to the corn crop. Not this time.

By August, it barely brushed Henry's knee. They cut it to feed the cattle—maybe the steers would bring a good price at the sale barn. They had a good, uniform set of steers, but by then Connor had very little hope. Hardly anybody in the country, maybe the world, had the money to eat steak four years after the stock market crash.

August 15, Connor dunked his head into the stock tank on his way to the house for dinner. He wondered what the cows thought of that. They'd stopped drinking and stared at his dripping pate. In the house, he toweled his hair while he and Henry listened to the news. The Carpenter State Bank had closed. When it reopened that Friday, it would pay ten cents on the dollar to its depositors.

"Well, that's that."

"Maybe next year," his mom said. "It's gotta rain sometime."

"Maybe."

SEE WILLY SEE

He helped his mom put the garden to bed that fall. Still no rain. He picked the few apples their trees produced and stored them in the storm cellar for winter.

Damn, he thought, as his father walked back from where he'd patched the wire. No plant breeding. Looks like it's livestock—turn this place back to grass like it should have stayed. God, I hate cows. Maybe I'll go fight the Germans for a while. But he really didn't want to do that either. Cows versus Germans. He couldn't decide which would give him more trouble.

Well, of course, I can.

Connor started stapling the newly stretched wire.

"We'll finish here," Henry said, "and I'll go back and stretch the last strand so I can get back to that wagon. Get it greased up and oiled before the snow flies."

"Okay Pop."

His dad hammered in a staple. "I worry about it all the time."

"What? That damned cow? I can shoot her this afternoon and get her hung to age."

"No. About college. I know you don't want to be a farmer any more than Nora wants to be a farmer's wife."

"Aw, maybe with both of us working, I can play around with some different kinds of plants in my spare time—when I get back."

"You're really determined to go?"

"I'll be honest. Harry really set me back. I mean he's a mess."

"He's not the only one, Connor."

"I know, Pop. He gives me the willies. Sometimes when I become conscious in the middle of the night, I don't know if I'm dreaming or just remembering. It's always that name-calling."

"Name calling?"

"Yeah. Dead people's names. People Harry served with I think. When I left, he'd got into a rhythm—Phil's dead and Scott's dead and Earl's dead and Billy's dead. When I closed the door, I could still hear that flat voice droning on and on, over and over, naming the names."

"I've heard him do that. It *is* spooky."

"I don't want to be like that, Pop. I just want to get over there and get this over with before Nora gets hurt or worse."

"I don't see what you can do to help Nora, Connor. They'll surely bring 'em home soon."

"I dunno."

"Look, soldiers have to eat. You can do as much for the war effort right here helping me produce food for the troops as you can carrying a rifle or driving a tank."

"Maybe so, Pop, maybe so."

His father hesitated a moment. "Prices are way up now." He squinted at his son's back as Connor hammered in another staple. "We're getting plenty of rain."

"Yeah, I know Pop."

"I'm thinking maybe you could go to college next fall if things keep going the way they have been."

Connor stood up and stared at his father.

SEE WILLY SEE

"You'd probably have to work—part time at least. Like Nora."

Connor couldn't believe what he'd heard. He'd given up on college six years earlier when the banks closed. He couldn't quite get the idea back into his brain. A long silence stretched out while Connor took in the new thought.

"I'm guessing you still have some of that money from your job down in Grand Canyon and that CCC job at Tahoe. I don't think you've touched the money the government sent to us while you worked there."

Connor nodded, thinking of his two years with the Civilian Conservation Corps in Tahoe National Forest. What a great job that had been. Connor thought Roosevelt had to be a genius to hire out-of-work youth to spruce up the park instead of getting welfare.

"I know you gave some of it to Nora . . ."

Connor interrupted. "Only $200. She didn't need as much as we thought."

"Anyway, between that and a good year here—and a part time job—I think you could do it."

Connor froze. *Really? After six years? What if it's too late? Could I learn to study again? HA. Nora would have something to say about that. Can't imagine myself in a classroom with a bunch of hot-shot kids. Always wanted to do something like Bessey and Burbank, but can I? What if I fail?*

He wanted to do it, he surely did, but his imagination stalled on the threshold—blank for once. He slumped.

"Pop, I certainly would not be essential farm labor if I went back to school."

His father shrank. Normally, he stood his full five foot-eight, but his spine turned to rubber. Connor had grown taller than his dad by the time he reached fourteen, but that afternoon Henry looked tiny and fragile. Connor wanted to comfort him, but he didn't know how.

"No, you wouldn't," Henry said. "No, you surely wouldn't."

November 19, 1940 – Willow Grove

As the sun set, Connor sat on the front step with Freckles watching the golden glow of the reflected sun moving over the valley east of the house. He caught a glimmer on a little pool of water left in the intermittent creek. He absently scratched a chigger as he considered his dad's proposal yet again. Of course, he'd have to give up his deferment. It probably wouldn't keep him out of the war anyway. He'd planned to enlist. But the option of college put him in a quandary.

"What do you think about it, Freckles?" He looked into the dog's brown eyes and scratched her deep golden fur.

The dog wagged a tentative tail. Freckles had been his mom's dog since she'd been a pup. Claire had trained her on chickens and Freckles hung around the house while Claire worked inside.

"I could sign up for classes next fall—if I don't get drafted first."

He wanted to get started before something he couldn't control snatched the chance away—again. *But the draft could get me before I finish.* He ran an absent-minded hand down the dog's back.

"Or, think about this," he said to the dog. "Maybe I should go ahead and get my service over with first. I could get out before we go to war. Then I wouldn't get interrupted."

He sighed. "And then there's Pauline to think about."

He remembered what his mom and dad had said. He agreed. She wouldn't wait for him, and he couldn't decide if that mattered.

Looking at the bridge in the bottom, Connor remembered sitting on the wooden timbers with their neighbors, the Green kids—Ian, Dylan, Agnes, Rory, and Pauline. Pauline had looked fetching even in overalls and flannel shirts. They'd sit on the edge of the bridge on fall evenings and dangle their feet, talking and laughing, until one or the other of their moms called for them. He grinned thinking about how his mother rang the old school bell she'd bought when the country school closed.
That neighbor girl still troubled him. They'd been going around together for almost a year—since he'd got back from being a bum. He just couldn't feel sure of her. He'd known her all her life—he'd been five when his mother helped with her birth. He couldn't quite see having the kind of relationship with her that he saw between his parents. For one thing, she always seemed a little annoyed with him and a little defensive. If he helped her with her coat, he never seemed to hold it right and she'd remind him she could do it herself.

Nora had maneuvered them together as soon as he'd returned home the year before.

He remembered walking into the farmyard after five years on the road. He'd left for California right after his sister's graduation in 1934, taking a few clothes and the Brownie camera he got for his own graduation. He'd worked and bummed and snapped pictures all over the West, picking olives and fruit that first year in the Sacramento Valley.

SEE WILLY SEE

Then he got the job with Roosevelt's alphabet agency, the Civilian Conservation Corps in Tahoe National Forest. After Tahoe, he'd jumped a freight and ended up wandering from one national park to the next with another bum he met in a boxcar. They'd trapped squirrels and marmots, caught a few trout, picked berries, robbed nests, and worked some short-term jobs between parks. They'd separated in the winter and Connor had worked his way down to the Grand Canyon alone the following summer. He took a job there at a resort on the canyon floor.

At the end of the season, he'd walked and hitched his way home. He kicked up Route 66 to Tucumcari and detoured onto U.S. 54 through Dalhart into Kansas. At Pratt, he'd turned north on U.S. 281 across ravaged farmland, just beginning to recover.

He'd spent a day with his dad's brother near Smith Center, looking over cropland that grew a thin crop of oats.

"I left the stubble to hold the dirt," Uncle Billy told him. "Just disked it down and planted into the debris. Seems like the residue anchors it down."

"Good idea. Guess I don't know why we disk it up every fall anyway."

"Aw, to make a nice, clean seedbed, keep the weeds down, buncha stuff, I guess. Hey." Billy walked to the pasture fence, leaning on a post. "Lookit this pasture. I grazed ten head on it this year. Just moved 'em over to the cool season pasture."

"Did you keep your cattle all through the dust?"

"Naw. Just a milk cow for the young'uns. Look at all this land and that's all I could grow—enough to feed one cow and some chickens."

Connor spent the night with Billy's family. The next morning, he slung his knapsack over his shoulder and started walking. He crossed the border in mid-afternoon and swung into the yard at dusk. He stepped through the porch and into the kitchen. It was 1939. He'd been gone five years.

"Hey Mom, what's for supper?"

"Connor, you can see I'm frying chicken and—Connor!!"

"Hi Mom." He stood, grinning at her as she flung herself into his arms.

"We didn't know you was coming." She leaned her head back and looked into his eyes. "I think you've growed."

"Didn't have a phone to call you. Spent the night with Uncle Billy."

She turned back to her chicken and flipped it over in the hot grease, feeding another few cobs into the cook stove. "How're they getting' along?"

"Okay, looks like. He grew some oats this year. Pasture looks pretty good—thin—but he grazed some cows. Where's Nora?"

"She's out watering the garden. Still doin' it in buckets, although we've had some rain now."

"Dad?" He sawed off a slice of bread that sat on the baker's shelf cooling. He grabbed a table knife out of the drawer and dipped into the butter crock, smearing a layer of fresh homemade butter on the bread.

"Currying the horses, I expect. Go out and see your sister. She's been missin' you."

Chewing his prize, Connor stepped out the garden door and spotted Nora straddling the green beans, skirt tucked up into her waistband, pouring water from a five-gallon bucket onto rows of plants. He noted that she'd grown taller than he remembered and nearly white-blond. She must have spent the whole summer outside in the sun—probably with her skirt pulled up, because her legs sported a deep tan, too.

"Hey Nora," He grinned at his sister and strode across the yard in her direction.

"Connor!" She squealed, dropping the bucket and charging him. When she slammed into him, he took a step back to keep them both from falling.

"I'm glad to see you too."

"Oh, Connor, I've missed you so much! I thought you might be back pretty soon, though. Your last letter said so."

"After I got out of the canyon, I hitched into Kansas . . ."

"Your pictures!" she interrupted. "They're fabulous. We got them processed all at once this spring when we sold the heifers. You sent a whole bagful of them, you know."

"I had no idea how many rolls I sent. Just dropped them in the mail when I could."

"I want you to tell me about all the places and . . ."

"Hey, I'll be around a while. I haven't seen Pop yet."

"He's in the barn. Come on. I'll go with you." She grabbed his hand and pulled, dragging him along.

They met their dad coming out of the barn carrying two full buckets of grain, his hair shining blue-black in the sun. The horses munched behind him.

"Pop."

"Hey." His dad stood looking, eyes traveling over his much taller son.

Connor noticed a quiet smile in the sharp blue eyes. "You home to stay?"

"If we can make a living."

Connor leaned down to take the buckets. "You okay?"

"Yeah. Just surprised. Um," he paused. "I think we'll be fine. We've had some rain. Not as much as I'd like, but no dusters for—a while. I don't just remember when we had the last one."

"Where we takin' these?"

"Chicken house. Thought I'd help your mom, since I was down here anyway."

"Hey Pop," Nora said as they walked across the yard together. "Don't you think he's taller?"

"Aw, I dunno, seems like he's always been taller'n me. Both of you." He looked at his daughter over beetle brows.

"Mom too," Nora reminded him.

"Hmph. Say Connor, I'm glad you're home."

"Me too, Pop."

After delivering the water to the chickens, Connor opened the porch door and his father stepped through, removing his hat and gloves, placing them into the familiar cubbies to the right of the door. This time when he stepped into the kitchen, Connor took a good look around. Nothing much had changed. The ceiling-to-floor cupboard divided kitchen and dining room. The monstrous flour drawer in its middle still hung open an inch because it wouldn't slide shut and Mom couldn't wrestle it. The cook stove sat in the back corner, partially recessed next to the cupboard.

He dipped a pan of water from the reservoir on the far end and carried it to a basin on the counter across the kitchen.

"Table's set," Claire told them as the three washed their hands.

"I can't wait. I'm ready for a good home-cooked meal. I been eatin' a lot of beans and bologna."

Connor relaxed with his family while he and his dad discussed the farm operation over supper. Eventually talk turned to the war.

"What's goin' on over in Europe?" Connor crunched the crispy skin on a drumstick. "I been seein' enlistment posters in the Post Offices. Has Hitler taken over the whole continent?"

Nora and Claire exchanged glances as the men talked about the war half a world away.

"You think we'll get in it?" Claire whispered.

Connor glanced at her. "I dunno, Mom, I don't see how we can avoid it."

"Well, let's not worry about that right now."

She stood, picking up the chicken platter. "Anybody want more chicken?" Both Connor and his dad hooked a piece as she held the platter.

"Green beans?"

Connor spooned some onto his plate and she walked off with the two serving dishes. Connor served himself with potatoes and milk gravy as Nora picked up the bowls.

"Pauline just broke off her engagement," she said when she returned with rhubarb pie.

"Didn't know she'd got herself engaged." Connor hadn't forgotten the neighbor girl. They'd spent a lot of time together in high school. But he hadn't thought about much for five years except the next meal and finding or making shelter.

"Some guy from over by Ong."

Connor noticed that Claire exchanged a glance with Henry and grinned. His parents had always liked Pauline.

A few days later, Nora called Pauline, who had become a secretary for Dutton-Lainson in Hastings. When her friend dropped by, Nora remained in the kitchen while everyone sat down at the table—so Pauline could sit by Connor, giving her a chance to chat about his travels.

The first time they sat down together, Pauline turned to Connor. "Nora showed me some of your pictures. It looks like you've been everywhere."

Connor grinned. "I did see a lot of beautiful country. Never got east of the Missouri, though."

Nora sat on Pauline's other side. "What about the winter with Uncle Ollie and Aunt Ella in Glendive."

"Oh yeah. Barren country."

"Tell her about Charlie."

Connor served himself some roast beef and passed it on. "I met this Irish guy, Charles Seamus Shank. Met him in a boxcar and we hit it off . . . Say, you're not interested in all this."

Pauline took a slice of meat and passed the platter. "Sure, I am Connor. You should write a book." she took the bowl of pickled beets, added a few to her plate and passed it. Mischief in her eyes, she grinned. "I'll type it for you."

Connor laughed. He knew that look. Next thing he knew she'd have him traveling all over the country signing books. "I have to write it first, Pauline, and I've got my hands full helping Pop catch up."

It felt pretty good to talk and laugh with his family and that neighbor girl he knew so well.

After supper Sunday, Connor gave Nora a suspicious, eyes-narrowed look when she suggested he and Pauline walk down to the creek bridge. "How about you?"

"Oh, I let Mom do all the work this weekend. I'll stay here and help her with the dishes. Pauline has to leave pretty soon, so give her a nice send off. Like old times."

Connor frowned behind Pauline's back and Nora stuck out her tongue.

As Connor and Pauline strolled down the hill east of the house, she reminded him of their childhood together.

"Remember, Connor, when Dylan thought he saw lights bobbing across that field?"

Connor chuckled. "And then your dad came up with that old story about the Carson brothers and the murder."

They'd arrived at the bridge and sat swinging their legs over the edge.

"How many nights did we all come down here and watch for them lights?"

Connor grinned. "All summer. Every night, until one or the other of our moms called us in."

"Sometimes it got pretty dark and a little chilly—especially toward fall. Like now."

He wrapped an arm around her. "You know, I wrote to the University of Nebraska about them lights."

"You'd do that. What did they say?"

"They said it was something they call swamp gas. Said that old, dead plant material gives off a gas as it decomposes and, when conditions are right, it glows."

"Hmm," she said, snuggling closer. "What're you gonna do now, Connor? You gonna farm with your dad?"

"I don't know, Pauline. I've been wandering all over the country the last few years. Saw some beautiful places, but don't know how to make a living in any of them. I kinda decided to come home and farm with Pop—maybe take some courses in horticulture. Correspondence, you know." He trailed off, looking down the little dry creek bed. "What about you?"

"I've got a pretty good job now." She paused. "I'm not like Nora you know. I really want to be a farm wife. I love this place. I love walking around in the pastures and cooking for harvest crews and watching them sleep scattered on the dining room floor after they eat at noon. I love the smell of wheat dust and a milking barn and watching rows of little plants coming up." She hesitated. "Guess I should write a poem."

"It is kinda poetic. I know what you mean though. I just," he paused, "after the dusters, I want to do more. I want to help bring this country back on its feet and help figure out how to keep the big dust storms from happening again."

"You sound restless." Pauline sat up, looking into his eyes.

"I guess I am a little." Connor squeezed her hand. "You know, wandering around in the mountains, I got hungry sometimes and I don't think I'm cut out for a lifetime of that—not knowing where the next meal's comin' from. But it didn't keep me from buying film whenever I had money."

"Maybe you should be a photographer."

"God no! Now tip your head to the left and smile." He held his hands up in a little box to frame her face.

She laughed. "No. But have you ever heard of Ansel Adams or Dorothea Lange?"

"Yeah, it's a thought. I don't know. I'm not sure I want to wander around by myself like I have been. I had Charlie with me last year. We tromped Glacier and Yellowstone and the Grand Tetons—but it's not the same."

"Same as what?"

"Well, as having your own family."

"Connor, you've got a problem," she said, laughing. "I hope you solve it. But right now, I've gotta get back to Hastings."

Nora met them at the door. "Say. There's a dance at the Pavilion next weekend. Lawrence Welk. I just heard it on the radio. We should all go."

"We should," Pauline said over her shoulder as she headed for her car.

They watched her drive down the hill, raising a cloud of dust.

"So, Connor, did you see any ghost lights?"

"No lights. Just ghosts."

Henry stepped out of the house, almost stepping on his son, bringing Connor back to his current problems.

"You and Freckles seem to be spending a lot of time together out here on the front step."

Connor looked up from his view of the valley.

"Thinking about Pauline and school—and the Army."

Henry sat on the step next to his son. "Still not sure about her?"

"I don't know what it is, Pop. I've known her all her life. She's a good friend."

"She'll make a good farm wife."

"She really does love farm life, but I don't know."

"You could do worse."

"I just can't quite see having the kind of life with her that you and Mom have. I've never heard you fight."

"That's mostly because your mother is the most even-tempered human being I've ever met."

"She's not a wimp."

"No, but her way of standing up for herself is—unusual." Henry scratched the dog in silence for a few moments. "She had to train me you know."

Connor chuckled. "Are you trainable?"

"Let me give you an example. I used to drop my overalls on the floor when I went to bed. Your mother always had some mending, or something on the stove, or something else to do, so I went to bed a little before she did. She never brought the lantern in the bedroom. She didn't want to wake me up. In return I gave her one more little thing to do. She hung them overalls up every night in the dark."

"Yeah. She'd do that."

"Anyway, she musta got tired of trippin' on them overalls because one morning I got up and tripped on them damn things on my way to the kitchen to light the stove." Henry paused and grinned at his son. "I didn't get it the first time. Not smart enough. She had to leave 'em where I'd dropped 'em three times before I realized she was talking to me. After that, I took them damn overalls in the closet and hung 'em on a hook before I crawled into bed."

"I can't imagine Pauline doing anything like that, Pop. She'd probably pick them overalls up and throw them in my face. And I'd come up fightin' mad. Wouldn't want to be, just wakin' up sudden like."

"Not too many people smart as your mom, but you're pretty smart too. You could find a way."

Claire cracked the door. "Supper's ready."

Freckles stood and peered at Claire as the two men brushed off their overalls and stepped inside leaving all of Connor's dilemmas unsolved.

November 20, 1940 – Willow Grove

Pauline still occupied Connor's thoughts when the news came that Germany had invaded Romania and Greece. He had gone dancing with Nora and Pauline every weekend after that first Saturday his sister had set them up. When Nora headed off to Lincoln and the School of Commerce, Pauline and Connor had spent most Saturday evenings dancing or going to movies. They'd even gone ice skating on the mill pond at Crystal Lake. With bad news about the war in Europe escalating and the nation preparing to defend its allies, Connor looked forward to

SEE WILLY SEE

another night with Pauline, dancing to Lawrence Welk at the Crystal Pavilion.

A quick bath and he would be out the door. He wondered what Pauline would wear. She'd looked marvelous the last time they'd danced—in the ruffled yellow dress Nora had made for her. His mood darkened when he remembered what he had to tell her. He'd made up his mind. Army first and then college. Maybe she would understand.

As he dried off, he stopped for a moment, shivering in cold air that crept along the floor of the warm kitchen.

He thought about how he'd say it—maybe in the car on the way home. At least the whole evening wouldn't be ruined. "Pauline," he rehearsed, "I think I'm going to enlist."

No that would be a blast in the face. "Pauline," he whispered, "Pauline, they're drafting guys now. I've gotta go." He scrubbed with the rough towel until his skin burned red.

"Pauline," he tried again. "They're drafting guys now. We'll be in it before you know. I don't think I could get very far with my classes before the war catches up with me."

He yanked on his clothes, still talking to himself.

"Pauline, they passed the draft bill. I have to enlist. I can't let Pop live the rest of his life with all the parents whose sons he drafted while he kept me home."

He stood at the little mirror beside the cook stove and parted his wet hair on the left, slicking it down.

"Pauline," he said again. "I just can't live the rest of my life with the people who went while I stayed home."

He stepped through the swinging door into the front room, still muttering. Connor watched his dad, a new *Farm Journal* in his lap. He knew Henry only had a third-grade education, but he read quickly, although his speech combined his Appalachian slang with correct English.

Henry looked up from the magazine. "Sounds like you had a whole conversation with yourself in there."

"I gotta tell Pauline I'm goin' to enlist."

"You know she won't like it any better'n your mom does."

"Yeah, I know. I just can't hang around here while everybody else is out there doin' his part, even Nora—especially Nora. And when I go to school, I want to have the freedom and time to finish it. Nothing else hanging over my head."

"We could sure use you around here."

"I know, Pop, I know."

"Well, you know we want you here whenever you get back."

"I gotta go, Pop."

"Have fun."

He glanced quickly at his father. How could he have fun with his enlistment in the background.

"Bye Mom," he yelled and walked out the door onto the porch where he bumped into his mother. He took a step back.

"What're you doin' out here?"

"Checking on the chickens. It's supposed to get cold tonight."

"Chicken house buttoned up tight?"

"I think so. You going to pick up Pauline."

SEE WILLY SEE

"Yup. See ya later."

"Have a good time."

He closed the front door and headed for the car.

"Sure, Mom," he muttered. "Just gotta tell my girl I'm leavin' her for the Army."

He continued rehearsing as he drove. "Pauline, I know you don't want me to go, and I'd rather be here with you. But Pauline," the car made a little sashay when he pulled out of the driveway onto gravel, "what if I start school and then get drafted. I'd probably have to start all over and lose the money I'd already spent. I have to do this. I'm sorry. Will you wait for me?"

He pulled out of the driveway heading for Hastings and Pauline's house. "Aw hell, Pauline," he said. "You understand, don't you? I have to enlist."

When Pauline got in the car, she sat silent after a brief 'hello.' Connor hadn't decided what he would say, so he said nothing. They barely spoke during the short drive. When they arrived at the Pavilion, Connor's and Pauline's old neighbor, Jack O'Neill, home from basic training in his new uniform, swept Pauline away for a polka. Connor watched, trying to enjoy himself. He grinned and wondered how a big man like Jack, 300 pounds Connor guessed, could be so light on his feet.

Connor claimed Pauline for the next dance, a waltz. Gliding around the floor to the languid strains of The Whistling Waltz, Connor felt Pauline's slender waist bending into his arm.

"How's Jack getting along with the Navy?"

He turned a quarter to the right, turn, step, close; step, step, close; step, step, close.

Pauline smiled. "Oh, he says he's seen the insides of all kinds of ships. Says they're gonna let him shoot one of those big guns, 16-inch, I think he said."

Connor stepped aside to avoid jostling, turn, step, close; turn, step, close, step, step, close. "Does he know what ship he'll be on?"

"He says he's stationed on the U.S.S. Arizona."

"Where's he going?"

"The Pacific. Hawaii first."

"Lucky devil."

Pauline said nothing, but Connor caught a flash in her eyes, and he guessed their talk wouldn't go well for him.

She danced with a lot of men in uniform, back from basic or on leave. Connor talked to some of them, too, all eager to go "kick Hitler's butt." They knew the official line, that they mobilized to protect U.S. borders, but they believed, not so secretly, that they'd be at war before long.

As they walked out after the last dance, a group of friends couldn't stop talking about what a beautiful couple they made together and how in step they were. They smiled and went on to the car, but Connor knew something was about to put them out of step. As he turned onto highway 74 through Ayr, Pauline tugged at his sleeve.

"Could you stop here, please?"

He pulled over beside Ed Egan's bar in Ayr, moon reflecting a bright pallor off the stucco side. The car cast a long, dark shadow. They sat looking at each other in silence. Pauline spoke first.

SEE WILLY SEE

"I watched you with all those guys back from boot camp. You seemed excited. You guys act like it'll be an adventure."

Connor tapped his fingers on the steering wheel. "I've had my adventure, Pauline, but I think we're gonna have to help out the Brits or they'll go under, and Hitler'll take over the world, including us."

"Let's hope not, but you act like they can't win the war without you. Your dad is on the draft board. He doesn't have to send you."

"No, but I won't put him in that position."

"What're you gonna do?"

"I've gotta enlist, Pauline. I don't think Pop will be able to keep me out of it for good and I prefer to go with guys I know. I really want to start school right now but if I get interrupted, then what?"

She turned to him, her voice scratchy, but firm. "Well, here's what I'm gonna do. I'm not waiting for you if you sign up. I won't wait around wondering if you're alive or dead. I've got brothers I have to worry about. I don't need another person I love over there not knowing if he's alive or dead—if I'll ever see him alive again."

Connor's voice stalled in his throat. Neither of them had said anything about love. Did he love her? *Christ on a crutch. What the hell am I supposed to do now?* His brain froze. Well hell. He'd had his mind made up. He'd already accepted that she might not wait. He wouldn't even think about what that meant. He plowed ahead.

"Pauline, I don't have a choice. My only choice is when to go. If I go now, maybe I'll be out before it gets bad."

SEE WILLY SEE

"Don't tell me you don't have a choice. If you're worried about your dad . . ." she took a deep breath, "You know they don't draft married men."

Connor stared at her. Thoughts stuttered in his brain. As he stared into her eyes, he felt his own bug out. He caught his breath.

"Aw Jeez, Pauline. That's not a good reason to get married."

"Lotsa couples are doing it."

"But that's for life."

"So is the Army," she spat.

"No, it's not. It's only until we beat Hitler."

"Look, you big knucklehead, you could get killed. That's for life. What about your plant breeding? You could go to college—no interruptions—become a famous plant breeder and have that family you talked about."

He'd taken in as much as he could absorb. He had not been ready for the ideas of love and marriage. Pauline had lunged ahead without him. Marriage, family, college—death—all piled up in his brain. He'd worried about when, not if, to go to war.

"I. Won't. Get. Killed."

"You could. I love you and I don't want you to die," she said, tears glistening in her eyes, "and you're gonna go. Because you can't settle down. You're already bored with farming. You'll never love it like I do."

Connor reached over to hold her, but she pushed him away, tears spilling.

"That's not true, Pauline. I love it here."

"Then it's me you don't love. You want to see the rest of the world. Just like Nora. That's why you understood her when the rest of us didn't."

"Nora and I were kids together."

"So were we."

"You're right. We were, but I want to see and do more. There's so much wonderful stuff out there that I know nothing about, and I think I can make a difference."

"You don't have to see it from behind a gun."

"Granted. I'd rather see it through a camera lens, but I think we've got to stop the Nazis. We've just got to."

"Take me home, Connor and know I won't wait."

Connor crept in the door that night more confused than ever. He lay in bed, staring at the ceiling for hours, blankets tucked up under his chin. He just couldn't get warm. He kept hearing Pauline's voice, her cry, echoed in his head.

"Then it's me you don't love!"

Was she right? If he loved her, would he know it? Would he be sure? Would he quit dithering and just marry her? Was he some kind of adventurer? Worse, was he the kind of man who wanted adventure even at the expense of hurting people, endangering his own life? What kind of man was he?

When the sun rose, he had no more answers than he'd had when he crawled into bed.

SEE WILLY SEE

November 23, 1940 – Willow Grove

Connor and Henry sat on three-legged stools next to a pile of corn augured into the middle of the double corn crib. As they shucked ears, ripping husks with hooks in their palms, strapped around their hands, Connor thought about what Pauline had said. After a half-hour filled only with the shuffling of brittle corn husks and the thump of ears dropping into the slatted crib, Henry spoke up.

"How'd it go with Pauline the other night?"

He shook his head, looking down at the husks piled between them. "Not good, Pop. Not good at all."

"She's not going to wait for you, is she?"

"No, but it's not just that. She really threw me a loop."

"What kind of loop?"

"She . . . when did you know you were in love with Mom?"

Henry chuckled. "Your mom and I haven't told you much about that, have we?"

Connor threw another ear into the bin. "Not that I remember."

"Your mother's a beautiful woman. I took to her the moment I saw her." Henry smiled. "Nineteen hundred and twelve, when my brothers and me come to Nebraska to find land."

Connor had heard that part of the story, but he'd never heard how his mom fit into it.

SEE WILLY SEE

"Where'd you met her, Pop?"

"Right there in Willow Grove in front of Murphy's Mercantile." He paused. "Didn't meet her then, just saw her."

"Before you even found the place?"

"Yup. We was plannin' to keep goin'."

"What happened?"

"Your mother happened. I liked that calm look in her eyes."

"You never told me that. So, you persuaded Uncle Billy and Uncle John to stay here because you saw Mom?"

"That's about the size of it. I saw her laughing and joking with her mom and one of her brothers, and I saw her helpin' when they loaded their stuff—really puttin' her back into it, not just standin' by and watchin'."

"You musta watched a long time."

"Nobody payin' attention to me. Just another drifter passin' through. Didn't take much to persuade Billy 'n John. We was all tired drivin' them mules all the way from Wheeling. We didn't have nothin' so we had to work for a while an' save up some money. We agreed Willow Grove was good as any place."

Connor thought about that. "You got lucky when you got that job at the Flaherty's."

Henry grinned. "Well, I'm Irish an' I do have some luck, but I don't mind helpin' it along. Flaherty's Irish too, you know."

"Wha'd you do?"

"I just asked around and got her name and where she lived. Found out along the way that people thought a lot of her. Then I asked about people lookin' for hired hands. Brothers an' me went out and looked for them jobs, but I made sure I tried the ones next door."

"An' you got Flaherty."

"Yup." Henry nodded his head one quick time, "got there before my brothers." He ripped another husk.

Connor grabbed an ear from the pile. "So—love at first sight?"

"Nah. A lot of like at first sight. I wanted to know more an' that's where I got lucky. The Flahertys and the O'Neills exchanged a lot of work, so I got to sit at her table when we worked over at her place. She always helped serve the meal an' it was hot in that kitchen, so she always had a wisp of that golden hair driftin' over her forehead."

Henry looked toward the house as though he could see his wife inside working.

"She always laughed and joked with us. Didn't matter we came in all sweaty an' filthy." He paused looking at the hills. "Some of the others caught on I was interested in her an' when we finished eating, the guy next to me would get up and stretch out on the floor for a little nap, leavin' a place for her to sit—an' sure enough she sat."

"And after a while you started calling on her in the evenings." Connor remembered his grandparents, pulling chairs into the yard and watching the sun set. He imagined his dad there. "The whole family."

"Yup. The whole family. An' by the end of the growing season I'd made up my mind. Took me a year to get a grub stake together, but we was promised. Henry looked into his son's eyes. "So, son, Pauline said you wouldn't go if you loved her?" He dropped the ear he'd been holding.

"How'd you know?"

"Seemed pretty clear—you askin' about me an' your mom."

"I guess so."

They each picked up some corn from the ground, husks rustling. The smell of dust and corn made Connor sneeze. He wiped his nose on his sleeve.

"Then she did this other thing, Pop," Connor said, holding an ear in his lap unshorn.

"What's that?"

He paused, barely breathing. "I guess you could say she proposed to me."

"Proposed to you? Proposed what?"

"Marriage, Pop. Said if we got married, I wouldn't have to go."

Henry's hands stopped with a husk half ripped. "That's a hell of a reason to get married."

"That's what I told her."

He husked the ear in his lap while his dad watched his face.

"She said I could go to college and have the family I want and not get interrupted by the war."

"What did you say?"

"Said I would still go now. That I know I can't get out of it, even if I want to."

"But you're still struggling with it. So do you love her?"

SEE WILLY SEE

"I just don't know. I've known her our whole lives, and I like her a lot. I really want to go to school, and I wouldn't be interrupted by the war—maybe I wouldn't. Trouble is, that family. I want a family, but I keep seeing myself trying to study with a bunch of kids running around. That's what would happen." He picked up another ear of corn and ripped the husk. "She cried, Pop." They worked in rhythm—rip-thump, rip-thump, the ears dropping onto the wooden floor of the crib.

"There's something else, Pop."

Henry pitched another clean ear into the corn crib. "What's that?"

"She said I'm restless and that I just want another adventure."

"Like being a hobo?"

"Yeah." Connor dropped an ear into the bin, ripped and dropped another one. "Am I the kind of man who would go someplace where I will have to kill people just to have an adventure?"

"I remember when you shot your first pheasant. You took that bird in your hands and gazed at those feathers as though they were the most beautiful thing you'd ever seen."

They kept working—alternating rip-thump, rip-thump. "You been chewing on this since Saturday?"

"Yeah."

"Did you come to any conclusions?"

"No, Pop. Maybe I love Pauline, but so far, I just can't imagine livin' with her."

"Because of that stubborn streak?"

"I'm pretty stubborn, too.

"What if you just shut up and let her think for a while—give yourself time to think? You two are smart. You can figure it out. Give a little, take a little."

"I don't know, Pop. Hard to imagine. I can imagine us goin' at it like those big horn rams with their horns locked together in my pictures."

"I remember those pictures."

"Magnificent beasts but, if they didn't get those horns loose, they were both goin' to die."

"Any pictures of a ram and ewe locking horns?"

Connor smiled. "I see where you're going. No, I never saw a ram and ewe lock horns."

"Why do ya suppose that is?"

"'Cause the ewes don't fight over the rams. It's the rams do all the fightin'?"

"There ya go. You and Pauline could try to lock horns, but it ain't goin' to happen cuz you're different. Different can be hard, but it's also more interesting."

"Interesting all right. She snapped at me the other day because I held her coat wrong."

"Her coat?"

"When I helped her on with it."

Henry smirked. "She always wanted to do everything for herself, even when she was a little girl. How about you let her do it?"

"Might work, Pop. This other thing's what's got me riled up the most, though—the fact that she thinks I could go someplace to kill people for an adventure. Now I'm questioning myself."

"Probably just said that to make you think."

"Well, I'm thinkin' all right. Am I that kind of man, Pop?" Henry stopped with an ear of corn in his lap.

"That's not the man I see, Connor, but that's not something I can know. You get bored easy, always have, but I don't see that kind of disregard for life—any life. I'm more worried about you getting into it to save a life."

"Nora?"

"Yeah. You can't do anything about that. They'll bring 'em home if the Germans take the rest of France."

Connor continued to think about Nora's situation, only with Pauline's words in his mind. Could she know him better than he knew himself? Was war an excuse for him to have an adventure.

When his mother called them in for dinner, he welcomed a break from his thoughts. Not a long break, it turned out.

That afternoon, he and Henry sat side by side next to the corn pile when Pauline's brother, Dylan, came walking up the hill. He squatted next to Connor, grabbed an ear, and began ripping husks with his bare hands.

"Heard you're gonna enlist," he said.

"Yeah."

"When ya goin'?" He tossed the ear into the crib.

"Dunno, Coupla weeks probably."

SEE WILLY SEE

"Think I'll go too."

"Your dad's gonna need you around here." Henry ripped off a husk and pitched the ear into the crib.

"Pop can't pay the taxes. He don't need no help. He needs less mouths to feed."

"Dylan, your father's a good farmer and he works hard. You all do. I can help him out."

"He told me you'd say that. Said he'd be grateful, but he's just tired. Got through them dust storms and no money for nothin'. Watched the gover'ment kill them fine big Duroc hogs. Broke his heart."

"Prices are goin' up now," Henry said, "He can buy more."

"His heart ain't in it anymore."

"How about you, Dylan? You could take it over. I've got a little cash. I'd like to help you."

"Tell the truth, I'm sick a' farmin.' Maybe I go in the Army, I can learn to do somethin' I can do when I get back."

"I'm gonna go talk to Charlie. I hate losing good neighbors like your family."

Henry gave his hook to Dylan and started walking down the hill. The two younger men worked and chatted.

Connor pitched an ear. "Pauline's not too happy with me."

Dylan chuckled. "She's livid. Stormed around the house all Sunday talking about us war mongers."

"You too?"

Dylan held a clean ear in his lap. "Hell yes. Says if we didn't all line up to fight there wouldn't be no fight."

"I suppose she's right—if we could get the rest of the world to quit."

"That's what I told her."

"You sure you want to go in the Army, Dylan? Pop's right. Prices are good now. You can make some money. Folks are gonna need to neighbor more than ever when we get into this. It's a good neighborhood. People help each other out."

"Yeah, I'm sure. Sick a bein' poor all the time and watchin' Mom and Pop work themselves to death." He ripped another husk and tossed the ear. "Sick of it."

"How about Rory and Ian? They want to farm?"

"Rory might want to take a stab at it, but what's the use? 'Nother ten years and the bottom'll fall out again and he'll get smacked down."

The two worked until Henry came trudging back up the hill.

"What's he think?" Connor asked.

His dad gave him a crooked smile. "I just bought a farm."

"You what? You can't even keep up with this one."

"I know. I told Charlie I'd lease it back to Rory and Ian until they finish high school."

"That might work."

"They can decide if they want to buy it back. If they don't, maybe you'll want to raise a family there when you get back." Henry paused and looked at Dylan. "Your folks will be able to buy a house in town, Dylan. They can stay where they are until spring. Aileen seems to have her heart set on moving though." Henry hesitated a moment. "This is if Claire thinks it's a good idea."

"You know she'll agree," Connor said.

Dylan's face creased with a broad smile. He reached out to shake his neighbor's hand. "Thank you, Henry. This means a lot."

Henry smiled. "I'm gonna miss neighboring with your pop."

"You've seen Rory scoop grain and Ian's getting so he can keep up, too. They'll be good neighbors." He turned to Connor. "Can I ride along when you sign up?"

December 1940 – Willow Grove, Nebraska

Connor stood next to the mailbox holding a letter from his Uncle Sam. Until that moment, his enlistment hadn't seemed quite real, even when he'd passed his physical. But on December 15, 1940, he got his orders to report to Omaha on February 3, 1941, for induction. He would go from there to basic training.

I guess I'm in the soup now. No way out.

Throughout the Christmas season, Connor saw his mother become increasingly agitated. As he packed his cardboard suitcase, she hovered at the bottom of the stairs. All that day, she hung close to her son. He felt her eyes on him almost constantly. When his father took him to the train station, Claire said goodbye at the house. As they started for the car, she stood by the door like a sentry.

She pulled him down and took his face in her hands. "I want you to live," she said. She held his glance as though she were holding him with the sheer force of her will. He knew that will—quiet, unassuming and rock solid. "And I want you to remember you're a human being." She stood, still, "and I want you to remember, as much as you can, that the man trying to kill you is a human being too." She held his gaze for another moment then dropped her hands to her sides. "I love you," she whispered.

Connor embraced her while the car engine rumbled and his dad waited. He felt the warmth of her body seeping into his as he continued to hold onto her and her comfort. "I love you too, Mom." He got in the car without looking back.

As Henry pulled out of the yard and turned onto the road into town, he glanced at his son. "Your mom sure gives you a lot to think about."

"Pop, if somebody's trying to kill me, I can't think about what a great guy he might be."

"Just," Henry paused for a long moment, "stay alive, Connor. Just stay alive. We'll deal with the rest of it when you get home."

They picked Dylan up at the bottom of the hill and rode the rest of the way to the railroad station in silence. Then the two boarded a Burlington Northern and Santa Fe passenger car with several other local boys.

Connor found a window seat and stared at the drab, brown countryside streaming past. After his years riding trains the hard way, he found an actual seat inside a passenger car downright luxurious. He wriggled his butt a little on the soft upholstery, smiling in satisfaction.

"Hey Conroy," someone shouted, "what's an old duffer like you doing in the Army?"

He looked around for the voice among a carful of youngsters less than a year out of high school and spotted his high school buddy's younger brother.

"They need people with some maturity to keep you young duffers in line."

"Ha!" yelled another recruit, "you're so old, you'll be down on your face on the obstacle course gasping for air."

"Oh really? And you think workin' in a soda fountain hardened you up?"

All the joshing and carrying on distracted him and his mother's words faded from his thoughts. He soon had plenty to think about anyway. In Omaha, the Army sent Dylan to basic in the south somewhere and Connor stepped onto a Union Pacific car headed west. A couple of days later he got off in California at Camp Roberts where he spent four months hauling full packs of gear over brown hills, and shooting every kind of gun he could imagine, including a .30 caliber semi-automatic M1 Garand rifle. It had a 15-round magazine, and he knew how to use every one of those rounds.

When he wasn't shooting or running or belly crawling in mud, he met some other victims of drill Sergeant Underwood's abuse. He and Earl Miner, another older Nebraska farm boy, buddied up and helped each other when they could.

SEE WILLY SEE

PART TWO: PANAMA CANAL ZONE

June 14, 1941 — Fort Clayton, Panama Canal Zone

By mid-June, Connor had become an infantryman. He stood on the deck of a ship headed for Panama. Rain fell so hard he couldn't tell where the sky ended, and the ocean began. He watched several fellow soldiers leaning over the rail and vomiting into the ocean.

Gagging at the sight and sound, he headed below to write a letter to Nora.

> Dear Sis,
>
> Remember in grade school how we used to fold up pieces of paper and cut snowflakes? That's what your letters look like. Since you can't get any real news out of France, I'll tell you about me. I'm on a boat, but instead of heading for Europe, where I hoped I could find a way to see you once in a while, I'm going south. I hear we're going to guard the Panama Canal, unless the Army thinks of something else for us to do.
>
> I'm not sure where we are, but I went up on deck to blow the stink off and just about drowned. Somebody told me this is the dry season, but I've never seen so much rain. Could have used some of it back home.
>
> You remember that first big dust storm? This is the direct opposite. The sun shines in the daytime except

for squalls, but at night the noise of rain pounding on the metal deck is deafening down below.

I hope we get off this tub soon. We're stacked three deep in hammocks, and we can barely get a breath of air. We're below water line, so there are no portholes. It stinks and it's noisy and you hardly take a step without stepping on somebody's gear. It'll be terrific to get some air, even if it's filled with water.

I guess they've got yellow fever and malaria there, so we got shots before we left Camp Roberts. No shots for malaria, of course, but don't worry about me. They gave us pills to take and I understand they're very effective.

Just remember to take care of yourself, Sis. Even though your area is not occupied by Germans, I worry about you all the time. DON'T TAKE ANY UNNECESSARY RISKS.

Connor

Later, sitting on the deck, leaning against the bulkhead, Connor thought about the dust storm he'd brought up in his letter. It had started one evening six years before, in February. His mom and pop had been off playing cards with his aunt and uncle—a Saturday night ritual; Nora'd been sewing a new dress; and he'd been reading Teddy Roosevelt's book about roping lions in Grand Canyon. When he went to the cellar to get apples the wind had begun to kick up a little dust. He heard it whistling around the corner of the house when he made popcorn. He and Nora were munching and reading when a gust sent a tumbleweed flapping against the window where it scratched and squealed before ripping off and lodging against the fence.

Connor paced from window to window, peering out at the dust swirling on the ground. He stopped to listen. "Damn!"

"What?"

"Hear that banging? We must not have got that granary door latched when we fed the hogs this afternoon."

"So go close it before it blows off," Nora, back at her sewing said, clipping a thread.

The wind gusted when he opened the door, blowing a thick cloud of dust into his face. "Ach," he yelled as he pushed outside, wrestling the door shut.

By the time he made it to the granary, the wind had risen to a gale that howled around buildings and tossed tree limbs in a frantic, clattering dance. Tumbleweeds scudded across the farmyard without tumbling at all. Pushing against the wind on his way back to the house, he could barely keep from getting pushed off his feet.

"Shut the door!" Nora yelled as he slammed back inside. Her fabric fluttered onto the floor. "What's goin' on out there?"

Connor chewed the dirt between his teeth. "The air's plumb full of dust. I could hardly breathe. I got a mouthful." He grabbed a dipper of water and spat into the wood-burning range, making it sizzle.

She looked at the pile of dirt that had come in with him and grabbed a broom and dustpan. "Help me sweep this up."

Connor held the dustpan while Nora swept, but just as they put it away, another gust shook the house and Nora started sneezing.

Connor checked the windows. "Look at this." He pointed at a pile of dirt on the sill. "It's sifting in around the windows."

SEE WILLY SEE

In a few moments, the air had filled with dust. Nora grabbed some scraps of the fabric, and they covered their mouths and noses. "I'll grab some sheets to cover the windows."

She got the sheets and Connor went to find tacks and a hammer. That helped. At least they could breathe. Dust piled up on the floor at the foot of each window.

The wind finally quit screaming at about midnight and their parents weren't home.

"I'm goin' to bed," Connor said.

"What about Mom and Pop?"

"Probably decided to stay at Edna and Carl's. Pop wouldn't have taken Mom out in that mess. Couldn't see to drive anyway."

The two took lanterns and headed upstairs. Connor got to his bedroom first. "Argh!" He stood staring at bedclothes turned black with good topsoil.

"What's wrong now?"

"Come take a look at this."

"Looks like somebody dumped a bushel basketful in the middle of your bed."

"Any clean sheets left?"

"We'll have to take these outside and shake 'em."

Connor bundled his sheets and carried them downstairs where he draped them over the clothesline and beat them with his hands. Dust rose in a cloud.

"That'll have to do."

"Mine too?"

He repeated the performance, and they went upstairs, made their beds, and climbed into them.

They were sweeping up dust piles when their parents arrived, coughing, at about ten in the morning.
"Where's our car?" Connor wondered as he watched Uncle Carl back out of the yard.

"Wouldn't start," Henry explained. "Carl's was in the garage, so he helped me tow ours into town to get the dust cleaned out of the motor." Henry sat and leaned on the table. "You been outside yet?"

"Nah."

Connor looked out the window while his dad described the countryside. "Looks like a dirt blizzard. Fencerows drifted, drifts around the house and buildings. We even had to go over drifts on the road. Not very big yet, at least."

"This ain't gonna stop, is it?"

Henry shrugged. "We get much more of this, and the cattle will just walk over the fences. If it don't stop, I don't know what we'll feed 'em."

It didn't stop. They planted a crop the following spring, but the wind covered it almost as soon as it broke ground. Connor got a job helping build the new library, but that didn't last long, so he'd gone on the road.

Earl interrupted his retrospection. "Hey Conroy, Whachu doin' just sittin' around here? We're about to land this wonderful vessel."

"Nothin' Earl. Just thinking."

"Let's go on deck and watch her pull into port."

Connor and Earl followed a string of men onto the deck where they watched the green shoreline approach.

"I thought there'd be more sandy beaches," Earl remarked.

A narrow strip of sand edged mounded hills covered in a wall of jungle. Connor had never seen anything so green, even at Tahoe. An intense blue sky crowned the trees with tall puffy clouds. That at least, reminded him of home. A slight breeze cooled his soggy fatigues and lifted a sodden lock of hair off his forehead. A few hours later, they watched seamen tie ropes to massive cleats on the dock while others dropped the gangplank.

"I guess this is about the end of our little ride," Connor said as he turned from the rail and went below to gather his 100 pounds of gear.

By the time they stepped off the gangplank they faced another rain squall.

"D'ja ever see so much damn rain?" asked Earl.

Connor flinched against the cold water streaming down his neck. "I ain't never seen so much green."

Water ran down their backs and off their noses. Their boots squished through standing water. Ten minutes later, before the companies formed up, though, the sky cleared to a high, vibrant blue and the sun raised steam off their fatigues.

Earl whispered out of the corner of his mouth as they stood at attention, waiting for orders. "My mom used to talk about stewin' in her own juice. Think we're gonna do a lot of stewin' 'round here."

SEE WILLY SEE

Once organized, the recruits boarded Panama's light rail trains and headed to the Pacific side of the isthmus.

"Just like the Army," Connor remarked, as they rattled across to Fort Clayton, "train us on the West Coast; put us on a train to the East Coast; put us on a boat 'n take us to Panama; and then put us on another train and take us to the West Coast."
He peered into the jungle, trying to spot the source of a deep howl like the hollow sound of wind moaning through a barely open window. Vegetation grew in a canopy over the rails, nearly touching the sides of the cars that rattled across the narrow strip of land connecting continents. A flock of parrots startled out of the trees as the train chugged higher into the spine of the isthmus.

Connor continued to stare. "Even the birds are green!"

Before they dispersed to their barracks at Fort Clayton, they listened to a talk about the challenges they'd face in Panama.

"Don't any of you guys go wandering off into the jungle until you get your orientation. There are all kinds of snakes around here. There are several kinds of pit vipers and some coral snakes and there are sea snakes and there's that cute little eyelash snake. They blend into the jungle, so you don't see 'em until you step on 'em. Stay in the barracks tonight or right around 'em. If you step out for a smoke look the hell where you step—they do sometimes wander in here at night.

"Some of you'll probably have some little pets before morning. We call 'em sand fleas. If you don't have any, you shouldn't feel left out; you'll get well acquainted with them in a day or two.
"Do not forget your Atabrine." He paused for a couple of beats and looked around at all the recruits. "I said do not forget your Atabrine. This place has mosquitoes about as big as eagles and there's malaria 'n fevers you never heard of. Make sure there are no openings in your mosquito nets when you settle down for the night.

"Your biggest challenge will be keeping your feet dry. You'll learn more about that tomorrow but be sure you hang up all your wet gear because it can mold before you even turn around. So that's it. Go get settled in, write your letters and fall out at bugle call in the morning—and welcome to Panama. You're gonna love it here."

"No doubt," Earl muttered.

"It won't be so bad," Connor said as the men wandered around waiting for their bunk assignments. "We'll sure see some stuff we never seen before."

"If we don't get bit or carried off by them mosquitoes."

"We'll be all right. Just gotta watch what we're doin'. Snakes'll do their best to get away whenever they can."

"How do you know that?"

"Spent a lot of time trying to get close enough to take pictures of wild critters—even snakes. Mostly I saw their backsides."

After dark, Connor listened to the jungle settling down, just as he'd listened to the Sierras five years earlier. The sounds of nocturnal wildlife reminded him of waking up at Tahoe.

The roar of another squall soon obscured every other sound until it stopped abruptly as it started. He finished his letter to Nora in the sudden silence, listening to the spaced bubbles of a whippoorwill's whoop . . . whoop . . . whoop, and a cacophony of frogs sawing away for a few moments—then stopping for three or four seconds to resume at full volume as if celebrating the break in the downpour.

>Dear Sis,
>
>This sure is a noisy place. When it's not raining like nothing I ever heard before, all the animals are screaming. There must be ten million frogs right

outside the camp, all hollering at once—parrots squawking and 'poorwills whoop, whoop, whooping and some kind of monkeys howling. They say it rains more than 120 inches a year here but, since we're up in the hills, it's cool and fairly dry. We only get it at night.

The only danger I have to worry about is stubbing my toe—well I guess there's a selection of poisonous snakes, but you just watch out for them. You're in a whole hell of a lot more danger than I am, so be careful. Please. If anything happens to you, the folks will kill me for getting you interested in the Foreign Service.

I've written Pauline several letters but haven't heard a single word from her. She said she wouldn't wait, but you'd think she could at least write a letter, wouldn't you? We have been friends for a long time. Anyway, I don't know much about this place yet. I'll keep you posted.

Connor

Connor scribbled off a note to his parents, similar in contents to the one he wrote to his sister, and then settled down to sleep, smiling.

This won't be so bad. I'll get to know something about jungles. Maybe I'll spend the war here. Maybe I'll get some great pictures like that Ansel Adams guy.

August 31, 1941 – Fort Clayton, Panama Canal Zone

At dawn, diffuse light filtered through the canopy a particle at a time, turning a little patch of sky faint, rosy, pink. Connor searched that sky, but saw faint little through the broken canopy, cut years before to build the fort. After the big skies at home, he felt a little claustrophobic. He'd already noticed that, although Panama had plenty of sun, the fort resembled Grand Canyon with just the sky directly above visible.

He didn't know if he'd ever adjust to the green. The air even smelled green—in a bouquet of damp soil. As he surveyed the jungle, a howler monkey cried—like a hollow wind blowing through a narrow cave. He heard an answer from afar. They broke the weighted silence, seeming to echo off the very air. A whole troop of Capuchin monkeys chattered in the trees at the edge of the fort, their white faces peering through dense leaves. Unlike howlers that stayed deep in the jungle, the Capuchins liked to hang around the fort, stealing any shiny thing they could grab.

The jungle seemed enormous in a completely different way from the big skies of the open plains. Never had he imagined that he could miss the wind, but he could use a little breeze. The air felt like a weight that pinned him to the earth. Sometimes during a rain—almost all the time—he thought he might drown.

When he stepped into the jungle during a rain squall, the roar became a quiet rustle of drops dripping from leaf to leaf, sliding down from a canopy of green shingles. Vines as thick as his arms festooned the trees, arcing to the ground amid blade-like buttress roots that supported gigantic shallow-rooted trees. Beneath his feet the ground was a loose amalgam of decaying material. As he ambled deeper, he heard little rustles and murmurs as well as howls and squawks far above his head.

For lack of anything better to do, he photographed everything that would stand still long enough. He'd sent home as many pictures as he thought he could get by the censors—prints instead of film. He figured the Army would want the enemy to know they guarded the Canal, just not things like troop strength, defense facilities, military activities and such. He sent close-ups of hermit crabs and iguanas in all stages of development from the little, bright green ones to the huge olive drab ones. He snapped all varieties of palm trees, some with coconuts, some with clusters of dates, and some with red trunks. He'd taken photos of them silhouetted on the seashore, when he could get to the seashore, and in the soft light of morning. None of his photos had any background to give away his location or anything about the canal or the fort.

He made friends with a green parrot that became attached to the scattered bits of food the men dropped. Connor spent hours, sitting in the shade of the barracks, watching the bird watching him.

Gradually he placed little treats closer and closer to where he sat. He watched the parrot, cocking its head to peer at him and waddling a step or two closer. It would stop to peer some more before lunging for the snack and flying off. It took him a month of off-duty hours to coax the bird to take peanuts from his hand.

He named it 'Peanuts' and before long it would squawk an answer and fly to his shoulder when he called it. It often perched on his shoulder during his forays into the rain forest.

Besides adjusting to his new surroundings, he tried to keep track of Europe. He'd barely moved into the barracks when the Germans invaded Russia. He guessed that would end their little non-aggression pact—not that it mattered much to the Poles.

The pact had surprised him in the first place, given Russia's and Germany's history of repeated wars. He recognized the futility of hoping the Russians would keep Hitler too busy to mess anymore with France.

He opened Nora's snowflake letters with care, as if written on fragile bits of ancient parchment. He grumbled when they contained no news and he tried to keep in touch by writing letters every couple of weeks. He told her about the parrot and about all the pictures he'd taken. He never knew what the censors took out of his letters after seeing his sister's missives out of France, but he wrote what he wanted and hoped for the best.

>
> Dear Sis,
>
> My pictures are a crap shoot. By the time I get them processed, I've forgotten what kind of conditions I had.
>
> I've made a pet of a green parrot. (Everything's green here.) I call him Peanuts. He eats out of my hand and accompanies me on my forest perambulations.
>
> I've taken pictures of the Kuna laborers they've hired to work in the camp here. They don't speak English, but they speak Spanish and I'd picked up a fair bit from working the fruit harvest in California, so I get along pretty well. They're beautiful people, Nora, with wide faces and high cheekbones—like the pictures we used to see of Geronimo and Sitting Bull. I'll try to send you some photos, but the Army's pretty touchy about anything that might give away our location—as if the Germans can't guess that we would be here to protect the canal.
>
> By the way, I've been in town a few times when I have a pass, I've heard some new music. I love the rhythms and it's fun watching those senoritas dance.
>
> I've learned some new steps we can try if we ever get back home.
>
> Connor

By the middle of August, Connor had the days counted until his enlistment ended, but then Congress extended enlisted men's tours to eighteen months. He counted up again. He worried his dad couldn't hang onto his cattle and the rented land for that long. He knew his absence had been tough on his parents. What news he heard, when he got news, made him wonder if they'd extend him again. He wished he could get to Europe and look out for Nora. Maybe help get the war over with.

Maybe the U.S. really won't get into it and I'll get out. He peered the barracks. *Fat chance.*

At the end of the month, off-duty, he hung around the barracks, waiting for someone to start up an interesting crap game. When he heard the company clerk yell for mail call, he hustled to HQ. He returned shortly with a much-anticipated letter from Nora. He opened the envelope and read, eyes bulging after the first line.

> Connor,
>
> I'm in love, I'm in love, I'm in love!!!

Connor paced the aisle. Holy shit!

> Here I am in the middle of this god-forsaken war and I've met this wonderful man. His name is Daniel. He's kind, quiet, and gentle like Pop. He's brave like you. He understands what I do, and we're interested in the same things.

"Oh shit," Connor muttered. "What does he understand? What interests? I suppose the guy's smuggling people out of France. Leave it to Nora. He's probably in the French Resistance."

"What'd you say, Conroy?"

Connor glanced at the man he hadn't seen lying on a bunk, reading. "Nothing. A letter from my sister. She's in France with the Foreign Service. Afraid she'll get herself shot."

"France huh? We're not in it yet. She should be safe."

SEE WILLY SEE

He grunted and went back to his letter.

> He waited for me after work one night and offered to take me to dinner. We sat in this café almost all night, talking. He's tall like you and dark. Says he loves to dance, although there's not much dancing now.
>
> He comes and finds me whenever he's in Vichy. We usually go to the cabarets and end up in my room. Don't tell Mom and Pop.
>
> My God, Connor, I hope we both survive this war! I don't know what our lives would be like, but I'd like to hope we'd spend them together.
>
> Nora

Connor flopped on his bunk, thinking about Nora and how vulnerable she was. He just knew she'd found someone who would put her in even more danger. He sat down to write immediately.

> Dear Sis,
>
> Wow! I'm so happy for you, but please, please be careful. I want you to live to see that future you're dreaming about. I guess I kind of envy you, too. I still haven't heard a word from Pauline. Guess I'm not going to. Makes me kind of blue, but I guess I'll live.
>
> For me now, it's the boredom. After six months, the novelty's pretty much worn off this place. I'm tired of being wet and I'm tired of looking at guys with yellow/green faces and taking that damned Atabrine every morning. I'm tired of the damned mosquitoes. (They carried Earl off the other day and nearly drained his blood.) But mostly, I'm sick to death of feeling useless. I know you're under a lot of pressure

and it's got to be frightening in the middle of occupied France, but at least you're busy.

Well, I guess I'm done. A soldier's got to reserve his right to bitch you know, but I'm even tired of that. It's raining (Surprise!) so I can barely hear myself think and I've got the watch. So, in a few hours, I'll go out and watch for Germans—and get waterlogged. Maybe Peanuts will keep me company.

Connor

Over the roar of rain, he noticed quiet music playing on Earl's wind-up phonograph.

"How about turning that thing up?"

Earl complied.

"All the way!"

"*In the Mood*," he muttered as he stood. "I'm in the mood for something—anything."

He strode outside, followed by seven or eight others. Always alert to a change in atmosphere, they'd noticed Connor's determined stride. He knew they hoped to see something interesting. Connor stood looking up into the downpour until water soaked his hair and his fatigues and began streaming off him in sheets.

Just like a damn turkey. Ain't got sense enough to come in out of the rain. Look up with water runnin' up your nose 'til you drown.

He started to jitterbug, splashing mud all over himself and the soldiers standing around watching. Another soldier joined him—grabbed his hand and started dancing as well. More barefoot men joined in a gyration that shook water out of their fatigues like dogs stepping out of a pond. When Connor's partner tripped on a foot poked out by one of the bystanders, he took Connor down with him. The other two tripped over Connor and plowed, laughing and sliding, into the lineup of clapping, stamping, whistling warriors, upending them like bowling pins.

The soldiers picked themselves up, one by one, grinning. They stood, spread-eagled and allowed the rain to wash mud off them and their clothing. When it stopped, they brought out camp stools lined them up in the shade and sat, waiting to dry, like a row of crows on a clothesline.

December 7, 1941 – Fort Clayton, Panama Canal Zone

At 1300 hours Connor lay on his bunk in his skivvies, sweating and reading a pocketbook from home. At 1321, sirens all over the base blasted him onto his feet. Before he could step into his pants and grab a shirt, he heard the distant buzz of interceptors followed by the roar of the bombers taking off from Howard Field. Certain of an imminent attack, he glanced around the barracks at a scattering of other off-duty soldiers scrambling into fatigues. He snatched gas mask and rifle, running to the parade ground, his partially buttoned shirt flapping loosely around him.

Men stampeded into the compound in rough formations. Within seconds, the loudspeaker whistled and screamed. Someone at the mike yelled out the news.

"The Japanese Navy has mounted a surprise attack on the U.S. Naval Base at Pearl Harbor." He paused. Connor could hear the man catching his breath. "That attack is still in progress. We have no damage or casualties estimates." He hesitated again. "We have no idea whether they're continuing on to Panama. They may already be approaching the isthmus." He scanned the parade grounds. "Your company COs will have orders for you in minutes, so stay in your formations." He looked them over again. "That's all."

In twenty minutes, captains and lieutenants, hair standing in tufts, boots unlaced, found their units and gave out staccato orders. By 1430 hours, Connor had climbed into a jeep, headed for a battle station at the mouth of the canal, gas mask hooked on his belt, sweat pouring from every pore. His mind ran on a creaky wagon wheel.

Damn. Last I heard Jack O'Neill was at Pearl Harbor. Hope he's okay. Sounds bad.

He spent the rest of the day and most of the night, walking the beach with a walkie talkie and binoculars, looking for subs or aircraft carriers. He listened for Japanese Zeros. Guard duty doubled immediately. Wake Island, Guam, and the Philippines had sustained attack. No one would know about the outcomes of those battles for days. The Army scrambled to augment fortifications. At night, off-duty soldiers fell onto their bunks, exhausted, without bothering to strip.

The dry season had begun but nighttime squalls covered any sound that might warn of approaching enemies. The men strained, in troubled sleep, to hear anything unusual. Fortunately, days remained mostly dry.

At night, Connor shot off notes to Nora and his parents. He didn't know how much of them would be blacked out or cut out by the censors, but he was too distracted and exhausted to try a code only his family would know.

Anybody who's been monitoring communications out of Panama will know it all anyhow. I won't mention anything about troop strength or air bases. None of that stuff.

    Dear Sis,

    Since the attack on Pearl Harbor—I'm sure you've
    heard about it—we have to carry our gas masks

everywhere. The Air Corps has been buzzing around non-stop and the artillery guys have plenty to do.

We've got officers running around here like a bunch of Mexican jumping beans and they've got us jumping too. I guess we'll be shipping out in a couple of days. I don't know where we're going, but I'll try to let you know where we land.

> Connor

He shook off his lethargy and moved with a newly sharpened sense of purpose.

Now we're in a two-front war with inadequate naval power. Pearl killed us. We need the canal to get everything from one ocean to the other.

Sometimes when he stalked the coastline, he stopped and stared out to sea. *Come on you sneaky little bastards. We're ready for you.* He wished he could feel ready. The twenty bases scattered around Panama could scramble pursuit planes with enough warning, but he'd seen those locks and dams. One Japanese bomber with a phalanx of Zeros to defend it could wipe out a lock or blow out a dam. Radar might spot 'em, but maybe not in time to scramble those old P26s and P36s. *Even the P40s lack range. If not, the Navy'll be running all the way around Cape Horn. Don't know if it's iced in during the winter.*

Earl, who always seemed to be up on the latest scuttlebutt, said that a Japanese fleet had steamed toward Panama, and that an aircraft carrier had been sunk near the mouth of the canal.

Not likely. We've had men out there every day. We'd have seen smoke and fire. We'd have heard explosions. Surely the interceptors would see a carrier. They fly twenty-four hours every day.

With the element of surprise gone, he thought Japanese attack posed less of a threat than sabotage by one, or a cadre, of

SEE WILLY SEE

Japanese, German, or Italian immigrants who lived in Latin America. Or maybe a merchant ship would blow up in the canal. He hoped the canal agents searched them.

Ordered to guard against sabotage, the soldiers watched any nationals of the Axis countries—fishermen, merchants, shop owners. People from those countries had scattered all over Central and South America. The regulars told him the Army had monitored them for a year or two anyway. Sometimes, the long timers said, they'd slipped into Colombia and Guatemala. After Pearl, the Army sent soldiers to capture any Japanese people they could find in Panama. Connor and Earl helped round up Japanese fishermen to be held prisoner indefinitely. Connor hated that duty—hanging around the beaches, waiting for the boats to come in, then arresting the men and dragging them, along with their crying wives and children, to temporary internment camps in the highlands. He'd heard they would send most of them back to Japan.

Really? Piss them off and send them back to Japan where they can map out all our airfields, all the locks and dams? Stupid idea.

At Christmas, he wrote to Nora, this time thinking about encoding his thoughts.

I can let her know we're getting more troops. Sure. She'll remember Jason and the Golden Fleece; sowing dragon's teeth to grow warriors. No numbers anywhere, though. That'll be cut.

> Dear Sis,
>
> Everything has changed with the Japanese attack. The entire isthmus vibrates with determination.
>
> Anger seems to sink into the soil and sprout like dragon's teeth. We're not preparing for war anymore. We're at war.

SEE WILLY SEE

I can't wait to get into combat, Sis, so I can kick some Jap ass. I heard some guys on the ships at Pearl Harbor burned up or drowned. I wonder if anyone's heard from Jack O'Neill.

Anyway, I want to give the Japs a taste of their own medicine. It's hard to sleep wondering where we'll end up and what kind of new country I'll see. I think of all the thousands of miles of ocean out there. It's just empty water, waiting to swallow us. It's kind of intimidating, looking out at the Pacific and knowing how far away everything is. And then I think about Uncle Harry and wonder how I'll take it.

Meanwhile, if I'm not standing in the rain with a rifle, I have a choice. I can drink all by myself or I can sit around camp and play cards or shoot craps. I can drink and smoke cigarettes. (I don't do that yet, although I might as well, since there's enough smoke around those games to suffocate a man.) I can go to the Kuna workers and maybe get some hemp to smoke. That stuff'll knock your socks off. I got the idea I was Jesus one night and tried to walk across the canal to prove it. Darn near drowned myself.

Connor

I don't guess anybody'll care about any of that. Maybe make the Japs think we're all lotus eaters. That's all I can think of anyway.

After Christmas, everything stalled. Nobody got orders to go anywhere; they just kept drilling, working their way into the jungle and setting up bivouacs. Lethargy set back in. Connor wrote a reassuring letter to his mom and pop.

Dear folks,

Well, there's no use worrying about me. I never heard of anyone dying by just wanting to get into action. I'm tired of itching. (The damned sand fleas just

about make a guy crazy.) We're doing a lot of
marching around and I might sprain an ankle or
something, though, so keep me in your thoughts. Oh,
and I might itch myself to death.

Connor

After the first of the year, Connor heard the Arizona National
Guard had reopened the old Camp Paraiso at the foot of the
mountains, pitching tents down next to the canal. Mainly
Indians—Pima, Maricopa, Navajo, Hopi, Tohono O'odham, men
from twenty-two tribes—and Mexicans, with a few cowboys
thrown in, the Arizonans already had a tough reputation. Some
of the regulars had loaded into jeeps to watch the newcomers set
up their tents, but Connor remained in the barracks. He lay on
his cot reading when Earl came in swearing.

"D'you see that one guy, Connor? He must be seven feet tall."

Connor chewed on a matchstick while he read his latest
paperback from home. "Ain't been down there."

"My God, what'd they send us?"

"More soldiers, I'd say. Maybe reinforcements for when they ship
us out."

"A bunch of Indians and Mexicans."

"So what, Earl. They're soldiers like you and me."

"Why ya wanta associate with them savages? First it's them
damn Kunas..."

Connor sat up, feet thudding on the floor. "Now look. You don't
know what the crap you're talking about. If you'd bother to get to
know folks, instead of spoutin' bullshit, you'd learn we're not all
that different."

SEE WILLY SEE

"You sayin' I'm like a blanket ass or a wetback?"

Connor scowled. "I'm sayin' you're a fuckin' narrow-minded ass and if we ever get into this war, I want one of them blanket asses or wetbacks watchin' my back, you dumb fuck."

"I ain't servin' with 'em."

"Looks to me like you'll do what you're told, just like the rest of us. And someday soon, you're gonna be glad to have them beside you. Think about the Northern Cheyenne—starving, sick with malaria, men, women, and children running from Oklahoma to Fort Rob before the Army could catch them—and that in a blizzard. They've had to survive on land I wouldn't give a dog. That's tough. That's the kind of men I want to fight with me."

Earl stomped off. "I'm real disappointed in you, Conroy."

Earl had raised Connor's curiosity and later he jumped in with a bunch of guys heading down to the new camp. Barely parked on the edge, he heard somebody snicker. "They oughta be pretty good at settin' up tents."

"Maybe they're gonna shoot Japs with bows and arrows."

The new troops kept working in silence until Col. Prugh Herndon strode over to the bivouac area. "Ten Hut!" Everyone snapped to attention.

"That'll be enough," he growled. "You regulars, get the hell back to Fort Clayton. I don't know what you're doing here anyway."

The critics shut up, broke up, and jumped back in the jeeps. Back on his bunk, Connor smiled into his book.

At 0330 hours the loudspeaker at Fort Clayton blasted reveille. While the regulars marched off on a fifteen-mile hike with full packs, the newcomers remained in their tents down at Camp Paraiso, dozing.

"Fuckin' Indians," Earl growled after about ten miles.

Connor grinned. "I hear them fuckin' Indians used to take twenty- five-mile hikes across the damn desert, with full packs and no water."

"Bullshit!"

Connor smiled and kept walking.

Hours later, when they returned from their little hike, Connor learned that he had orders to report to Herndon's office. After his regulation salute and greeting, Herndon put him at ease.

"You've been here six months, Conroy," said Herndon. "I've heard that you spend a lot of time in the jungle taking pictures."

"That's true, sir."

"I also understand you spend some time with the Kunas—and that you speak Spanish."

"Some, sir."

"We need men who know something about the jungle to train the new desert troops."

"Yes, sir."

"What do you know about the jungle?"

"Not a lot, sir—I avoid snakes."

"Have the Kunas told you anything about what to eat and what not to eat?"

"A little, sir."

"I'm promoting you to staff sergeant and attaching you to the 158th Infantry Regiment. That's the Arizona Guard unit that came in yesterday."
"Yes sir."

"Report to Captain Cochran, Second Battalion, Company G. I want you to tell him what you know about the snakes and whatever the Kunas have told you that might be useful to a soldier fighting in jungle territory."

"Permission to speak, sir?" Herndon inclined his head.

"Are we moving out soon, sir?"

"No, Conroy. Not until we've trained these men. I want to take the best jungle fighters in the world into the field against the Japs."

"Yes, sir."

"Dismissed."

Connor snapped a salute and left. Within an hour, he'd packed up, camera and all, and hopped in a jeep for the ride to the lowlands. Once off the paved road, the driver navigated a one-lane track closed by jungle on both sides and overhead.

At Camp Paraiso, Connor reported to Captain Cochran, a short, muscular man who had arrived in the Canal Zone with the Arizona Guard. A Spanish-speaker himself, he planned his own meetings with the Kunas and expected Connor to make introductions. All business, he consulted a clipboard and assigned Connor to Lieutenant David Carpenter's platoon. The lieutenant assigned him a tent and pointed in its general direction.

SEE WILLY SEE

When Connor located his new quarters, he found his first sergeant, Russell Jakes already in residence. Connor often towered over other men, but when Jakes stood, Connor had to look up. *That must be the guy Earl hemorrhaged about.*

Connor's counterpart, Staff Sergeant Stan Peters, and another first sergeant, Jesus Lopez, occupied the remaining two cots. Lopez interrupted his knife sharpening long enough for introductions before he returned to his work. Peters went back to the Infantry Field Manual he'd been studying, and Jakes lay back on his cot.

Connor dropped his duffle and flopped on his own cot. For the first time, he had time to think about his changed circumstances. *This is a fine kettle of fish. A promotion. Not just a little one either— corporal to staff sergeant. I think that's about double pay.* He raised his head and looked at the three other men. *But that makes me responsible for thirteen other guys. Done that before, but not when I could get them killed with a stupid mistake.* Pauline's accusation about seeking adventure flashed through his mind.

We won't fight on familiar ground. We'll take desert rats into the heart of darkness—like in Joseph Conrad's book. I'm having a hell of a time adjusting to the humidity and I've been here six months. It saps a man's strength, destroys his ambition, and leaves him gasping, sweat pouring from every pore. What'll happen to these newcomers when they have to hack their way through ropes of vines and brush on the jungle floor? Can they carry their rifles and field packs and stand upright at the end of the day? Hope Herndon's training lasts long enough for them to make the adjustment. Me too, for that matter.

He felt pleased and proud that Herndon had singled him out, but the more he thought about it, the more he hoped he could live up to the responsibility. *No Pauline. This is no damned adventure.*

SEE WILLY SEE

January 15, 1942 – Camp Paraiso, Panama Canal Zone

Pay day. It appeared to Connor that would involve plenty of alcohol, but then, it always did. He'd soon learn how the Indians handled booze. He began the afternoon in his tent with Peters writing letters. But first he wanted to quiz the more experienced man.

"Hey, Peters, how do these men handle alcohol?"

Peters chuckled. "It's likely to get a little weird."

"Weird how?"

"You'll just have to see for yourself. There's no pattern. No more than the regular Army." He paused for a moment. "Believe me, if they couldn't handle it and still soldier, they wouldn't be here. Herndon believes in marching, and he especially likes long marches the day after payday. If they couldn't stand it, they'd be gone. Don't worry about these men, Conroy. This unit has been around, on and off, since 1865. That patch they wear? Cuidado means danger. They live up to it."

Peters went back to his letter and so did Connor.

> Dear Nora
>
> About the first of the year, they sent us a National Guard unit from Arizona, all Indians and Mexicans— and a few cowboys. I got a big promotion . . .

Hell, that'll never get by the censors. He balled up the paper and stared at the wall, canvas puffing in and out in a little breeze. He started again as Peters folded his letter, stuffed it into an envelope and left the tent.

> Dear Sis,

SEE WILLY SEE

Things just keep getting curiouser and curiouser. First, I got moved and Peanuts didn't come along. I hope the guys take care of him. He's got himself pretty domesticated. I'm gonna miss having him on my shoulder trying to pilfer my snacks.

Second, I've now got a bunch of Riders of the Purple Sage types in my unit. They put me in charge of a squad. We're bivouacked next to a squad headed up by Stan Peters. We're kind of a Mutt and Jeff pair.

She'll get that. The whole family read Zane Grey in the winters. She saw Mutt and Jeff in the Sunday funnies. He considered what more he could say. I can describe individuals. That shouldn't get censored.

Peters is short, but he weighs a little more than me. He joined the Guard about three years ago and thought about joining the regular Army so he's a lot more go-by-the-book than me. He's part Navajo but mixed with two generations of white missionary teachers, his dad and his granddad. He's real quiet and reserved and efficient. Peters, our first sergeants, and I share a tent. He and First Sergeant Russell Jakes are my mentors when it comes to dealing with the Indians and I'm glad to have the help. Jesus Lopez, the other first sergeant, seems pretty tight-lipped. I'll have to earn his trust, maybe more than the others.

I don't know anything about these guys. One of the first things I think about is names. We grew up with cowboy-and-Indian movies and history classes that had Indians named things like Tonto, Squanto, Sacajawea and Pocahontas, but all the guys here have "regular" names.

Keep in mind that these are all first impressions. We've only been out in the jungle on maneuvers once but let me tell you about the two. Ben Hayes is my

> scout. He's one of the shorter men, maybe five-foot-four. He's strong as a mule. He's an athlete and I love watching his elegant way of moving through the jungle. I'm sure his size helps, but he barely disturbs a leaf and hardly makes a sound. When I try to imitate him, I feel like a cow. He really keeps to himself. Whenever we have to be anywhere near the regulars, the old-timers are malicious. Apparently, his size makes him a great target.
>
> Russell Jakes is my first sergeant. He's a few inches taller than I am and he's heavier. He seems able to adapt to almost anything and gets along with everybody in the unit. Maybe that's because of his quiet sense of humor. Like most of the guys, he's very self-contained. Like me, he spends off-duty time in the jungle. It's like he wants to learn everything he can about this new environment. I hope eventually, he will let me tag along. Maybe he'll notice stuff I don't. He can see a lot farther than I can and pays more attention. He'll probably save my life some time. That's if I can convince him, all of these guys really, to trust me enough to care. None of the Mexicans or Indians has any reason to trust or care about an ignorant white man like me.

Laughing and shouting outside interrupted his letter writing. He followed the noise to a group of soldiers crouched on the dark side of a tent playing poker. As he turned the corner, he nearly stumbled on George Green, Giles Cormac from Peters' squad, and a couple of other troops.

"Want in?" Green asked, thick-tongued and barely balancing on his heels.

"Nope. I'm goin' to wander around and see what's up."

He stood and watched for a few minutes, grinning at Cormac's beer-fueled humor—most of it about cattle and scat.

SEE WILLY SEE

Cormac saw him as fresh meat. "Hey Sarge, what do you get when you sit under a cow?"

"Hell, I don't know."

Cormac grinned wickedly as he threw in his hand. "A cow pat."

Connor groaned along with Green.

While Green shuffled, Cormac set off on another story. "Hey Sarge, did you hear about the rancher bringing a new bull onto the ranch?"

"Guess I didn't."

"The other bulls heard about it, and they weren't too happy. They wanted to keep all their cows, of course."

"Of course."

"Well, they made a pact. They were going to be real tough about it." He picked up his new cards and took a look.

"When the truck pulls up, though, the biggest bull they've ever seen steps off and the older bulls concede that they could give up a few cows—all except the newest, youngest bull. He's pawing the dirt, shaking his horns, and snorting."

Cormac bids and continues. "The old bull says, 'now son, don't be foolish. Let him have some of your cows.'" Cormac looked around. "'Hell,' says the young bull, 'he can have all my cows. I just want to make sure he knows I'm a bull.'" He glanced up at Connor. "You really oughta get in this game—contribute to the increase of my cattle herd."

Connor grinned and walked away. He could easily imagine Cormac regaling the crowd at any old county fair while he served barbecue beef with his beefy paws. He continued walking down the grid of tents.

Inhaling moist air heavy with the scent of green decay, he remembered cold nights in the mountains and the crisp smell of pine and spruce. He strode off in the direction of Charlie Company where he watched a circle of shirtless men dancing around an oil drum. The metallic thumping and moving shadows gave him an eerie feeling of dislocation.

This must be what it feels like to be Indian—on the outside looking in. Except I get to go back to what I know and control. He turned and went back to his tent thinking how much he'd like to understand and how presumptuous it would be to ask.

Next day, as everybody else sobered up, Connor got back to his letter. This time he focused on the men in the circle.

> I'm back, Sis. We all survived a long night. One of my guys, Ferro Gordon, grew up on the Gila River Reservation where he worked in a gas station. More importantly he's what you'd call a shaman. I don't get to see what he does, but some of my guys say they go to him when they're feeling bad—I don't know if that includes brown bottle flu. If it does, he's pretty busy today.
>
> Gordon has a squarish, dark copper face and long, slender fingers. He's really quick. He could be a card shark if he wanted. What impresses me about the man is his eyes—quiet, deep, and attentive. A glance can make you feel revealed down to the bone. Like everybody else around here, he drinks plenty on payday, but he's very quiet about it. If anybody goes down during our marathon marches, it will be Gordon. I could see him suffering this morning when we took our post-payday hike. This morning sweat streamed off his face. I noticed his boots dragging and he stumbled a few times. I thought he would go down, but he kept walking. I've never seen anybody

eat as much as Gordon, but Peters says he never gains a pound, and he's always sucking on his canteen.

Tayo Reese is one of my guys too. He has a big, bulbous nose, thick lips that always turn down, big meaty hands, a large belly, and a temper. He weighs about 225 pounds I'd guess, and he's a few inches shorter than me. His brown eyes turn black when he's mad and I hope I never have to tangle with him. He's Apache like another guy in my squad, Sterling Menardo.

Menardo's my height, but he outweighs me by fifty or sixty pounds. He's clean limbed and very broad across the shoulders and chest. He says the nasty scar on his forearm comes from fighting with the Indian agents when they took his children from him. Indian School. He doesn't like us white folks much, and I'll need to earn his trust. As it is, he salutes and stands at attention as a kind of sarcasm.

Connor lay back on his cot and listened to rain roaring through camp. He watched shadow rivers slide down the pitch of the canvas roof like shushing down a ski slope. The previous night had been rare. Clear skies, no rain, but the Panamanian sky sure made up for it as he wrote.

Enas Moore, our gunner's assistant, can shoot just as well as our machine-gunner, George Green. He works hard and I'm sure he'd be a corporal before long if he weren't Indian. As it is, I'm not sure what his chances are. The Army doesn't like to promote people who aren't lily white. Jakes and Lopez are exceptions, and the regulars are pissed about it. Back to Moore—his granddaddy was a missionary, but his mom is Pima/Maricopa. He's mad at his granddad for mixing up the races and his anger seems to make it hard for him to accept friendliness as anything but a trap.

SEE WILLY SEE

Last night I saw him smile for the first time. Mostly he scowls. He cleans his side-arm obsessively and it's not unusual to find him sitting on his bunk, muttering to himself as he works on his pistol. Do you remember Cousin Doug, how he had such bitty short legs and a long body? That's Moore.

Hey, it's time for me to go on guard duty.

Connor

He folded the letter and stuffed it into an envelope, figuring he'd take it to the PX the next day. Then he grabbed his rifle and headed into the downpour.

Walking to his guard-post, he thought about the men he'd described to his sister. He'd had only two weeks to get acquainted, but so far, he'd found them quiet and self-contained. Gaining their trust would require up-front honesty. He had a hunch they could spot the most minor evasion before he realized that he was being evasive. He also figured the time would come when their mutual trust would mean life or death. He planned to earn it—and hoped he could trust them.

April 5, 1941 – Camp Paraiso, Panama

The Arizona National Guard again became the 158th Infantry Regiment as it had during World War I. For the next ten months, they became a unit of guinea pigs. They tried out "jungle hammocks," complete with mosquito netting. They received jungle boots—lightweight, rubber-soled footwear with vents in the instep, and canvas uppers to provide ventilation and drainage of the inevitable water and sweat. They ate C rations specifically designed to provide 4,500 calories a day. The ration tins included raisins, dried apricots and milk, peanuts and dehydrated beef. Mostly they liked the innovations.

SEE WILLY SEE

They took 20-mile marches with varying loads in their packs and varying amounts of rations and water—to see how much punishment they could take before they collapsed.

Connor really couldn't call their movements marching. They floundered through rain forest dense with understory. The ferns made his mother's spreading Boston fern look anemic. These were tree ferns that grew taller than him, spreading like leaky umbrellas. Puddles filled the square foot here and there not overgrown with plants. In dim light, they skirted buttress roots and lianas draped from canopy to floor in gigantic loops. They slashed at flowering shrubs and small trees that resembled gigantic versions of their mothers' houseplants and tripped on debris hidden by the green profusion.

Their training took place in five phases. They learned to stay off any existing trails, to spread out, to avoid open areas, and suspicious vines that sometimes turned out to be snakes. In combat, they would be fighting in small units, so they tried moving around in platoons and squads. Since stream crossings made them especially vulnerable, they learned to cross and disappear into the undergrowth before regrouping. They filled their canteens, one by one, after crossing. They set up camp in the safest, though not the most pleasant, places—in swamp or dense jungle. Sometimes, the whole battalion turned out for Herndon's marches—fifteen to twenty-five miles with full field packs—slogging their way with machetes, hands raw and blistered, through dense jungle, wading chest-deep streams with rifles hefted under their chins. They'd march up and over the Continental Divide. At least the high country didn't swelter with heat and humidity and feel so claustrophobic.

Connor considered the men of the 158th a lot more interesting than the regulars. Over time, he learned that more interesting wasn't always a blessing, like when they gave the 158th responsibility for building outposts. He'd done plenty of manual labor on the farm and in the CCC. The 158th installed bunkers and gun defenses, and strung miles of barbed concertina wire, all while watching out for poisonous snakes and frogs. At Camp Pina, they carved an outpost with nothing but machetes and their bare hands, slipping and sliding in the constant rain.

Then, they got an assignment he considered nothing short of abuse. The Army decided it needed outposts in some of the most remote parts of the isthmus—places they couldn't reach by jeep or mule train. The 158th got the assignment at Camp Pacora to build a garrison, packing all the lumber and supplies through five miles of swamp. Mules hauled materiel as close as possible. Standing at the edge, Connor looked between trees across a fetid swamp. The water extended as far as he could see, interrupted by hummocks of vegetation. Jungle canopy muted light and vines hung into their pathway. In spots, the surface looked soft, as if fog were forming right on the water.

"It's wood. It floats," growled someone behind Connor.

"Can't build anything with sodden wood," said Peters.

"Be sodden in a week anyway."

Connor heard a hum of low grumbling that spread among the men shuffling around piles of supplies they'd soon carry on their shoulders.

Stoft came up to the forefront. "All right men, I don't care how you do it. We need to get that lumber through this swamp and keep it dry as you can. Peters and Conroy, your squads will take the lead. Open a way through this mess. The rest of the battalion will follow with the lumber. We should be able to transport everything before dark."

Connor looked back at his squad and started into the algae-covered muck, gradually sinking waist deep. Peters and their two squads followed, hacking vines and brush as they progressed, machetes occasionally catching a stray bit of sun that penetrated the canopy. As the hours passed, Connor heard only a low mumbling and an occasional shout, followed by a splash when someone stumbled.

Like a flock of geese, the men traded off lead positions, watching for snakes, severing vines and limbs, and hoping they weren't working in a circle. It took them all day, but they dropped the boards on dry land before the sun set. Days later, with the outpost completed, the soldiers returned to Camp Paraiso.

Lying on his cot listening to the endless roar of rain, Connor dreamed of dry climates. That week he'd hacked his way through God knows how many miles of wet vines and brush. It didn't matter whether it rained or not. Although water didn't pour on him by the barrelful, it dripped constantly. Between his sweat and water that brushed off vegetation, he'd been wet for a week, even when he got out of the swamp. He always managed to get dry at night and he made liberal use of the Army's drying powder. He'd written home during his first few weeks asking for socks and Claire had sent enough to outfit the entire squad. He'd eaten capybara meat and palm nuts, as well as those special C-rations. He'd waded streams and swamps, water squishing through vents in the arches of his boots. Sand fleas had fed mercilessly on his skin. He itched everywhere. He had one spot of what the medics called jungle rot behind his right ear. He'd tried the powder there, but the rot persisted.

Jakes, lying on the next cot emitted a low growl and kept his hands pinned under crossed arms.

"Sand fleas?"

"Grrrrrr."

"Don't scratch 'em."

Jakes turned his head and gave Connor a scowl.

Half dozing, Connor remembered his years on the road. After his last assignment, it didn't seem so bad—not like it had been for a lot of people he'd met on the road. The rain pounding on the tent and bare soil in the compound sounded a lot like a freight train bearing down at full speed.

Slipping into a deep, exhausted sleep, he dreamed of a drier time. After they kicked him out of the Civilian Conservation Corps, he'd been in the rail yards at Roseville, California, looking for a boxcar to jump in and head home when he'd spotted a hard shadow thrown by bright lights. A security guard. Hoboes called them bulls. Standing over six feet, Connor towered over a lot of men, but the bull appeared larger and much heavier. Connor didn't want to get close enough to take his measure.

He poked around in a cloud of coal smoke and fog, eyes watering in the fumes. The growl of several steam engines felt more like pressure than sound. The squeal of wheels on steel rails, and the thunder of cars slamming together one-by-one as they made up trains made him jumpy. He couldn't hear the bulls over the noise.

He clambered over the coupling just as an engine up the line roared to life and the couplers slammed tight in a rhythm of thundering metallic clanks. He leapt from between cars as they started moving and watched them go by, while the guard watched him in gaps opening between cars streaming past, gaining speed.

He needed to get away. He looked for an open door. When he spotted one, he started running. The engine whistled its deep-throated steam cry. The wheels already spun faster than he'd like. With his rucksack slung bandolier-style across his chest, he reached for the bottom rung of the ladder—and missed. He dug in and sprinted like he had in track. He'd almost reached the door when hands reached out for him. He grabbed them and they pulled him safely aboard.

He lay panting on the boxcar floor for a moment, then rolled over and looked at his rescuers as he got to his feet. "Thanks for givin' me a hand. The bulls've been chasing me all night. You can call me C. Willy C."

A tall, cadaverous-looking fellow reached out his right hand.

"You can call me Skinny."

"Pleased ta meet ya," said the other, a big youngish-looking man with a flaming red hair and a bushy beard. "Charlie."

A third man stepped out of the shadows. He looked pretty tough with cuts and bruises around his face and a missing tooth in the front.

"Let them damn bulls get the best of me," he explained. "People call me Shillelagh."

"Shillelagh?" Connor said, thinking for a moment. "Isn't that some kind of Irish beatin' stick?"

"Walkin' stick."

"Yeah. But it's stout and it works for other things."

"You Irish?"

"My pop is. I'm a mongrel."

"Might as well settle in," said Charlie. "Gonna be a long night."

"Yeah," said Skinny, settling himself cross-legged on the floor, "but at least no bulls for a while—unless they're crawlin' around on the train right now. They'll throw ya off at sixty miles an hour as soon as look at ya."

"Not if we throw 'em off first," said Shillelagh, glowering.

SEE WILLY SEE

Over a game of cards, the men talked about the rail yards, the hobo jungles, the best places to get a meal and the sights they'd seen.

"Hey! You wanna see somethin,' go up in Montana. It's a national park, Glacier National Park," Skinny said. "There's these glaciers—just huge sheets of ice look like they're flowin' down the mountain only real slow, like syrup."

"Or there's the Grand Tetons," said Shillelagh. "Those mountains just jump up out of the flats like somebody poked them out of a crack in the ground. There's no foothills."

Shillelagh stared at the boxcar wall in silence. "One of the businesses in our little town had picnics in the Grand Canyon," he murmured. "Take a mule train down. God it's beautiful down there—Colorado River rushing and curling over itself."

"I gotta see those things someday," Connor said.

The train whistled and slowed. The men stopped for a moment to listen to its rattle and clatter.

"Do you have anything better to do now?" Skinny asked when the train picked up speed again.

"Better'n what?"

"Goin' up to see the mountains. It's spring. You oughta head north and work your way south during the summer. You learned all that stuff in CCC. We get to Salt Lake City, you get off this train and head north. Look at all them things."

"Maybe I will. How 'bout you, Shillelagh?"

"Oh, I'm goin' home. Better or worse."

"I'm headin' home for a job, kid," said Skinny. "Things are pickin' up a little bit in Cleveland. They got that Roosevelt program now, I guess."

"How 'bout you, Charlie?"

"Maybe I will. I ain't seen none of them things neither."

As the train rattled on, the men murmured back and forth for a while. Connor noticed the two older men had drifted off to sleep. Maybe I will go north. Drop a note to the folks and spend the summer wandering around the mountains. Strange times. Just dropping everything and heading off into the boonies. No plans. Just keep movin.'

"Hey Charlie, you serious about goin' up North?"

"Aw. I don' know. I don't know nothing about building no shelters or catching little critters or startin' fires with sticks."

"Personally, I use matches," Connor said, grinning. "Seriously, though, I know how to do those things. I'll take care of you."

That night Connor had drifted off to the rhythmic rattle of the car, shaken by wheels jolting over joints tying rails together across a continent.

In Panama five years later, the roar remained constant, and in the middle of the night, Connor awoke to a drip falling directly on his forehead. In the darkened tent, he realized his roof needed waterproofing. He moved his cot slightly to the right and went back to sleep, wet again.

May 12, 1942 – Camp Paraiso, Panama

SEE WILLY SEE

Slow day—only regular guard duty. Jakes, Connor, Peters, and Lopez hung around inside their tent staying dry while rain roared outside. Connor no longer noticed the wet smell of mold or the feel of skin that never dried in the damp air. The rain only drew his attention when the tent sprang a leak. He didn't even realize anymore that, when he spoke, he shouted to be heard over the din of water pounding on canvas.

The compound remained empty except when they had to tramp to the mess tent—no point in running. Raining or not, they usually, but not always, slipped into their fatigues and boots and slopped through mud that splattered up their calves and soaked their pants. If they were lucky (April is the dry season) they walked in bright sunshine between neat rows of tightly pegged tents.

Connor lay on his cot reading a Jack London pocketbook. When he finished, he closed the book and laid it on his chest. After a few moments, he sat up, glancing around at his tent mates. Peters lay on his cot next to Connor in his regulation undershirt and shorts studying the Infantry Field Manual as usual. Connor wondered if the man intended to memorize its contents. The metallic swipe of blade against stone drew his attention to Lopez who sat with a whetstone in his lap, sharpening his favorite dagger. Heavy breathing attracted Connor's gaze to the other side of the tent where Jakes lay. Connor watched the chest rise and fall as the man chugged air in and out. He looked back at Peters.

"Peters, what did you do before you joined the Army?"

Peters turned black eyes on Connor, hesitating as if deciding whether to speak.

"I taught at an Indian school for a while," Peters said, ". . . until I saw what they were doing to those kids."

Jakes's rhythmic breathing silenced.

SEE WILLY SEE

"What do you mean?"

"Ask Jakes."

Jakes sat, feet thudding on the floor. "Nothin' to talk about." He looked away.

"I don't know about this stuff, Jakes," Connor said. "Is it still going on? What did they do to the kids?"

"My father hid me from the agents. I learned from my grandfather eleven summers. Then they found me."

"Who found you? What did they do?"

"Nothin' worth talking about."

"See what I mean?" Peters asked. "They treated those kids brutally. I wouldn't talk about it either."

Jakes stared at the far wall where they could hear rain spattering into a puddle.

Connor looked from one man to the other. "Brutal how?"

"They tried to erase the Indian in the kid." Peters stopped and looked at Jakes who remained silent.

Connor felt like he watched a tennis match with frozen players, looking back and forth between two men who stared at a canvas wall. He cleared his throat. "Erase the Indian? What does that mean?"

Peters shifted his stare to Jakes. "Should I tell him?"

Jakes shrugged.

Peters sighed. "They had a slogan. Kill the Indian—Save the man."

"What the hell does that mean?"

"For one thing, they weren't allowed to speak their own languages, even among themselves."

"How do you keep someone from speaking his own language?"

"You punish him. You beat him. You lock him up."

"They changed our names." Jakes stared at the wall. "Called us Billy or Johnny or Sam."

He glanced at Connor. "I'm no fuckin' Harry."

In the silence that followed, Connor wondered how the man got his "white" name, Russell Jakes, but decided not to ask.

"They separated brothers and sisters. They were never allowed to see each other or speak to each other. They cut off their hair and took away their Indian clothes."

No one spoke while Connor took it all in. Lopez's knife blade rasping across the stone made the only sound.

"Then why teach there?"

"I had no idea until I got there. My granddad was an Indian agent, married a Navajo woman an' broke her heart. I don't know. Maybe I thought I could make up for it."

"You white boys'll never make it right," Lopez snarled.

Peters glanced at him. "I can try."

Lopez tested his blade, shaving a bit of hair off his forearm. He went back to sweeping his knife.

"Grandpa lost the job. Bureau said he wasn't "stern enough," so he went back to Philly. To his credit, he took Grandma and the kids with him—there were two by then. But Grandma couldn't stand it—too many people, too much noise, no open spaces. He took her back to the reservation and they lived separate mostly. Grandpa and the kids—my dad and three others in the end—lived in Philly during the school year and they lived with Grandma on the reservation in the summers. I guess I thought I knew enough about Indians, being quarter-blood and spending a lot of time with Grandma and Grandpa and all."

"But you didn't?"

"I'd passed for white all my life except with my grandparents. Didn't realize how our system ate them alive. I thought I'd be helping them."

Jakes turned away from the wall.

"You ask too many questions, Conroy." He speared Connor with a look. "What did you do?"

"Yeah Conroy," Lopez prompted. "I'll bet you had a nice white-man life. Get drafted, did you?"

Connor ignored the remark and lay back on his cot, looking at the ceiling. He didn't know what he'd just heard, but he wanted to think about it later.

"Well, it could have been worse. Was a hobo for a while. Met a man in Montana once called himself the luckiest son-of-a-bitch in the world," he began. "I guess that describes me, too. Did a stint in the CCCs, 1935 to '37. When I ran out of time there, I hopped a freight."

Connor couldn't help himself—he just liked to talk. He described everything in exhaustive detail.

SEE WILLY SEE

"When first light started coming through the boxcar seams the second morning, I slid the door open and sat with my legs hanging out, watching miles of salt flats turning pink. I always tried to take time alone like that to suck up the clean morning air. I could sense dawn approaching, even in my sleep. Like a newborn before it defies its mama—full of wonder and possibilities—morning favors me.

"When the train approached Great Salt Lake, I yelled at the others. There were the onion domes of the old resort, dry and isolated from the lake that used to lick its pilings. No more pleasure palace. No more crowds.

"Charlie, Charlie Seamus Shank, eased down beside me. The guys had been telling me about all these great parks up north and I thought I'd go see them. I asked Charlie to go along. Charlie scratched his chest for a moment, looking at the floor. 'Hell, why not?' he said. 'I ain't got nothin' better to do. Guess we can starve there easy's here.

"We jumped out at Salt Lake City on a wild hair . . ."

The two men had said hurried goodbyes and tossed their rucksacks in the weeds by the tracks. Then they dropped themselves, tucking and rolling. Back on their feet, they waved, gathered up their belongings and started walking north with a cacophony of quacks and honks off to their left.

"I guess we're migrating too," said Charlie, stopping, hand over heart, breaking into song. "When Irish eyes are smilin,' sure 'tis like a morn' in spring."

Connor stood staring. "Yeah, I guess so."

"Guess what?"

"You said we're migrating too."

"Oh. Hey, Connor, I could use some breakfast. You got anything to eat in that pack?"

"Yeah. Guess I'm getting a little hungry."

Connor swung his rucksack to the ground and started digging around for food. He found an onion almost peeled from rolling around in the bag, a bag of macaroni nestled in a little cookpot, a can of ham, and a can of pork and beans.

 Charlie had a can of tomatoes and a bud of garlic in his own bag.

"Anything else?"

"I got some beans."

Connor pulled out the pot with his macaroni and a cup nestled in it. They laid all their ingredients on the blanket Connor had spread on the sand.

"Say, that's some outfit you got there," Charlie observed.

"Yeah, Aunt Emily donated this to me when I left to ride the rails home."

"It'll sure come in handy."
"Mmmhmm."

Charlie pulled a pack of matches from his pocket and lit the dry grass he'd bunched under his pyramid of sticks, while Connor dipped some water from the lake and poured it from his cup into the pot. He rigged forked sticks into a tripod to hold the pot over the fire.

 Charlie nodded at the tripod. "That something you learned from CCC?"

"Nah. Just seems sensible."

He looked around as they waited for the water to boil. "This sure is a noisy place."

"Yeah, we must be hitting the height of spring migration. Wish I could catch one of them fat mallards."

Connor dumped some macaroni into the boiling water and stirred with a handy stick. He added a little bit of onion and garlic he'd chopped up on a rough piece of driftwood and let it all boil. Charlie sliced the canned ham and laid the slices on a forked stick, which he held over the fire.

"This stuff is better hot," he remarked, watching it drip fat.

"Say, you got any more food?"

"Just them beans."

"I still got my last pay from CCC. They sent most of it home to the folks, but I got five bucks a month and, since I don't smoke, I kept 'most all of it. Let's see if we can find some place to get canned stuff before we hop a train goin' north."

Once they'd fed their faces, they doused the fire and scattered it. Connor rolled his bedroll and strapped it to his back, stowed his washed-out pot and cup, and slung his rucksack.

"Connor, you got too much shit to carry. Never seen no bum carry so much shit."

"Got used to carryin' a bunch of stuff in CCC. It ain't heavy and I get by okay."

They headed eastward. Since the lake blocked the west and the city blocked the south, they knew the railroad and highway had to follow the valley between lake and mountains. Connor wanted to stick close to the lake for a while, though. He wanted photos of the waterfowl.

SEE WILLY SEE

"Pitchers!" Charlie said. "How you gonna get pitchers?"

Connor patted his pack. "Oh, I'm kind of a camera bug. I've got my little Brownie in here."

"Jeez, Connor, don't that thing get heavy? How 'bout carryin' some food?"

"The camera and film don't weigh much."

"You carryin' a book and now you got a camera and some film. If you've got a Packard in there, you better trot it out because I'm not crazy about walking."

Connor grinned and kept walking. "Ya know," he said, "you're probably right, but it gives me somethin' to think about—show the folks back home where I been, find the best angle to show what it's like. Makes me feel like I'm doin' something that's worth something, not just stumblin' around."

Connor stopped and dropped his rucksack and bedroll in the sand. "You comin'?" He stripped off his shoes and socks and rolled up his pants.

"Naw, I'll watch."

Connor dug out his camera, dropped a couple of extra rolls of film in his pockets, crouched down, and began working his way toward the sound of ducks.

After crawling around on the marshy shoreline for a couple of hours, he made a wrong move. In an instant, the marsh erupted with pintails and mallards, teal and goldeneye squawking and flapping into the sky. A few white-fronted geese jetted into a bald, blue sky, gabbling their squeaky alarm. He spotted avocets among the crowd, along with a variety of other shorebirds—willets, sandpipers, and Godwits.

SEE WILLY SEE

He stood and walked back to where he'd left Charlie stretched out in the sun with an arm over his eyes. Connor stowed his camera and started stripping out of his pants.

"My God, you stink," Charlie grumbled, peeking from under his arm with one eye.

"Rotting vegetation."

"What's rotting?"

"It's the marsh. Gotta find some sandy beach where I can wash out my drawers."

"Ya gonna go around naked? 'Cause I don't want to see that."

Connor started rummaging around in his bag. "Nah, I got a change in here."

Charlie sat up to watch. "What ain't you got in there? You're like a traveling medicine show."

"Just stuff I need."

"Need, hell. You don't need no camera and film and books and what all else."

"Bread and roses, my friend. Bread and roses."

"What?"

"Ya gotta feed more than just the body, Charlie."

"Jesus! I'm travelin' with some kind of Socialist or somethin'." He shook his head.

Connor chuckled and slipped into fresh pants.

"So'd ya git any pitchers?"

SEE WILLY SEE

"Hope so, got close enough."

"Ya wanna git goin'?" Charlie asked, "I'm gittin' hungry."

"We just ate." Connor slung his knapsack.

"It's been a coupla hours."

Connor grinned. "We better get some food then."

They followed the lake until they found a road, which they followed to a neighborhood with a grocery store. They bought some canned goods. Connor splurged on a dozen eggs for eighteen cents and a pound of bacon for thirty-eight. He finished his purchases with a loaf of bread for eight cents. At check-out, Charlie just watched the cashier ring up Connor's purchases.

"Eggs!" he exploded as they left the store. "What in hell're you gonna do with a dozen eggs?"

Connor grinned. "Eat 'em."

"They'll be all broke! An' then they'll rot and you'll smell like . . ."

"A marsh?"

"Yeah."

Connor grinned, sat on the curb, fished around in his knapsack, and pulled out a metal ammunition box. He lined it with some socks and an undershirt, packed the eggs, and secured the lid as Charlie watched, open-mouthed.

"You got a damn kitchen stove in there—or a bathtub?"

"Nope. Just a buncha folks' leftovers. Uncle Earl got my little box and the duffle during the World War."

"They won't keep," Charlie said.

"Nope. You'll hafta help me eat 'em." Connor laid the bread on top of his load.

Charlie walked off shaking his head and heading for the gas station down the block.

Connor jumped up and followed him. "We ain't got no car, Charlie. What're you gonna do at a gas station?"

"Ask for information."

"What kind of information?"

Charlie answered Connor's question with a question. "How're you set for money?"

"I've got a few bucks."

"I'm broke. I heard some guys talkin' in that store there. Said there's work in a cannery over on the east side, over by the tracks."

"What're they cannin' this time of year?"

"Peas, I guess. Maybe we could get on there and get a few bucks before we head north."

"Good idea."

"People in gas stations know stuff. I want to know where that cannery is."

At the station, they met a young fellow who had a little time between pumping gas.

"Yeah," he said, "they're hiring over there. You go up north a little ways. The tracks run right next to the road. Cannery's next to the tracks—for shipping, ya know?" He stopped and looked them over. "There's a jungle along the tracks just east and north of the cannery."

They easily found the cannery and got jobs starting the next day. A little more walking brought them to the hobo's jungle. Once set up, Connor laid out his bedroll. With the little time before dark, he could write a letter to his folks. He'd post it on the way to work in the morning. He fished a Big Chief tablet out of his bag, located the pencil that had migrated to the bottom, and retrieved his pocket-knife from his pants. Before he started writing, he cut open a can of beans with his buck knife and sliced bread—a luxury he didn't have very often. He sliced some bologna from the ring he'd bought earlier and scooped some beans out of the can with his knife blade, spread them on a slice of bread, added some bologna, and topped the lot with another slice of bread.

"Here ya go, Charlie," he said, handing his knife to his friend.

"Have at it."

Then, with his sandwich in his left hand, he settled the tablet on his right knee and started writing.

"S'prised ya don't have a desk in there," Charlie mumbled around a mouthful of food.

Connor started writing. Nora would want to know about the waterfowl and the pictures he'd taken of the marsh and the mountains, so he started there. He told her about the swans, too. He took a bite of the sandwich and scribbled.

"Think I'll go see what ev'rbody else's up to," Charlie said when he'd eaten and cleaned up the fixin's.

"Okay," Connor said, looking up for a moment.

SEE WILLY SEE

As Charlie wandered off, Connor remembered that his mom always wanted to know about the plants. So, he wrote about the bushy plants that look a lot like sage. He would send his film home, of course. They'd have it developed when they could. His dad—Henry would probably tell him he should have gone off with Charlie to get acquainted, but he'd spend some time looking at Connor's pictures—especially the mountain shots and the scenic pictures of the marsh with the Great Salt Lake in the background. Henry'd be glad Connor got to do things he never got to do, growing up dirt poor in Ohio.

Connor took the last bite of his sandwich.

"Guess I'm dirt poor too," he reminded himself as he put his writing materials away and followed Charlie to one of the other campfires. But this ain't so bad.

By the time he finished talking, the rain had stopped, and he returned to reality. The other guys had all lain idly on their bunks while Connor talked, but Peters sat when he took a breath.

"So that's where you got the camera bug, huh?"

"Well, back in Tahoe. Those two years in the CCC were just great. Beautiful country. But yeah. I wanted the folks to see the great stuff I saw."

"And all the letters. You know most of us just scribble a note once in a while to let 'em know we're still alive."

Connor studied his boots lying on their sides on the floor. "Aw, I guess I have to write it all down—so I don't forget anything."

"Your memory's pretty damn good. You got people betting on it."

"Yeah, I know, but it's the detail, Stan. It's the soft rosy glow of the light coming over the jungle in the morning . . ."

Peters laughed. "Yeah, I get it. You're a poet, don't know it, feet show it—Longfellows. But it's about time for chow. It's not raining right this second, and I'm hungry."

Connor and his bunkmates arose from their various states of repose and tramped off to fill their bellies.

August 7, 1942 – Camp Paraiso, Panama

Connor hadn't heard anything from Nora in four months and he worried. Surely, she could have at least dropped a postcard—unless she were in real trouble. For lack of anything he could do for her, he started yet another letter.

> Dear Sis,
>
> Haven't heard anything from you in a while. I hope you're all right and staying out of trouble. Anything either of us writes will get chopped by a censor, but at least let me know you're okay.

Jakes found him in their tent.

"Hey, Conroy, what about Herndon's hammocks?" Connor laid his pencil down and looked up at Jakes.

"Have a seat," he said, gesturing toward Jakes' cot. "Tell me about the hammocks."

"Netting keeps mosquitoes out. Keeps us in."

"Yeah? What's wrong with that?"

"Zzzzzzip."

"Noisy zippers."

Jakes nodded. He made a two-handed stabbing motion. "Bayonet us before we get out."

"Not much of a choice between malaria and Japs, is it? How about the boots?"

"Good as anything we got."

"Foot rot?"

Jakes shrugged. "I don't have any better ideas."

"How's everybody gettin' along with those rations?"

"Peaches be nice. But we're not starvin'."

"I thought you guys were all about fry bread."

"That's about all you can make with white man rations. Peaches are better."

Connor studied the paper in front of him. He'd given up saying sorry. He sighed. "Okay. I guess we all weigh in at the end of the week. Then we can go back to the mess tent. I'll talk to Carpenter about the hammocks."

Jakes shrugged and left.

> The 158th is the guinea pig unit. They want to see how much a man can stand. None of my guys have passed out yet but they're suffering. I can see them struggling, pulling on their collars, trying to get air— that is, when I can lift my own head. Even when it's not raining a drop, we're soaked through within the

> first half-hour of march. The water we squish in our boots is our own sweat.

Connor looked at what he'd written. He guessed the censors would take the whole paragraph, but he shrugged and kept writing.

> These guys are hard. None of them will give an inch so the regulars have something else to gig them about. It's sheer will keeps us on our feet. I sure don't want to go down and humiliate myself.

Wilson wandered in, wearing only his government-issued undershorts.

"Christ Wilson, you got any flesh that's not tattooed?"

Wilson grinned. "Not much." He sat. "We're gettin' up a poker game. You in?"

"Nah, I lost all my shekels already."

"I could bankroll you 'til you win somethin'."

"I'll pass."

Wilson shrugged and headed out. "Suit yourself."

> A bunch of the boys are getting up a game of poker, Sis. Dan Wilson came in here recruiting suckers.
>
> Wilson's like a portable art gallery. We all call him Tats because every visible inch of skin's covered. For a boxer, his face is in pretty good condition, except for a jagged left eyebrow. As you might expect, he has heavily muscled shoulders, arms and chest, so he's our ammo carrier. Besides his pack, which is eighty or a hundred pounds, he carries bandoliers of ammo slung across his chest ready for action and a box in

his left hand. He's a real sight when he's loaded for bear.

Before the war, he was a contractor in Tucson. His wife has taken over the business. His foreman is 4F—can't see past his nose without glasses Tats says. He runs the jobs, and she does the books. Hope it works out for him. He says the draft is crippling his business.

Green stepped in, grinning. "Hey, we got us a bet going. I got a hundred bucks riding on the Yankees for the 1939 World Series. Eisler's betting on the Reds."

"Green, that's not a fair bet."

"Eisler shook on it."

Eisler's mop of white-blond hair preceded him through the tent flaps.

"Eisler . . ."

He shrugged, palms up.

"Who won?" Green demanded.

"You know who won. The Yankees won. Next time try for somethin' with a little challenge —maybe a point spread." He turned to Eisler. "Why would you bet on the Reds?"

"Aw, my dad's from Cincinnati."

"Jeez," Connor said as the two guys took off. He turned back to his letter.

Our machine-gunner, George Green, just dropped in here on a bet. See, the guys have figured out that I can remember all kinds of worthless shit, so they bet on it. Whatever I say, they pay off. Weird, huh?

Green is one of the cowboys. He's a little shorter than me and built kind of average. He was a bull rider and bronc buster before they sent him here. He's a towhead, and his hair is always bushy. He claims he's descended from a prospector and a prostitute. Says his daddy always wandered off looking for the Lost Dutchman mine. He's a knucklehead about betting on stuff, like who will see the first Jap, who will shoot the first tree kangaroo, how many gold medals the Americans won in the 1936 Olympics.

One of Tat's former employees came with Green. His name is Chet Eisler. He ran Wilson's framing crew. He has monstrous, hairy hands, blue eyes, and a shock of sun-bleached blond hair that stands out all over the place. It's like a halo. If he doesn't keep it covered up, he's a beacon when we're out in the jungle—that's what the guys call him—Beacon.

Green stuck his head back in the tent. "Mail call."

Connor dropped his pen and tablet on his cot and hustled out.

"You lucky dog. Two letters."

He grabbed his mail. One from Nora and one from the folks. He set the one from Nora aside and opened the one from his parents. A newspaper clipping fell out. He picked it up and spread it out.

"Damn!" he said and sat. "Damn."

He sat a moment, head bowed, then stretched out on his cot, head resting on his left arm. *Well, Connor Conroy, she told you. She said she wouldn't wait, and she sure didn't. Damn it, Pauline. You always were a stubborn woman. That's part of what I liked about you—and what worried me about you.* He reached for the engagement announcement on the floor and looked again. *I don't know this guy. He's not local. Probably a 4-F. I suppose,* all the 4-Fs and all the "essential laborers" will marry all the girls while we're wandering around over here with our thumbs up our asses, marching until we collapse and—maybe—fighting some Japs. I wish we could get this damned thing over.

"Hey Conroy."

"What?"

Green walked over and looked at Connor. "Whatsa matter'th you?"

"Aw, I got a letter from the folks with my girl's engagement announcement stuffed inside. Prob'ly some 4F SOB."

"That's tough."

"I shoulda known. She said she wouldn't wait. Hasn't written. Just told myself . . . Just thought she'd . . . Aw, I don't know what I thought." He sat up, swinging his feet to the floor with a thud. "Guess I'll live."

"Well, Cochran's got something else for you to think about. He wants all the noncoms in his tent. Now."

"Damn it. I ain't even read my letters."

Green raised his eyebrows. "I don't think Cochran gives a shit."

"Crap." Connor folded his letter, stuffed it back in the envelope, and headed for Cochran's tent.

Cochran stood at his map board, laying out the course for another march.

"At 0400 tomorrow, I want all squads front and center with full packs. I want the machine-gunners armed and a full load on every ammo carrier. Take no rations and no water. Any questions?"

"Tomorrow's payday," Connor reminded him.

"We're well aware of that, Conroy. Herndon wasn't too pleased with the ruckus after last payday, so he wants everybody too exhausted to go to town."

"But . . ."

"Dismissed."

A quick salute and the men departed.

Jakes walked out grumbling. "We'll just get drunk day after tomorrow."

"I know," said Connor.

"Humph," said Jakes. "I'm gonna get me a full bottle of Johnny Walker and a six-pack of Bud and curl up with it like a mama with her baby."

Back in his tent, Connor sank onto his cot and read the letter from his parents.

> Dear Son,
>
> The wheat brought in thirty bushels to the acre and the corn looks good. Steers and heifers are going for $11.75 a hundred weight, and we have a dozen weighing about 1200 lbs. Your Mom and I will take them to the sale barn Saturday. Your herd accounts for about half of that.
>
> Mom says to take care of yourself and keep your head down.
>
> Pop

Connor did some calculating in his head. That's almost $1700.

SEE WILLY SEE

Of course, Mom still worried about him—and Nora. Apparently, the Army had censored his location, so she didn't know he remained safe in Panama. Nora, on the other hand; he worried about her too.

As usual, Nora scribbled a quick note to let him know she was okay.

> Dear Connor,
>
> We hear some nasty rumors here about what the Nazis do with all the people they've rounded up with nothing but the clothes on their backs. They put them on trains—often in boxcars—and send them who knows where. I don't know what to believe. Sometimes I just like to think about home.
>
> I just told Daniel about the time Freckles got to snooping under the woodpile and found that nest of baby rabbits. Remember how we took them out of the dog's very mouth and hid them in the feed room? I look at the woods here and imagine all the baby rabbits hidden in them.
>
> Gotta go.
>
> Nora

Connor smiled as he pictured the old dog and the damp little rabbits he'd teased out of her mouth from time to time. He'd accompanied Nora on her many rescue missions, saving helpless little creatures—a baby bird fallen from its nest, a bunch of naked field mice, a nest of bunnies whose mother got caught in the mower—he never knew what would come next. He remembered looking over the hill at the greening prairie and the lattice work of spring willows by the creek and hoping Nora's rabbits would make it.

Then he realized his sister was talking to him in code.

"Jesus!" He exploded, scrubbing his hands through his already-rumpled hair. "Why can't she just do her job?"

Standing alone in the tent, overcome with pride in his little sister, he tried to swallow his terror for her. She remained indeed the same person as the little girl who rescued baby rabbits right out of the jaws of the confused dog, bandaged up their wounds, and cried when they died or, when they survived and she could release them, watched them hop off, laughing and clapping her hands. In France, her rabbits were people the Nazis wanted for whatever awful reason. He guessed she'd adopted Daniel as her new sidekick, and he hoped the Frenchman he'd never met wasn't some knucklehead who would get her killed. He didn't have it in him to be philosophical about how—if she and Daniel got caught—they'd die doing what they were meant to do.

November 24, 1942 – Panama City, Panama

Connor knew Cochran had to issue passes eventually or he'd have had a mutiny, so he tried to be patient. When he and Peters got theirs, they headed directly to the bars in Panama City along with most of their squad members. The two staff sergeants tried to stay close to keep their men out of trouble because they always seemed to end up in the guardhouse at Fort Clayton. Connor knew the drill, but it never stopped pissing him off. Any time the Arizonans had to be around regular Army, the regulars engaged in covert harassment they thought they could get away with—a foot stuck out to trip someone, an accidental shove, or an elbow to the ribs. The two noncoms knew their men never started it.

The platoon stayed together. They had at least some safety in numbers against the regulars. The career men resented recruits like Connor and Jakes getting rank when they were in line for it. Connor had noticed scowls and grumbling from the career men as soon as he got his stripes. But it wasn't only that. Many career men hated serving in the same country with the mixed-race unit. They had to be careful on base—Herndon wouldn't stand for their shenanigans. Off-base, though, the Arizonans were on their own.

They ducked into a rickety bar with ten or eleven tables and a few waitresses. They barely got seated and ordered drinks before a couple of regulars, started taunting them.

"Hey you blanket asses. Where are your feathers?"

"They shouldn't let you into a civilized place like this."

One sauntered over to Connor's table and flicked a couple of newly arrived drinks on the floor with a crash and a tinkle of glass.

"Shoulda got my Daniels and Bud and hung out in my tent," Jakes muttered while the rest of the platoon kept their heads down and their mouths shut.

"They shouldn't serve you blanket asses and wetbacks, you just get inta fights."

Connor stood. "You need to replace these drinks."

"Sez who?"
"Sez me." Connor took a step closer.

Like a snake striking, without windup or warning, the soldier punched Connor in the face. Startled, eyes burning with rage, Connor stood dumb for a second.

Jakes stood, toppling his chair. "Damn." He sent the soldier sprawling with a backhand.

Before Connor or Peters could react, the bar erupted with men jumping to their feet toppling chairs and tables. Drinks spilled everywhere, making the floor a river of slop. Men who went down dry returned to the fray saturated in beer and blood. Connor noticed the sharp smell of spilled beer and spilled blood. He glanced around realizing he and his men had been set up. They'd stepped into a nearly empty bar, but regulars seemed to come walking through the walls. Outnumbered nearly three to one, the two squads formed into a rough circle, back-to-back like they'd done this before, and tore into their enemies. Connor looked over his shoulder at Peters who'd been trying to shove his guys out the door. Instead, his counterpart ended up in the circle duking out with the rest of the platoon.

Connor barely heard a jeep motor over the din. In moments, MPs came storming through broken doors. They waded in, swinging their nightsticks, as their immaculate puttees and crisp white MPs on their black armbands became smeared with sludge.

By the time the last weary member of the platoon rose to throw one last punch, the men looked like they had been through a prairie cyclone with torn shirts, bloody hands and faces, even missing boots. Connor looked around for the regulars. Quite a number lay on the floor. He'd left a lot of blood there himself, so had the rest of his men. He touched his throbbing nose and straightened up, throwing his shoulders back. He winced. Probably re-broke those ribs he'd broken in football. He shook off the hand on his collar. The second grab proved stronger.

"You're not going anywhere, soldier," snarled an MP. "So whadaya White boys doin' with them fucking Indians?" he growled, hauling Connor and Green off, none too gently.

Neither spoke. "I said . . ."

"I heard what you said." Connor twisted so he could look into the other man's eyes. "Them fuckin' Indians are my friends."

The MP smirked. "How 'bout you, squaw man?" He looked at Green.

"Least they know how to fight," Green looked pointedly at the regulars still lying on the floor.

Wilson, in the process of allowing himself to be manhandled by another MP volunteered his own comment with a grin. "Look what they did to your guys."

Mr. MP turned a deep shade of reddish purple and Connor watched him sizing up Wilson. He had to admit his ammo carrier looked invincible. Mr. MP wound up and took a poke at Connor instead. He ducked before the blow connected, leaving the man to scramble for balance.

"I'll get you busted so low the snakes crawl over you."

"That's okay," Connor said, "Maybe you can get me on KP. I really like KP. I like peeling spuds. It's soothing."

"I'll have you cleanin' latrines."

Connor grinned as much as his battered face allowed. "Kinda like cleanin' horse stalls, ain't it? Consider the warm, sweet smell of shit."

"Fuckin' Indian lovers."

"Yup, that's us. Remember us. We're the Bushmasters."

After a couple of days lying about the guardhouse looking at bare walls and sleeping on hard bunks, the men had sobered up. Boredom started a conversation—nothing else to do. "You ever been in jail before?" Connor asked.

Jakes cocked an eye at him. "Often."

"Barroom brawls?"

"Nah. Walking around bein' Indian."

Connor sat up. "What do you mean?"

Jakes looked at Peters and the two other white men.

"I'd be walkin' along route 160 into Tuba City and some cop'd need his grass mowed or a fence built. He's arrest me for trespassing or some damn thing—to get his work done."

"They can't do that."

"They can. I was properly grateful, though. They coulda shot me and left me for the crows."

"He's not lyin'," Peters said, "not a damn thing you can do about it."

"Say Conroy. You got purtier stories to tell," Green interrupted. "What'd you do after cannin' them peas?"

Connor looked at Jakes, who shrugged at him. He hesitated a long moment, studying Jakes' face. It betrayed nothing. He turned to Green. "Charlie an' me hopped another freight north out of Salt Lake. Rode it all the way to Canada almost. In a couple of days, we were in Glacier National Park. We had a little money in our pockets and knapsacks full of food."

"An' stuff," Wilson contributed, "clear out in the middle of nowhere."

"Best place to be," Jakes grumbled.

"Yeah. I taught Charlie to make a shelter. Gettin' late by then, so we crawled in and curled up for the night."

Connor lay back with his hands behind his head, looking at the ceiling.

"Next morning, I grabbed the Brownie. While Charlie laid a fire, made coffee and heated up some beans, I wandered around looking for camera angles—already havin' a good time."

Fed and packed up, the pair walked deeper into the park, hiking into rougher, higher country. In a little copse of cottonwoods, Connor paused to wander around stumps and dead logs, picking up mushrooms, explaining when Charlie asked, that the morels would make a good side dish.

"If we can find some bird's eggs, we can fry 'em in batter."

Occasionally, he picked leaves from a weed or two—a dandelion here, a young lambs quarters there or some watercress from the stream—and poked them in his bag, explaining to Charlie that they'd have a salad to go with their mushrooms. In a sandy area near the little stream they'd been following, Connor noticed a killdeer playing broken wing, just as Charlie broke out in song again.

With his hand over his heart, he set off in a high tenor. "Sure, the Hudson looked just like the Shannon . . ."

Connor swept his hand back against Charlie's chest. "Shshshsh."

"What?"

"Shshshsh!" Connor crouched and gestured for Charlie to do the same.

"See that little bird over there?" he whispered. "She has a nest close by somewhere."

"So?"

"Eggs, Charlie, eggs."

SEE WILLY SEE

Connor scanned the sandy area where he'd first spotted the killdeer. He walked a slow grid, careful not to step on what he sought. When he finally found the nest, he carefully stole two of the five eggs and nestled them among the greens.

"This won't be enough to batter those mushrooms, but it's a mouthful of protein for each of us."

"Where'd you learn what to eat out here?"

"Oh, my Pop grew up in the Appalachians, pretty much living off the land and mom's folks—I guess you'd call 'em pioneers. They kept moving ahead of the frontiers. So, they knew this stuff."

"And they taught you."

"Not so much taught me. I just followed 'em around . . . watched what they did. Sometimes mom'd show me something and say, 'Now that's poison, Connor. You leave that alone.' I used to sit and watch the critters I saw on the farm—figurin' out what they were doin'."

They walked in silence along a stream of snowmelt coming off the glaciers. Charlie kept peering into the water. Finally, he took off his hat. "Be nice to have some fish with those mushrooms and eggs."

"Would, wouldn't it?"

Charlie stopped and unwound his string hatband. "Let's see if there's some trout in this river."

"What're you gonna use for bait?"

"I know some things, too," Charlie said, reaching into a pocket and pulling out a cardboard with a couple of flies attached. "This ain't fly fishing, but my brother Robbie, tied some flies for me and my brothers when we left Pittsburgh."

SEE WILLY SEE

He gave Connor a sorrowful look. "Wonder where they're all at now."

He went back to rigging his line on a piece of willow and threw a fly into the water. Almost instantly, the stream bubbled up and a sleek form streaked away with the fly. Charlie waited a few seconds, then jerked the line and brought up a glittering cutthroat trout, flopping on the bank. In about fifteen minutes, Charlie had a couple of little trout to add to their evening meal.

"Maybe we can catch some more tomorrow."

Sitting around the fire that night, they listened to the crackle of fire and moved now and then when a light breeze blew the smoke in a new direction. Connor had cultivated silence as a youngster on the farm, sitting in a tree observing a nest, or on the ground watching a burrow, but Charlie seldom lapsed into silence.

"Ya know," he said finally, "them sons-a-bitches closed the mill between shifts like—the night shift headed home and before we could get in the gate, they slammed it shut." He stared into the fire.

Connor waited to see if he had more to say.

Charlie shook his head, a slow back and forth movement. "I was so mad." He looked at Connor. "Me dad died in them mills." He studied the fire for another moment. "Then all four of us brothers was workin' there." He lapsed into a thoughtful silence. "Then boom! All four of us was out of work in one day. No money. No nothin'."

Charlie peeled a stick, throwing the green bark onto the fire. "I got to drinkin' and fightin.' Then me friends quit buyin' drinks an' I'd fight 'em over that."

Connor poked at the fire and added a couple more sticks. "Don't s'pose that made you feel any better."

"Spent the days lookin' for work—anything to keep food on the table—and the nights drinkin' and fightin'."

"How'd ya get by?"

"Christ, I don't know. Me younger brothers and me, we hung around a while, then we all took to the road."

"Think they're all right?"

"Hell if I know. Hope so, but I got a bad feelin.' How about you?"

"Aw, folks are all right. Pop grew up scratchin' out a living. He don't owe nobody an' gran'pa owns the farm. Got a good well an' Mom can grow food—bucket water to the garden, eat lotsa beans. . . at least they'll grow. If they can scare up enough to pay the taxes—that's the problem, folks losin' their land to taxes.

"Mom's got chickens an' there's plenty of grasshoppers especially in a drought. Ain't nothin' else. Anyway, she sells eggs an' they were managin' to feed a couple of milk cows, so there's cream an' butter to sell." He gave the fire another stir. "They'll be all right—I hope. Worried a little 'bout Mom. Them dusters. She had a bad cough when I left."

"Whadaya think you'll do, Connor, if it ever rains again an' we can get jobs? S'pose you'll go back to the farm?"

Connor leaned back on his elbows, gazing into the sky. "Just look at all them stars, Charlie. D'jou ever see so many stars?"

Charlie stared into the black sky with its thousands of light chips strewn from the black silhouettes of mountains on one side to the mountains on the other. "Not in Pittsburgh."

Connor's eyes got dreamy as he stared at a little sliver of moon. "I thought I'd go to college and be a horticulturist and learn to make new plants. Now I guess . . . I always thought I'd have a family." He got up and moved to the other side of the fire. "My mom and pop. They're just so . . ." He poked at the fire again, moving coals and adding fuel.

"So what?"

"Hell, I don't know. Agreeable. I mean they never fight or even exchange a cross word. They're just so good together."

"All lovey dovey?"

"Not like that. Not at all like that. They don't go around kissin' and huggin.' But sometimes there's just a touch or you see 'em exchange a glance an' it's so full of . . ."

"What?"

"I don't know—tenderness maybe. Gives me the shivers." He stared into the flames. "I want that."

After a few more moments' star gazing, Connor decided to turn in, standing and dusting off his pants. "Let's get some shut-eye." Charlie got up and scattered the fire, scooping sand over it, then the two stowed their belongings and crowded into their shelter.

Connor glanced around their cell to see if the others were bored yet.

"Not too bad a way to be broke and jobless," Wilson said.

"I got pictures of some of the most beautiful country in the world— an' we had a few adventures. That's what my used-to-be girlfriend woulda called them."

"We were climbing up, following a little stream and I spotted a big rock in the middle. I jumped on it. I slipped around for a few seconds, then steadied myself, an' took a picture right up the middle of that glacier. Charlie had a conniption.

SEE WILLY SEE

"'Are you crazy?' he said. 'You coulda broke your leg with that stunt 'n I don't want to cart you back outa here.' We had a lot of discussions about my risky behavior.

"By the end of May, we'd wandered the park for a month. I taught Charlie how to make a string trap, so we trapped and roasted a rabbit here and a pine squirrel there. Sometimes we ate trout, but when we failed to catch anything, we ate canned meat or beans.

We left the park with most of our provisions in our bellies. We wandered into Hungry Horse late one evening—knocked on a farmhouse at the edge of town. An old man stuck his head out the door.

"I asked if we could sleep the barn and if he had any chores we could do in exchange for meal or two."

Connor closed his eyes and pictured the little house and the old couple who put them up for a while.

"Well, it don't rain here much," the old guy said, "but I'd be obliged if you healthy young fellas would nail them shingles up on that roof." He pointed at some blocks of shingles stacked on the porch. "Ma here'll get you some grub and you surely can sleep in the barn."

They stayed a couple of days, crawling around, shirtless, on the roof yanking off old shingles and replacing them with new. As they sat around the table after supper the last night, the old man leaned back in his chair while his wife cleared the dishes. "I sold my ranch just before everything went bellyup," he said. "Getting' too old to run it an' all the kids wandered off. Anyway, I guess I'm the luckiest son-of-a-bitch in the country."

Connor grinned. "How's that?"

SEE WILLY SEE

"Well, I bought n' paid for this place'n I took the rest of the ranch money in cash. Don't rightly know why. I was a'goin' to put it in the bank, but I never got around to it . . . you know lotsa little things needed fixin'."

"And the banks closed. And you still had your money."

"Yup. Wan't worth much, but we don't need much. I'd already bought them shingles, but nobody knows how long this'll last so I didn't want to spend any more'n I had to. Really appreciate you boys nailin' them up there."

After Hungry Horse, the pair worked their way down to Yellowstone. They wandered and grazed there. Connor got his pictures, and they spent a couple of nights bedded down next to the mud pots.

One morning in mid-July, picking berries at the edge of a wooded area, Charlie heard it first.

"Huff, huff." It sounded like some big animal's heavy breathing or snuffling.

Charlie shot nervous glances over his shoulder. "She's right close," he said.

"Sure is."

"Shshshsh, she'll hear you."

"Don't want to surprise her."

"Oh, right." Charlie relaxed a little bit, still watching for movement in the direction of the sound. "I think that's a bear, Connor."

"I expect it is."

"Don't you think we oughta get out of here?"

SEE WILLY SEE

"She already knows we're here and we can't outrun her."

The baby's squall made both men's hair stand on end. The sow—they assumed it was the mama—huffed off to their left, the baby cried off to their right—and they were right in the middle. They started to back away, but here she came, fire in her eyes, rumbling out of the bushes. Connor, scrambling backwards, tripped and fell on his back. Charlie turned to run, then stopped and spun back around to face the bear, standing beside his helpless friend.

"Hey you! Get out of here," he yelled, standing on tiptoe and waving his arms.

The sow reared up on her back legs, roaring, her lips flapping and spit flying. Connor started shooting off exposure after exposure, cranking film ahead as fast as he could, until he ran out. The three didn't move for a few seconds until the cub squalled again. The sow dropped down on all fours and ambled away.

Charlie collapsed onto his knees. "I knew I was gonna die."

"Me too."

"But you kept on clickin' that damn shutter." He looked over at Connor. "You nuts?"

"I figured if I's gonna die, I'll get me some great shots. Somebody'll prob'ly find the camera eventually."

"Connor, yore one crazy nutcracker."

Connor grinned as he turned over and stood. "Maybe so—thanks for protecting me."

"Yeah, I must be as nuts as you are."

SEE WILLY SEE

"Good to have comp'ny."

Charlie just shook his head and stood up, watching the bears amble off. "That sow had the smelliest breath. I'm glad that's not the last thing I smelled in this life."

"Maybe ate a kill that wasn't too fresh. Hey, what made you think of standing up and yellin' like that?"

"Damned if I know. Not thinkin.' Too scared to think."

Peters ended Connor's reverie. "That's more'n luck," he said. "That's . . ." he paused, ". . . that's I don't know what it is."

Connor grinned. "Yeah. I didn't always have that kind of luck."

Before he could tell his next tale, the MPs came with keys and they headed back to camp.

A couple of days later, Connor wrote his sister.

> Dear Sis,
>
> I've been in another barroom brawl. Someday I'll tell you all about it. I promise you it's not an experience you need to envy. Got my nose and my ribs taped. Buncha other guys wandering around with miscellaneous bandages, too.
>
> The good news is I've got a squad of men that look out for each other. Being all mixed up the way they are—Indian, Mexican, and cowboys—they could divide up into groups, and they do to some extent. But when someone challenges one of them, including me, all their antennae go up. Maybe on second thought I should say their fists go up.
>
> Nora, are you all right there? I'm in no danger here, and I worry all the time about you. It's not fair that

you're the one in jeopardy. I'm supposed to protect you. Since I can't be there, you take care of yourself. I want to see you and that Daniel guy back in Nebraska when this is over.

That's an order.

Connor

Connor had no more than posted the letter than he received one from his parents.

Dear Son,

Halleluiah! Nora's coming home! We got a call in the middle of the night. Scared us to death. Henry tried to get to the phone without waking me, but I sleep real light with you and Nora in harm's way. All he has to do is twitch and I'm up.

Anyway, I jumped up and grabbed my robe, but Henry got to the phone first.

She said the Germans had ordered the entire embassy to the train station in Marseilles. Well, that scared me half to death, Connor. I just held on to your father to keep from collapsing while he told me what she said. She said the Germans are about to occupy the rest of France. She thought the Nazis were sending them home! She'll be here before you— just like I said.

Then she hung up before I could even talk to her. Wanted you to know right away.

Mom

Connor grinned. At long last. If the German U-boats didn't sink her ship, she'd be back in Nebraska soon and he wouldn't have to worry about her.

SEE WILLY SEE

Just a week later, at Fort Clayton on an errand, he passed a news-rack in the PX. He spotted a headline—Consulate Staff Taken Prisoner. He grabbed a paper.

"Son of a bitch," he murmured, reading fast. He reached in his pocket and dropped a nickel on the counter. "For the paper." The gist of the article told him that his sister had been taken by train from Marseilles to somewhere in Germany. He hoped the Allies weren't bombing that place—wherever it was.

"Damn it straight to hell!" He kicked the end of the counter where he stood reading. "God damn that Hitler straight to hell."

"Hey soldier. Take it easy. We all hate Hitler, but our business here is with the Japs."

Connor slammed the paper on the counter and punched his fist on it. "Not mine. Not anymore."

"What in hell's the matter with you?"

Connor held up his bleeding hand and looked at it without interest. "Fuck. He's got my sister and there's not a God damned thing I can do about it."

"What in hell are you talking about?"

Connor smacked the paper again. "See that headline? That's my sister."

"She's Foreign Service?"

"Yeah. Been in France almost three years."

"Holy shit! What do you think they'll do to them?"

"Hell if I know. Depends on whether they've figured out what she's been doing."

"What's she been doing for Christ's sake?"

Not naturally paranoid, Connor had to stop and think for a minute. They were thousands of miles away. Still, there were Germans in Panama, and it was his sister's life.

"Doin' her job, I guess. Typing out forms and filing—that sort of stuff."

The clerk grinned. "Can't get in trouble for that. She'll be all right."

"You may be right. I been worried about her since she got there."

He turned and left the PX, stomping and splashing all the way back to the jeep. Back at camp he flopped on his cot and grumbled to himself. When Peters wandered in Connor pretended to be asleep. He didn't want to talk.

November 27, 1942 – Camp Paraiso, Panama

By the end of November, Connor thought they would ship out soon. They'd trained for eleven months. They were as ready as they would get. His desert rats had adapted to the jungle—especially the humidity. Their eyes, evolved among long vistas, had changed their focus. Maybe more important, their minds had become jungle minds—now accustomed to the smells of green decay, the sounds of howling monkeys, squawking birds—and their absence. They'd adjusted to the sight of green, green, green and sorting out what they needed to see from the monochrome. Their skin knew the oppressive feel of wet that never evaporated. They could function when every breath filled their lungs with moisture. Connor felt confident in their transformation. They'd earned their title—Bushmasters.

Herndon said that they'd trained the best jungle fighters in the world. They would have to be. News coming out of the Pacific made that brutally clear.

The news had gone from bad to awful. During the first few months of that year, the Japanese had taken Hong Kong from the British. They'd captured Guam, the Philippines, Borneo, the Solomons, Java, parts of Dutch New Guinea and Bataan. Connor couldn't remember all the defeats anymore.

In May, the U.S. had its first naval victory in the Battle of the Coral Sea—but the Japs then completed their take-over of Burma. In June, the Allies won the battle of Midway, providing the first stepping-stone across the Pacific, but the Japanese invaded the Aleutian Islands—way too close to home. The next month, Japanese forces landed in Gona, New Guinea, starting the Papua Campaign, but within two weeks, the Allied South Pacific forces landed on Guadalcanal, Florida, and Tulagi islands in the Solomons while the Australians hung on by the tips of their fingers on the east end of New Guinea. Connor hadn't heard any more.

The Bushmasters were engaged in war games once more and his squad worked like a well-disciplined team. First Battalion, the opposition, dug in on the highlands, as the Japanese would undoubtedly be dug in all the way across the Southwestern Pacific. Second Battalion had to root out their artillery and machine-gun placements and take their base.

On December 1, Lt. Col. Mackey led Second out of Camp Paraiso toward the interior of the isthmus. He scattered squads along the way with orders to spread out and locate enemy emplacements.

Within hours, walkie talkies buzzed. The various squads had engaged. One squad in Easy Company ran into a machine-gun emplacement and a single Navajo warrior had climbed to the top of the canopy where he "fired" on the oncoming Second Battalion troops, pinning them down with two "dead" and four "wounded."

So well hidden among the leaves, he had Easy Company riflemen completely baffled for many deadly minutes before they located the source of the firing. Another squad had stumbled into a deep hole dug into the jungle floor and covered with limbs and leaves. First Battalion had netted four prisoners, including a first sergeant.

Connor and his squad headed for the highest spot they could see, hacking their way through vines and brush, stopping often to listen. He positioned Hayes in the lead as forward scout. He watched the smaller man who seemed to melt through the jungle. That's what made him such a great scout. Hayes disappeared and reappeared at intervals, always close but often out of sight. Connor found it a little spooky the way Hayes would suddenly appear at his elbow without warning. He had seen the man run and he thought that his scout could set records. He probably wouldn't run much in the jungle.

They hacked their way upwards for three hours before they came on a trail already punched through the understory. Their predecessors—First Battalion, of course, had not broken it quietly or carefully.

"What do you think?" Connor asked Jakes.

"Old trail. Maybe two or three days old. See, the breaks are dry. No sap."

"First Battalion?"

Jakes shrugged and nodded.

They moved faster, shoving through undergrowth that rebounded across the cuts, stopping more often to listen and look. Hayes stopped, pointing with his head as the men following nearly tumbled over one another.

Connor crept up beside him. "What?"

"Flash."

Connor peered through the leaves of the canopy. "I don't see it."

"There. Something moving."

"Monkey?"

"Too big."

"Go out around him. We'll follow. I'll bring up the rear." He motioned the squad to follow Hayes.

They moved left off the trail. Mendez stopped where Hayes had noticed the sniper. He crouched behind a small palm, indicating with his eyes the muzzle of a sniper's rifle. The rest of the squad took cover.

Connor crept up. "He's spotted us."

"Yup."

"Suggestions?"

"I'll catch up with Hayes. Climb that palm behind the sniper and throw my knife. Out."

Connor grinned. "Make sure you don't kill him. We need his intelligence."

The squad stayed in place, poking up a head from time to time to keep the sniper's attention while Mendez crept around behind him. Connor spotted a gold flash when Eiseler took his turn tempting the sniper with his mop of hair.

"Damn it, Beacon, Connor whispered, "get a helmet on that halo of yours."

About fifteen minutes later, they heard a thunk and a "Damn."

"Get the knife," shouted Mendez as he and his mark climbed down.

The sniper headed back to Camp Paraiso, and Hayes led the squad on up the mountainside. At a little broader disturbance, Hayes went ahead to reconnoiter.

Half an hour later he returned. "Machine-gun emplacement."

"Can we get behind it?"

Hayes gestured a wide circle.

"OK, let's go."

They came in behind the emplacement, snuggled under a rock overhang. Connor sent Gordon and Trigg to drop a couple of dummy grenades over the edge. They disappeared. Connor hadn't quite made up his mind about Trigg. Could he trust him? Trigg had robbed a jewelry store and chosen the Army rather than prison. He looked like a weasel with his narrow face and small, close-set eyes, although Connor knew better than judge a man by appearance.

Connor and the rest of the squad hunkered down in the clearing they'd hacked to wait for the "all clear." He heard Trigg yell, "You're out," and motioned his men ahead. Irritated that the man had made enough noise to alert the whole First Battalion, he grumbled and tried to decide how to approach Trigg.

The defeated machine-gun crew disappeared down the trail and Connor's squad spread out, stopping more frequently. Connor sent Hayes ahead again. Going by the maps, he thought they would soon get close enough to converge with the rest of the battalion on the highlands.

"First base camp is about five miles ahead. Well-fortified. On top where they can see everything."

"Any other squads?" Connor couldn't get how Hayes could snake his way through the rain forest without messing up his fatigues. He glanced around at the rest of the squad. Some of them would be sewing on a lot of buttons. They all looked dirty, sweaty, and tired.

"Captain Cochran and the rest of George Company, about a mile to the right. Fox Company coming up behind."

"Orders?"

"Catch up with George and clear out in between."

"Anything to clear?"

"Sniper about a hundred yards." He pointed ahead and to the right with his chin. "Machine-gun emplacement between there and Cochran."

"Can we get 'em?"

"Sniper's not well hidden. Machine-guns harder."

"You wanta take out the sniper?"

Connor sent Mendez ahead again. The man grinned. He crouched and disappeared as Connor and the rest moved out in the direction of George Company. They met Mendez, and the sniper heading back to Camp Paraiso. They caught up with Hayes, who sat on a rock watching a line of army ants crossing the trail.

"Okay, where are the guns?"

Hayes gestured toward an opening. "See? They're dug in. It's open all around. Can't sneak up on 'em."

"How about behind 'em?"

"Lookout at the edge of the trees."

Connor gestured for Mendez. "You go with -0-9972677-4-7 and take out the lookout."

The men moved off just as a rain squall began, giving them the cover of sound and a veil of water. A few minutes later, Hayes signaled from the tree line. The squad moved out and took the position, losing two men—Reese and Mendez—spotted before the squad got into position. The rest of the squad joined Captain Cochran's command for the remainder of the exercise, a hard-fought "battle" that cost many men but ended in a slim victory for the Second.

SEE WILLY SEE

PART THREE: SOUTHWEST PACIFIC

January 6, 1943 – Aboard Ship

The regiment loaded equipment and supplies, lugging boxes of ammunition and crates of rifles, mortars, bazookas, and flamethrowers, tents, hammocks, and C-rations. They walked up the gangplank of a converted passenger ship, the Dickman, in the dark of a new moon. It seemed appropriate to move in the dark, although Connor could see by starlight. He and the squad had set up radar outposts, so he knew about radar. He hoped the Japs didn't have the new technology yet.

Connor found Pacific distances daunting with nothing to see but water, fish, an occasional bird—and men hanging over the rail. His dad always characterized the earth as a living thing and on the ocean, Connor could see it—a vast expanse of water heaving and breathing, rolling and sparkling beneath the drab, gray behemoth plowing along its surface. Certain that the scent of man sweat, crotch rot, and sour feet below decks could strangle a horse, Connor spent as much time as he could on deck.

If Panama had bored Connor, enforced idleness aboard ship left him lethargic. Cooped up in the hold of the Dickman, he saw some money change hands, including his own, in games of blackjack, stud poker, craps, and any other damn thing the men could think up.

They kept betting on his answers to their random questions, too. Anything for a bet.

SEE WILLY SEE

Some days dolphins escorted them, rolling along by the nose of the ship. Once, a pod of whales breeched, blowing air, water vapor, and mucus. He knew whales breathe through blow holes in the tops of their heads, but to hear the great beasts undulating on the surface inhaling into their monstrous lungs made him breathe more deeply, in synchrony.

He wrote letters, thinking he might not have much opportunity after they landed. He answered Nora's letter, knowing his might not get to her for months—if at all.

> Nora,
>
> I can't tell you where I am 'cause the Army would just cut it out of my letter anyway, but I'm okay. It's so boring here, I've started smoking. Everybody else does already and I need to see the breath coming out of my lungs to make sure I'm alive.
>
> I gotta tell you about one of the guys in my squad. Name's Martinez and he pitched for the minor leagues before this war started. He's a real ladies' man. Whenever we go into town, he flirts with every female he sees, but there haven't been any towns for a while and he's pretty much off his feed. He consoles himself by laughing and joking around with the others. He has a great sense of humor. He carries a rock around in his pocket and I see him sometimes weighing it in his hands—tossing it from hand to hand, especially when he's under pressure. We call him Fast Pitch.
>
> Another guy, Sterling Menardo, is a convicted felon. They gave him a choice of Army or prison. Here's the deal, though. They were dragging his son, kicking and screaming, to the Indian school and he just lost it—tried to fight the officer abducting his kid.
>
> Someday, Nora, we're gonna have to pay for what we've been doing to people.

SEE WILLY SEE

At night I see a whole different sky than you see.

Connor

On a moonlit night, he stood on the foredeck smoking a Camel and watching spray as the transport cut through water. Wandering back amidships, he spotted Ferro Gordon sitting, cross-legged, on the deck, peering at the sky, light hair stirring in the breeze.

Connor stopped, unwilling to interrupt the other man's thoughts. Gordon turned dark, quiet eyes on Connor. "Different from home."

"Sorry. I didn't mean to intrude."

"Don't know which way's home," Gordon repeated.

Connor took another drag on his cigarette, scanning the sky. "I sure couldn't find my way."

Gordon stood, his tall, slender body swaying with the motion of the ship. He pointed at a cluster of stars. "See. Four bright ones," he made a kind of cross, pointing at each in turn, "and one a little dimmer."

"I think they call that the Southern Cross," Connor said as Tayo Reese walked up and stood next to Gordon.

Reese craned his neck and rotated his body with his face to the sky, looking around and around for something familiar. Suddenly, he rushed across the deck and leaned over the rail.

"Not again," Connor muttered. He watched the Indian walk back, studying the wide face and bulbous nose. "Reese, I thought you was done being seasick."

Reese wiped his mouth on the back of a meaty hand. "Aw shouldna turned 'round like that."

The man's big belly had disappeared over the side of the ship, along with every ounce of food he ate.

"We get to Australia, they're gonna turn you around and send you home 'cause yore too skinny to carry a rifle."

"I be awright."

"Hmmmm."

Connor strolled back to the bow, leaving the others to their star gazing. He could see clearly in the bright moonlight. He squinted into the distance wondering what he would find over the horizon.

Green joined him. "How long ya s'pose we'll be on this tub, Sarge?"

"Damn 'f I know. Hope we see land 'fore we see the Japanese Navy."

"Me too." Green took a drag off his cigarette.

"All this water's sure different for this ol' farm boy."

"Yeah. We settled in the desert after my granddaddy wandered down into the Superstitions sometime 'round the end of the last century—lookin' for the Lost Dutchman."

"Find it?"

"Hell no. Rattlesnakes, tarantulas, saguaros, and a dance hall girl."

Connor grinned. "A dance hall girl?"

"Yeah. My gramma made her livin' fleecin' miners outa their gold dust in the Dutchman Saloon—until my grampa came in there without a pot to piss in and took her away from all that."

"Bet she was happy to see him."

"Not so much. Said she had a better life in the saloon."

"I'll be damned."

"So will I, Conroy. So will I.

"So'd *you* ever try to find gold?"

"Oh, yeah. I s'pose everyone in Arizona's tried one time or 'nother. I panned the streams a little when a spring rain washed down some new stuff."

"Find anything?"

"Aw, I got a few little nuggets tucked away at home. More a curiosity 'n anything."

Green finished his cigarette and flipped it over the rail, watching sparks fly down the side of the ship to the water. "I be pretty happy to stand on some dry land."

"Me too. At least we're not seasick like Reese."

"Yeah. Big wind could blow him away. Think he'll get his belly back?"

"Dunno."

"Guess I'll go get a little shut-eye."

"Not far behind ya."

Connor flipped his fag over the side but instead of going below, he stood leaning on the rail and looking out on the ocean. He wondered what lay ahead for the Bushmasters. Their regimental patch now depicted two of the snakes wrapped around a machete. They sported the word cuidado on their shoulders.

SEE WILLY SEE

Danger! He'd trained for a year with tough, dangerous men, but would they be tough enough? Would they all survive? Intellectually, he knew it was unlikely, but he had to hope. Even Trigg had his qualities.

Well, I guess this is about to get real. Never could picture it back home. I guess that's how we get into war. Nobody can picture it until it's too late. Now I've seen what a light machine-gun can do to a palm tree. That's real. But I still can't translate that into human flesh. Don't want to. Seen mortar craters and hills ripped up by howitzers. Still abstract, though. It's like the trig that allows artillerymen to drop shells in the right place when they can't even see the shell soaring over rain forest and exploding on the ground.

In a couple of weeks, I'll know.

He considered Nora. She'd had a different mission. *Will I have her courage, risking her life to save people she's never even met? Ha. My job's to kill people, not save them. We're supposed to save the world for democracy. I wonder what that means. Killing to save the world don't make much sense.*

The Japanese attack on U.S. personnel all across the Pacific had made him stinking mad, but standing aboard the Dickman, looking out at the vast expanse of water, he wondered what all those U.S. military personnel had been doing on all those islands. He knew the history but seeing the vast ocean from the middle made him wonder what his country could possibly want out there.

What possible use could some little island out here be to us? Why does anyone, except the natives, want this?

A school of tiny, luminous fish rose to the surface interrupting his thoughts. As he looked more closely, individual ocean animals sorted themselves out of the waves. Whip-like creatures undulated amid clouds of tiny, circular animals. He spotted something that looked like a chain of bubbles as it popped onto a wave, heaving with the moving water. The glowing silence of such peaceful, living things moved in stark contrast with his thoughts. Mesmerized, he stared at the shining sea surface. *I hope we humans won't destroy this while we're killing each other.*

Leaning on the rail, he realized how tired he felt—exhausted really.

Hell, I can't solve it and it's too late to do anything about it. I've already enlisted. I'm already on a boat. No choice but jump overboard. I just hope I can get through it and not go home looking and sounding like Uncle Harry.

He'd started below when he saw Reese heading for the hold.

"Hey Reese, how's the world treating you? You look a little better— not quite so green."

Reese frowned. "What do you care?"

Connor flinched. He knew it sounded like Army talk, but after fumbling around, he said, "I care about all the men in my squad." Connor stared at him for a few moments. Then he decided to just be straight. "What makes you so mad anyway?"

Reese's eyes darkened. He stared into Connor's eyes, speaking slowly. "Because I'm a fuckin' blanket ass."

Connor hesitated without breaking eye contact. "I've never called you that."

"You palefaces think you can just say you're not prejudiced, and it'll be all right."

"Well, damn it, what can I do? I treat you just like everybody else."

Reese continued to stare, his eyes hard black beads. Finally, he looked down at the deck.

"Yeah. That's true," he admitted, "you speak up for us sometimes, but that hardly counts in my life."

"What about your life, Tayo? What makes you so angry?"

Reese spat on the deck. "You wanna know about my life, white man? Let me tell you about my life. Your white grandfathers killed us and raped our women. You took our land, burned our homes, and scattered our food. Then, you took our children and tried to make them like you. You took the old ways and gave us English, and math-e-matics. You took our hope and gave us alcohol. Isn't that enough reason to be fuckin' mad?"

Connor pulled out a pack of Camels gave one to Reese and lit them. "You're right and I know I can't make up for it. But what about you?"

"What about me?"

"Can I do anything to make it better for you?"

Reese kicked the rail. "You can get me off this God damned tin can."

Connor sighed. "Would if I could." He paused a moment, thinking. "Think I'll grab a little shut-eye."

He and Reese crossed the deck together. Connor hit the steel stairs first, clanging his way into the dim belly of the ship. He'd become so accustomed to the growl of the engines and the hull's vibration that he barely noticed. He heard the clank of Reese's boots on the ladder behind him. The man stumbled with the sway of the ship. Connor hoped Reese could stop puking. He'd been a big guy when they left Panama, but halfway across the Pacific, his fatigues hung on him. Connor had noticed the end of his mesh belt flopped down his front. He shook his head listening to Reese's uneven progress across the hold and wondering if the guy could make another two weeks at sea.

In the stifling hold, he crawled in his third level hammock, thankful Green and Wilson hadn't retired to the lower levels. He had enough trouble creeping into the swinging bed without a couple of guys underneath. Cradled in his hammock, he crossed his arms over his chest and closed his eyes. Swinging with the ship's roll felt like floating and he'd started to drift off when he heard the screaming ahooga-ahooga-ahooga of the Klaxon. He knew that seamen all over the ship were scrambling to battle stations. He lay back and waited for the noise to stop, realizing he could do nothing to protect himself even if Japanese Zeros were bearing down. By the time the boat docked in Australia, he wouldn't care if he never heard that throaty sound blaring and echoing around the confined spaces inside the ship where they pounded against steel bulkheads.

When the horn stopped, he drifted off to sleep, dreaming of his days in Montana with his aunt and uncle near Glendive. He and Charlie had spent a month in Yellowstone National Park. Then they'd headed south again into the Grand Tetons. Connor used up a couple rolls of film on the east face of the shining mountains, then they walked right into the edge and set up a dry camp, sleeping out under the stars.

One morning Connor had started up a pile of rocks that had sheared off the cliff.

"Connor, damn it, you've lost a little weight, but you still ain't skinny enough for me to carry when you get all busted up," Charlie grumbled.

Connor looked back over his shoulder. "Shshsh."

He crested the edge and subdued a whoop. The bighorn ram he'd spotted going behind the rocks circled a second ram. They fought between the steep cliff face and the rough pile of stones he'd just climbed. He clicked off a few frames of the ewes that stood watching, then he settled on the rocks. The rams started a head-

SEE WILLY SEE

crunching battle with a resounding crash of horns. As he shot a roll of film and reloaded, he wondered how they stayed on their feet. They should have been unconscious. He hoped something would come out of the frames he snapped when the beasts stood locked together. He worried about motion blur.

What puny little things we humans are.

The rams fought their way closer and closer to where Connor squatted. Completely riveted by the animals, he stood and stepped back for a better shot, stumbling with his left leg jammed.

After a startled "Damn!" he said nothing, only gritting his teeth and trying to pull his leg free.

Charlie started climbing toward him. "Damn it, Connor."

"I'm all right," Connor mumbled.

Charlie kept climbing and swearing. At the top, Connor tried to move the rock that held his leg captive.

Responding to another crash of horns, Charlie peered over the rubble and stared. "So that's what you were doing with that damn camera."

Connor kept tugging on the rock. "Help me lift this thing."

Charlie turned back and Connor watched him studying the rubble. He found hand holds and lifted the one that had Connor pinned. The leg popped free, upsetting them both.

"Damn," Connor whispered. Sweat popped out on his forehead and his upper lip.

"Shit. You broke your leg. Just look at it swell."

"Nah," said Connor, "it's just bruised. "It'll be okay. Help me up."

When he tried to put weight on it, the leg screamed at him, and he realized Charlie was right. He eased back down.

"Okay. This is no big deal. I broke my arm playin' football in high school. Played the rest of the game with it taped to my side and then had it set."

Charlie stared at him eyes narrowed. "Well, we're out here in the middle of nowhere. There ain't a doctor or a town in hundreds of miles and I ain't even got a wagon to tote you around in. You can't tape yore damn leg to your side, you damned idiot!"

At first, Charlie tried to support Connor as he hopped from rock to rock, but Connor decided after the second hop that he risked breaking his other leg with a bad hop. He eased himself down and looked around as if a solution would magically appear. With his damaged leg thrust out ahead of him, he scooted his butt from rock to rock with Charlie hovering like a new mother.

When he reached a flat spot, he split his pants leg to the knee and looked. Sitting on the ground and gazing at his swollen calf, Connor tried to decide what to do next. He knew his shin bone remained intact. He'd fallen backward and the smaller bone would have taken the stress. He guessed he didn't have a clean break, maybe just a green tree break, because his foot and ankle worked, but it really hurt to flex them.

Charlie stomped off. "I'm goin' to look for splints."

Connor dragged himself over to where he'd left his rucksack and stowed his camera. He pulled out his extra shirt and began ripping the back into wide strips. When Charlie got back, they each took a stick and whittled it smooth and straight. Charlie examined Connor's leg, hands feeling the bump in the back of his calf.

SEE WILLY SEE

"I think we ought to wait until the swelling goes down before we wrap it."

Chastened, Connor patted the leg Charlie had elevated on a log. "Thanks, Charlie."

Charlie remained on his knees and they both looked up at the sheer rock face. "Purty, ain't it?" he asked.

"Beautiful," said Connor, working his way up onto his elbows. "Sorry to be so much trouble, but do you think you can find me somethin' with a fork I can use for a crutch?"

"Yeah. That'd be a good idea."

Connor watched him walk away, kicking at leaf litter as he walked. He wandered the sparse little copse of aspens where they'd decided to camp. Connor saw him pick up a forked stick and throw it down. Too short. He wandered a little longer and picked up another. Way too long. He found a third. He leaned on it, and it bent. Too weak. He walked this way for several minutes, head down, kicking at the litter. At last, he set a stout stick under his arm. His shoulder hitched up a few inches and he carried it back to camp. By time he got there, Connor lay stretched out in the waning sun with his head on his duffle.

Connor closed his eyes while Charlie set up camp. Connor could hear him muttering about how the hell they'd get out of the Tetons and how they'd get through the winter with Connor laid up. Damn fool kid and his pitchers. He warmed up some pork and beans, made coffee and poked Connor. "You hungry?"

Connor opened his eyes, feeling a little confused at first. "Oh, damn," he said, "that smarts."

"It's liable to."

Connor sat and started struggling to his feet.

"Just set. I'll bring you something—but don't you go expectin' me to wait on you."

"Never would."

After they ate, Charlie splinted the leg and wrapped it. "We'll tighten these wraps in the morning, but this should keep it steady if you move around in your sleep." He leaned back on his knees. "I been thinkin' . . ."

"Me too," said Connor. "We gotta get to Glendive."

"What the hell's in Glendive? Where's Glendive?"

"That's the problem. Glendive's way the hell and gone over on the east edge of Montana, all the way across this God-forsaken plain you see out there."

"So why in the devil's flaming hell would we go there?"

"My Aunt Ella and Uncle Ollie live there. They have a little stucco house, squatting on the lee side of a little knoll. It's just a square with a gabled roof."

"Wait a minute. It's out in the country?"

"It's a ranch."

"Out in the middle of this howling wilderness?"

Connor had heard the tone of Charlie's voice rising.

"The wind does howl sometimes, but it's a squatty, short house set behind a little rise, and the wind mostly blows over the top."

"Oh right. Over the top."

"It's shelter, Charlie."

SEE WILLY SEE

Charlie grumbled something Connor didn't hear.

"Ollie and Ella have a barn with a snug loft. We'll stay pretty warm with the horses' body heat rising through the floor. People used to live above their livestock in the early days."

"And how the hell're you gonna get up into that loft?"

"Slowly. I'll have to pull myself. Anyway, we can winter with Aunt Ella and Uncle Ollie, if we can get there. That's my plan. What were you thinkin'?"

"I thought maybe we should get to a rail yard and head south—fast, just so's we don't freeze to death. It'll prob'ly get damn cold around here before long. But I don't have nobody to look out for us."

Charlie got quiet. He stood and began cleaning up, scouring the pans and plates with sand and wiping them out with a rag. Connor watched him squatting next to the fire, hands moving with easy efficiency.

"Or we could split up," said Connor, "so's you're not burdened with me."

"Naw, that nice, tidy little barn sounds good to me. Let's head north in the mornin'. Maybe we can get back to the railroad."

The next morning, they headed back out to the road, hitchhiking north to southern Montana. Sunshine and bald blue skies followed them as Connor stumped along on his makeshift crutch. His gait and efficiency increased as the day passed, although his shoulder ached viciously.

Sometime around midday, a rattletrap old truck came up behind them. Connor looked over his shoulder, grinning at the weathered vehicle with its clattering wooden stock racks. It had no right front fender and the left one flapped.

SEE WILLY SEE

"Looks almost as bad as I feel."

They heard the brakes grind as the truck groaned to a stop. The driver didn't look much better off than they did. He wore a crushed felt hat with a torn brim and his denim work shirt looked like it had been in a battle with barbed wire and lost. His grease-spattered overalls flapped when he stepped out and reached for Connor's hand. The once blue stripes were only visible where the straps came across his shoulders.

"Where ya headed?"

"Nearest railhead," said Charlie.

"Hop on in. Name's Joe."

"Charlie, and this here's Connor."

"I'll get ya to Cody. The train stops there once in a while. You can maybe slip into one of them boxcars. I hear fellas do it all the time."

They climbed into the truck with Connor in the back where he could stretch out his leg. At Cody, they camped along the tracks for a couple of days before they heard a train coming from the south.

Made up mostly of cattle cars it stopped for water and Connor walk-hopped to the nearest empty car where Charlie wedged the door open a bit and shoved his friend through the opening.

"Damn!" said Connor as he scrambled through straw mixed with cow pies, dragging his leg.

"What?" asked Charlie, clambering up. "Oh." He crawled in with a bunch of skittish steers.

"Think we should try to find a boxcar?"

Charlie jumped out just as the train started moving.

"Damn." He clambered back in. "Well, ain't this gonna just be sweet."

"We'll smell pretty sweet," Connor said, wiping the manure off his hands with clean straw. "Wonder if it's worth changing this shirt."

He decided against it. It wouldn't do any good. Then he remembered his spare shirt was wrapped around his leg.

They spent a night and a morning with the cattle, each species keeping to its own space. Several times they heard a squeal of brakes and a jolt as the car's couplers slammed together. Often, they peeked through the slats to see nothing but open plains and the wooden platform of a water tower. They couldn't know where they were except for an occasional sign they spotted as the train slowed for some little burg in the middle of nowhere. Belfry. Bridger. Fromberg.

When the train stopped in Billings, Charlie jumped out. Connor sat just inside the door and watched Charlie sneak around the corner. About forty-five minutes later, the train started moving.

Damn it straight to hell. Where's Charlie? I don't even know where this train's going. Crap. can I jump out with this leg?

He'd eased into the doorway when Charlie appeared, fast-walking beside the slowly moving car. Connor scooted back and Charlie swung aboard. Before he could tell Connor what he'd learned, they stopped moving again.

Someone stuck his head in. "Hey, there's plenty of room in here. How many head you got?"

They barely heard the answer, "Just a dozen." "Bring 'em over."

Within minutes, another twelve head of steers had stepped, bawling and shoving, into the car as the men crowded against the front wall.

"Shit," murmured Connor.

"Plenty," said Charley.

The cattle bawled and milled about, crowding away from the two men. It came to a face-off with the cattle all facing front, watching Charlie and Connor.

"I snuck around the yards," Charlie said when they got moving. "Heard workers loading cars. Looks like this here train's headed east to Glendive."

They spent two days and a night with the beasts, wrapping up in their blankets at night and hoping they wouldn't get trampled. They heard the wind howling around the moving train and felt its fingers penetrating the slats in the car.

"You know," said Connor, "them cattle are probably keeping us from freezing to death."

"I don't think it's that cold," said Charlie, "but my eyes are watering from all the damn fumes."

Connor wiped his eyes with his sleeve.

The train made a long stop at the rail yards in Glendive, adding more cattle cars and giving Charlie a chance to jump out and look around. When he knew the coast was clear, he helped Connor climb out of the car and they walked into town.

"Where's this ranch?"

"It's out northwest," Connor said, leaning on his crutch and pointing.

SEE WILLY SEE

"How do we get there?"

"It's a pretty long walk and they don't have no phone."

They walked to the edge of town where the wind swept, howling, through heaps of tumbleweed piled up on a fence. It screamed between buildings and Connor barely made himself heard when he asked a local for the Post Office.

Charlie exploded. "Post Office! You gotta mail a letter now?"

"No, I'm gonna get a ride. The mailman delivers to the end of the driveway."

They hung around town until the next morning when they got a ride in the mail carrier's pickup. From the mailbox, they walked, heads down, leaning against the wind's embrace. Connor had gotten much more proficient with his crutch, but he struggled to stand.

"There's nothin' out here," Charlie snarled when they came to the dry creek bed.

When they finally spotted the house, sitting all by itself with its little barn, Connor nearly collapsed in relief. A horse nickered from the open barn door as they approached, and a bow-legged man stepped out onto the stoop.

"What kinda trouble brings you fellas clear out here?" yelled Ollie when they were close enough to hear over the wind.

"How ya doin,' Uncle Ollie?" Connor yelled.

"Uncle Ollie? Whose Uncle Ollie?" he stepped closer. "Connor? What the hell you doin' clear out here and what'd you do to yourself?"

"Fell off a rock pile."

"Well, c'mon outa that wind," he said as Ella followed him into the yard, grabbing her apron as it blew up in her face.

They all trundled into the house, doors slamming behind them.

They spent a couple of hours catching up on how the Leases were getting along with drought and impossible cattle prices.

Then Ollie cleared his throat. "You fellas need a place to shelter for the winter?"

"I hoped maybe you could put us up in the barn. We could help you with the cattle . . ." Connor paused and looked at his uncle with raised eyebrows.

"Like we been talkin," Ollie interrupted, "there ain't no cattle. Just a few breedin' heifers."

"I know that now, so . . . maybe you could give us a ride into town."

"Nah." Ollie glanced at Ella who nodded. "Yore kin 'n we got plentya food. Yore stayin' here. Just not sure where to put ya."

"We'll snuggle into the hay up in the loft."

"Not much hay there, Connor. Can't grow nothin' here."

Ella verbally worried about him going up and down the ladder, so they decided the "boys" would have to sleep in the main room. They'd have to fight over the couch, Ella said.

"Couch is too short," Connor said. "I'm takin' the floor where I can straighten out this leg."

"How'll you get up and down off the floor?" Ella worried.

"Like this." He pushed his leg in front of him as he slid off the couch onto his knee. He sat and then pushed himself forward until he lay flat. Then he quickly reversed the process. "I'm getting pretty spry at this."

As Connor and Charlie came to roost for the long winter, Connor got a look at Ella's well-stocked root cellar.

"How'd you grow all this, Aunt Ella, with no water?" "Buckets, Connor. Our well didn't dry up."

"Same at home," Connor said. "At least Mom can grow beans."

Connor and Charlie wrote their families before they settled in. Connor got an answer within a week, full of cheerful news, but Charlie waited more than a month. One evening after they'd developed a routine, they all sat around the coal-fired stove.

"What're you boys gonna do when it rains and people can get jobs again," Ollie asked.

They met his question with prolonged silence, staring at the glowing side of the stove until Charlie cleared his throat.

"We's seen some beautiful country an' I know now it's ours—yours 'n mine 'n everybody's." He cocked his head toward his friend. "Connor here's showed me how to live in that country 'n have enough to eat most of the time. Made me feel like a real man 'n not just a worthless old bum."

Connor said nothing and Charlie lapsed into silence, rubbing his palms together. Ollie also held his tongue, gazing at the younger man.

"Connor's showed me people'll share what they got, even when it ain't much." He looked up into Ollie's eyes. "You know I love this country. Couldna said that six months ago."

Ollie nodded.

"But ya know, I think I'll go back to the steel mills. It's what I know how to do."

Connor watched him frown and rub his hands together. He knew Charlie had been wrestling with his future and it was still uncertain.

"But now I know all this is out here—the mountains and the glaciers an' the great big skies. An' I saw that ocean glitterin' out there. Makes me feel like a rich man when I'm pore as a grasshopper." Charlie gave a head-down embarrassed snort of a laugh. "Listen to me speechifyin'."

"Them's pretty important words," Ollie said. "Somethin' like keeps me goin'."

"I sure got a better feelin' about the future since I met this here photo-snappy-shooter guy."

Connor grinned into his coffee, wondering how his blundering around the mountains could give Charlie such a good feeling. He'd learned his first lesson on how your most unconscious acts, just getting along as best you can, can change lives.

Charlie's letter from home came just a few days after his little speech. He scanned it quickly and handed it to Conner while he stepped outside.

> Dear Charlie,
>
> Your letter went to our house, but I don't live there anymore. It wound all over the place, going by the postal marks. I'm so glad to hear from you. I feared I'd never hear from any of my boys again.
>
> I'm here at your Aunt Mary Ann's house and I'm grateful to her and Todd for taking me in when Robbie went plumb screaming crazy. He did his best,

but he couldn't keep up with the rent. We moved several times, selling everything we had as we went. We used the soup kitchens several times.

Anyways, they've got Robbie locked up at Fairview now and I moved in here, but they can't afford to keep me for long.

I'm so glad you're all right and you have a place to stay.

Love, Mom

Next morning, Charlie grabbed his kit and left for the mailbox, so he could get a ride to town and jump a freight. When Connor couldn't see his friend anymore, he turned back to the house.

"He's gone," he said as he walked inside. He shut the door, head hanging, thinking about how much he'd miss Charlie.

They settled back into their winter routine with one less mouth to feed, and fewer interesting stories to hear. The wind tested every little seam in the house, blustering and shoving. It sounded like someone stood outside, throwing big handfuls of sand and gravel against the stucco. The occasional still day sparkled with ice crystals falling, but never with snow.

Ollie had kept one steer for winter meat and brought it in from the range to fatten on hay. Early one quiet morning, he stepped out with his 30.06 deer rifle. Connor watched him walk out to the corral where he'd left the steer the night before. Connor heard the rifle report and saw the animal go down.

He helped Ollie harness one of the horses to drag the beef into the barn where they pulled it up with pulleys on a single tree. They split the beast open and removed the entrails, saving the heart, liver, and kidneys in a basin. Ollie handed Connor a flensing knife and the two men stood in silence skinning the steer as it cooled.

For the next three days, they listened to coyotes prowling around the barn while the meat aged. They cut it into quarters and carried the quarters into the house, one by one. Crowded around the kitchen table, they cut them into serving pieces—mostly chunks for canning. They feasted on steaks and roasts for a few days and helped Ella can the rest. They also butchered and canned all but ten of the chickens—leaving ten laying hens Ella had bought grain enough to feed.

Ollie had a pitiful stack of hay in the barn, but he thought it would keep the horses and the pregnant cows till the grass greened in the spring—if it ever greened. Only fifteen cows on a thousand acres and they were lean. He had gathered them into the corral where he could feed them.

"You sure you can put me up?" Connor asked one night after they'd inventoried the hay.

"Hell yes," Ollie said. "Food ain't the problem. I don't know how long I can pay the damn taxes when I can't graze cows. We been holdin' out and holdin' out and cutting to the bone.

"Government come and slaughtered all but ten of my cows in '34. Bought 'em and killed 'em and buried 'em. It'll take me twenty years to build back up if we ever get rain and it better be soon.

"We got a coupla rains this fall so maybe . . ." he trailed off, looking out across the tan landscape. "There's a little bit of water out under the grass . . ."

Connor remembered standing there watching his uncle, knowing the man was stranded between hope and despair.

Rocking in his hammock aboard a ship to nowhere, Connor woke to a particularly loud snort from one of the men bunked around him. He lay awake thinking about time, amazed at the dream that seemed to last for months, but he knew he'd only slept a few minutes—forty-five at the most. The monotonous rumbling of the ship's engines gave him a sense of time out of time. He felt like he'd always rolled and swayed on the ocean, giving his whole life a dreamlike quality—like the song, "Row, row, row your boat . . ." Maybe he would always roll and sway on that ocean. The journey seemed less like a journey than a permanent condition. Rocking in his hammock, he listened to men stirring and snoring around him, disembodied, low level noise that seemed completely outside of time.

January 30, 1943, — Brisbane, Australia

In another two weeks, Connor stepped onto the docks at Brisbane in a downpour—mid-summer on the southern hemisphere.

Loaded on trucks, the 158th and their equipment pulled under the bleachers at Camp Doomben, a soaked racetrack where they sheltered from the rain in the bleachers.

Confined to their miserable stair-stepped camp, Connor joined in the grumbling. He'd thought when they landed, they would go to war and get it over with. By then the Allied Navy had already won some battles, stopping the Japanese push for Australia. U.S. Marines had also fought them to a standstill in hand-to-hand combat on Guadalcanal. Australians were holding the line in New Guinea.

Before they could mutiny, the Army moved them to Camp Coble in the Tambourine Mountains. They had no more than settled there, when the Army dragged Second Battalion back down to Brisbane to clean up a Javanese freighter, while the First cleaned up their camp litter. Connor began to wonder why the hell had they had all that jungle training. He hoped that at least

SEE WILLY SEE

that boat would get them into some action. When they climbed aboard, he assumed they were going to war at last.

As they loaded all the gear they'd moved on and off the Dickman back onto the freighter, someone yelled "mail call." They all stopped and surrounded the corporal with the mail bag, hoping for a last letter from home before they started another long dry spell with no news.

Connor'd already heard from his parents that Nora had called them. By the time he reached Australia, he knew the Germans had taken the embassy staff prisoner. In a way, he celebrated that Nora was a prisoner. Pretty sure they wouldn't kill diplomats, he figured she wouldn't be able to put herself in any more danger rescuing people from the Nazis. And yet, he couldn't stop worrying about how they'd treat her. He wondered where they'd taken her. Would the Nazis drag the Americans into one of the cities the Allies bombed every night? Nobody's safe while Hitler has military resources at his disposal.

They corporal finally yelled his name. He ripped open a letter from his sister as he pushed through of the circle of waiting men.

> Connor,
>
> I'm not sure what's about to happen. The Germans have ordered us to the Marseilles train station tomorrow morning, and I don't know where they're taking us. I called Mom and Pop, to reassure them, but I'm not so sure myself. Nazis have threatened to kill some of our people if anyone goes missing. I believe them. The friend I told you about is mailing this letter for me. He said I could go along with him over the Pyrenees, but I needed to stay with our staff. I don't want to be responsible for someone dying. I hope it won't be the last time I see my friend.
>
> Nora

"Sons a bitchin' Germans," Connor muttered. Another code. I think he offered to smuggle her out of France.

"'s up?" asked Jakes.

"Nothin' new. Just got a letter from Nora. I knew the Germans had taken 'em prisoner, but I hadn't thought about her sweetheart. I thought he was in the French Resistance and Nora just confirmed it. They may never see each other again. That'd break her heart."

"Best thing we can do's get this thing over."

"Yeah," said Connor stuffing the letter in a hip pocket and stomping off to the pile of crates. "Let's get this damn ship loaded and get outa here."

PART FOUR: COMBAT

March 17, 1943 — Port Moresby, Papua New Guinea

Steaming north, they landed at Port Moresby, where the Australians had held the Japanese Army off for more than a year. Soon, Connor thought, their training would pay off—but then they moved on to Milne Bay—also known as Death Valley because of air raids that often riddled the camp.

After every air raid, Connor would inspect the tent for holes from bomb fragments and flak from anti-aircraft guns. The fabric began to look like one of his sister's loose-knit sweaters. In addition to the endless mud, they continued to work as slave laborers.

Supplies still had to be unloaded periodically, of course, so mud-caked and sweating, in various stages of undress, some completely naked, they moved crates of fruit juices, canned peaches, salt, sugar, C rations, toilet paper, ammunition. The soldiers formed an assembly line, handing off the crates to a dump on the beach, like a line of ants, loads sometimes falling through wet, slippery fingers. Nobody spoke. Instead, they hustled to get unloaded before the Japs noticed the supply ship in the harbor.

The planes came in waves, tearing up the beach, blowing sand and shrapnel in every direction. Soldiers cringed when the planes swooped in barely clearing the trees but kept working. Connor'd gotten used to having bombs dropped in his general vicinity. Even bombing and strafing had become a bit of a bore, although a close one would wake him up. So far, Second

SEE WILLY SEE

Battalion hadn't lost a man. They'd learned safety lay more on land than on ships. The Japanese bombers focused on the ships where they could sink supplies and destroy the capacity to move them. Sometimes, though, bombs landed on the beach and, if not, flak from the anti-aircraft guns did the damage.

One sunny afternoon Connor and his platoon were helping unload. He heard the buzz of Zeroes first. Then, a siren screaming. He scanned the sky over his shoulder and stepped up the work.

"Hustle up," he yelled, "incoming."

In moments, the planes were overhead. He automatically grabbed the next crate without looking at the guys on either side. He turned to hand it up the line when an explosion flattened him and the crate he'd had in his hands. He struggled to his feet in a spray of sand, metal, and wood splinters, unable to hear his own scream.

"Corpsman!"

He knelt beside a guy he recognized from Fox Company. A rush of bile flooded his throat and he barely kept it down. The image of a hog suspended in the middle of the corn crib as his dad slit its belly came unbidden. He retched.

"Corpsman!" he screamed again holding a hand up.

He bent to hear the wounded man. Two corpsmen carrying a stretcher ran through loose sand, kneeling beside the injured soldier.

"Ed," the guy mumbled through bloody lips. "Get Ed," he said, "Right beside me."

Connor looked around, spotting another prostrate form in the bomb crater, and a dismembered leg farther along the beach.

"He'll be all right," Connor told the injured soldier as one of the stretcher bearers checked on the other man and shook his head.

"You okay?" asked the nearest medic. "Looks like you took some shrapnel."

Connor quickly checked himself feeling his torso with bloody hands. "Yeah, I'm okay."

As the stretcher bearers ran off towards the field hospital, someone handed Connor another crate and the work continued. Later that night, he wrote a note to his parents. He wouldn't sleep for hours, and then his sleep filled with bloody pieces of flesh. He hadn't known either of the men carried off on stretchers, except as he passed them in the chow line or wandered around on the ship, but they'd begun to appear in his thoughts.

In the letter, he worried that he would die of boredom.

> Dear folks,
>
> Here I am on the other side of the world, worrying about a stubbed toe. That's about the worst injury I'm likely to have over here.
>
> It's a good thing you taught me how to work, Pop, because that's all the Army thinks we're good for. We're stuck here unloading ships, making roads, and making room for more soldiers.
>
> There are a few natives who speak Aussie-English and I talk to them sometimes. I'm learning a few words of their language. The enemy has used them for slave labor, so they hate the Japs worse than we do. I'm learning a lot about the country from them, and I hope that will come in handy if we see any action.

SEE WILLY SEE

Mom, just remember, no bullet's got my name on it and I'll see you when this is over. Meanwhile, I'm seeing stuff I'd have never seen if not for the war. (I wonder if that means Pauline was right about adventures.)

Connor

Lying on his cot late one evening, Connor dodged a stream of water dripping from one of the many holes in his tent and tried to write to Nora. Damn air raids. Keep the duct tape companies in business.

Dear Sis:

Well, I thought I'd be reporting to you from the middle of the fray by now, but instead, the 158th remains a labor crew. Seems a waste to have crack troops. trained for jungle warfare, unloading ships. The Army won't allow my Indians and Mexicans to do what they're good at and trained for. Don't get me wrong, I'm not eager for combat, but it pisses me off they won't give my guys a chance.

I've got some good news, though. The jumpsuits they've given us have wide legs that can be strapped shut. It's amazing what you can drop in from the front zipper to retrieve back in your tent. We unloaded crates of fresh oranges yesterday. They were good!

Did you know you have to fill out a requisition form to get a roll of toilet paper? They fit nicely into the jumpsuits, too. You could think of it as stealing from the American public, but we really do need the TP and I think of it as saving the Army the cost of paper, typewriter ribbons, and carbon. I'm sure, if you were here, you'd approve.

To keep from simply exploding from boredom, I kind of slip out of camp sometimes. There are all kinds of critters here that you can't even imagine. I've still got my camera, so I hope I can get some pictures back to the U.S. I don't think they'll let them go in the mail now. I'm guessing if we ever get into action, the camera and film will have to go. I'm not sure how to save anything.

Anyway, I don't know if you'll get this, but I hope they're treating you alright.

Connor

Between labor details Connor finally received another letter from Nora. He couldn't tell where they held her because of words blacked out by German censors. At least he knew she was all right.
Connor

Well, here we are in our ███████ hideaway near ███████.

Food's short, but I think we get as much as they give themselves. Your dilemma has become familiar here too. Not much to do except supervised hikes or an occasional picnic—also supervised. Compared to the endless scurrying at the embassy this quiet is maddening, although a bit of a relief, I must admit. The country here is beautiful. You wouldn't know there's a war on except for the rationing. For lack of anything else to say, I'll close.

Nora

He began to feel better about his sister in a hideaway far from war. But he knew she wouldn't hesitate to make things up so the family wouldn't worry. He knew he was guilty of the same and he couldn't help thinking of the guilty secrets he and Nora had shared as kids. He hoped they weren't sharing this one. He wrote back immediately but didn't say much. The censors would cut it anyway.

Nora,

One of the more unpleasant, but efficient, members of my squad has just been snarling around here and I don't know yet what bugged him. Enas Moore's the gunner's assistant, a Pima/Maricopa, descended from missionaries, agents, and the Indians they were supposed to serve. I told you about him once before, I think. (It's been a long war and I haven't even been in it.) He's just mad all the time; works like a dog, always scowling, rarely laughs.

He's got blue eyes that'll drill right through you, and they make you feel like you've got a dirty secret and he knows it. I don't think he likes himself much.

Sometimes, when he talks about his dad, he refers to him as The Squaw Man. I don't know. We all get along here because we have to, but he seems to make everybody nervous.

              Connor

After a couple of months at Milne Bay, the First and Third Battalions peeled off to Kiriwina and Woodlark islands for more manual labor building airstrips and harbor facilities and to practice their amphibious landings.

Connor's battalion ended up providing security for General Walter Krueger's Sixth Army Headquarters at Finschafen—a far cry from fighting Japs in the jungle. The anti-aircraft guns and Allied Air Corps stationed there kept the bombing and strafing to a minimum. That was okay by him.

SEE WILLY SEE

He'd never been one to lie around, and he couldn't be still. He became acquainted with the little bit of New Guinea he could see or hear. Sometimes he stepped into the edge of the jungle, just outside the clearing of the compound, stood quietly, looked. He didn't always see the bird that went with the whirr, or the shshshshsh, or the tick, tick, tick, or even the bird that sounded very like a jay. One day he spotted a lovesick bird of paradise. He watched as the bird danced, spreading feathers around his chest and shoulders to make a wide crescent, ticking, and throwing his head from side to side, antennae swinging, and tail wagging.

Suppressing a laugh, Connor wondered if he'd have been more successful with Pauline if he'd put on a similar performance. He noticed the jungle sounded a little different from Panama. Instead of the loud, clear call of a bellbird like running a finger around the edge of fine glass, he heard the grunt of an occasional turkey-like cassowary that would wander into the compound with a chick. He learned to identify palm cockatoos when one of the island natives who befriended him pointed out a male courting with a twig drumming on a hollow tree. Not Gene Krupa, but it had rhythm.

Clearing roads, they sometimes encountered snakes as they had in Panama. Connor could have watched them for hours—smooth muscles rippling down long bodies. At the end of a long, boring day, when he wanted to run into the ocean and drown himself, the jungle would erupt with the rousing giggle of a kookaburra.

The natives, christened "Fuzzy Wuzzy Angels" by the Australians, had learned a little English. They had helped Australian soldiers who got lost in the jungle. They seemed likely to help the Americans. They'd rescued sick and wounded Aussies, and the Army from down-under had employed them as stretcher bearers. Again, Connor spent free time with the natives, learning what he could about the new territory.

He"d been on the southern hemisphere nearly a year when George Company got called into battle. The 112th Cavalry had pushed into New Britain by way of the Arawe Peninsula—right across the straight from Finschafen and the 158th's Second Battalion remained on stand-by. George Company had been outfitted and hauled to a tiny peninsula off the southern coast of New Britain where the cavalry held a line at the neck of the peninsula. Connor learned there that bombing and strafing on Milne Bay had served only as prelude. As usual, the Bushmasters unloaded their own supplies and weapons amid chaos.

December 20, 1943 – Arawe, New Britain

A dark hump appeared on the horizon—the Arawe Peninsula. This would be the Bushmaster's first real trial by combat. Through the rain, spatter on the ocean threw up a layer of fog. A long line of jungle appeared like a dark wall—a sinister black castle they would have to enter to slay a dragon made up of men much like themselves.

Connor stood at the rail, watching. *We've seen air raids, but there's not much you can do during an air raid except duck and cover. You either survive or you don't. This will be different. This time, we'll look into the face of the enemy, not through cockpit windows. Will we stand up under fire? Are we the men we think we are?*

Connor clambered over the side of the troop ship, letting himself down rope netting into a simple, topless, box-shaped landing craft where he and his platoon squatted in the bottom. They wore full packs on their backs, rifles gripped, butt down on the deck in white-knuckled hands, and helmets buckled on their heads.

Although he noticed Mendez clenching and unclenching his jaw, mostly the faces stayed rigid, eyes staring straight. He twitched to ease the straps over his shoulders and across his chest. Several others twisted or squeezed fingers under the straps to ease pressure and allow blood to flow down their arms. From the deck of the ship, all had seemed quiet on the landing beach. He could see little through the downpour.

Water cascaded over the front of the ramp as the craft accelerated and plowed toward shore like a truck loaded with livestock. So far, they'd been lucky. No enemy aircraft had greeted their landing. A thud jarred him when the boat hit the reef.

"Head for the trees," he yelled as men began bailing over the dropped deck like giant sea turtles, packs bulging with field equipment.

Connor hit the water running, knees high to clear the liquid hurdle. He gripped his rifle across his chest. He spotted Green, machine-gun balanced across his shoulders, and Tats Wilson right beside him, strings of ammo strapped across his broad chest ready to load and an ammo box in his right hand. He glanced up at the beach. Palm trees about ten feet from the water bristled with shreds of torn trunks and ripped leaves.

"Welcome to Arawe," yelled one of the 112th Cavalrymen lounging in the trees. "We're here to help you wimps set up housekeeping."

"It's about time you got here," yelled another. "We already cleaned out all the Japs."

Connor grinned. "That so? Then what are we here for?"

What a gorgeous day for a landing! He dropped his pack inside tree line and started to flop on the sand—maybe get the skinny from the men who had been there a while. Besides rain spatter on water, he could see broken trees and burned-out craters, and he knew his company had been brought up to reinforce troops who needed help.

SEE WILLY SEE

"All right," yelled Captain Cochran, "Off your asses and onto your feet. Get out there and help unload those barges."

A collective groan. Unloading yet another boat. That's all they'd done since they'd left Panama—unload supplies, build roads and airfields, and expand bases. They were trained fighting men. They handed off crates of food and materiel—fruit juices, canned peaches, salt, sugar, C rations, toilet paper, ammunition, and flamethrowers.

As he worked, he glanced around at a beachhead alive with activity—men unloading landing craft even as boats backed out to be replaced by others. They looked like water spiders skimming from ship to shore. He remembered an image brought to mind years before by a trapper friend of his father's—Old Bud Winslow.

'You know," the old man had said, "goin' by the number of animals I trap every night and the ones I see in my headlights when I go check my traps, the earth's crust must crawl with living things in the dark."

In New Britain in broad daylight, shuttered by rain, the narrow beach crawled. Trucks ferried the stacked crates to the front at the neck of the peninsula. When the Bushmasters followed, they passed the evacuation hospital with its crippled operating tent held together with duct tape and hope. It had taken a direct hit a few days earlier.

"Christ," said Green. "Just shoot me if I get wounded. Don't ever put me in one of them holes."

Connor peered into one of the slit trenches where wounded lay after treatment. White bandages stood out in the gloom. A pair of corpsmen hauled a stretcher out of the trench, jostling the bandaged soldier.

"Where you takin' him?"

"He's goin' on one of them ships headed for Finschafen. Home probably."

As Connor trudged toward the front line, he met several other stretcher-bearers, some of them hauling dead men.

George Company dug shallow foxholes as dark settled. They stuffed the wet bottoms with coconuts and leaves and roofed them with broken palm logs and thatch—all in a continuous downpour. Once the flamethrowers were unpacked, the nearly continuous sound of a hot wind, like the dust storms that had driven Connor away from home and onto the road a decade earlier, accompanied the work. Rain helped to muffle the screams of Japanese snipers fried out of trees where they'd tied themselves with ammunition, food, and water.

The heft of his shovel and the motion of lifting sand out of the growing hole gave Connor familiarity, a kind of tactile comfort as he tried to block out sounds of chaos and the smell of burnt meat.

During the last hours of daylight, in a period of calm, Connor retired to the mess tent where he could stay dry and write to Nora.

>Nora,
>
>We landed today on this little peninsula—one mile by three miles, I hear. I can't imagine what possible use it could be to us, but the generals want it, I guess. It's got a coconut grove right up to the beach, although the Navy and Air Corps have pretty much chopped it to pieces.
>
> You asked what it's like, Sis, so I'll give it to you straight. Soldiering is months and months of sheer boredom interrupted by moments of sheer terror. Today, we made our first landing into Jap-held territory. When we finally had a chance to eat, we stood in line and Jakes elbowed me in the ribs. He

pointed, like he does, kind of with his chin, at a little guy standing in the other line. The guy's uniform seemed much too big for him, so I nodded, and Jakes stepped over there. He grabbed the guy and sure enough—a Jap trying to get a good American meal. Somebody with the 112th hauled him off for interrogation. I don't know what they'll do with him after that.

It's been a rough day, unloading our supplies for this campaign in rain like you've never seen, but just know that I'm all right and no Jap's got my name on his bullet. You be sure you take care of yourself and don't give the Nazis too much trouble. Got an old newspaper in Finschafen before they sent us over here. I understand they're trying to trade you for some German prisoners, so I suppose you'll be home before me.

Connor

Darkness fell suddenly, like velvet curtains on a stage and Connor, back in his semi-dry foxhole drifted off into an eerie silence. Small arms fire startled him awake. Along with the rest of the squad he grabbed his rifle and prepared for hand-to-hand fighting.

"Don't nobody move," whispered platoon commander, Lt. Carpenter as he squat-walked, head down, along the row of soldiers.

"What's goin' on?"

"Dunno. But the sentries'll shoot anything that moves—coconuts, land crabs, people out to take a piss. Anything."

Jakes sat next to Connor in their mansion of a foxhole. "Remember them cliffs along the shore?"

"Sure."

"Japs dug caves in 'em. Come out at night."

"Fuck," Connor said. "So maybe they're coming in behind us?"

"Uh huh."

Despite the night's calm, Connor spent it listening to rats chewing on the coconuts he'd stacked in the hole underneath his body and trying to hear any movement above ground.

December 21, 1943

The next day, Connor had had very little time to orient himself to the camp before the bombing and strafing began. George Company had almost finished their foxholes when someone spotted the first speck in the sky.

"Here they come!"

Planes came in waves, a stray bomber barely clearing the trees, tearing up the forest. Men glanced over their shoulders and kept moving—maybe just a little faster, like frenetic puppets. They listened to the air battle above their heads and tried to get themselves underground.

The planes flew so low Connor could hear the bomb bay doors open—squeak, clang—and then the whistle of bombs. He hit the ground next to a cavalryman, rolling with him into a soggy crater next to some tree roots. The first of the bombs detonated, spraying metal fragments, along with sand, water, and mud. When the planes had passed and the rain of debris stopped, Connor stood, brushing his fatigues. The other man remained curled in the bottom of the crater, trembling and twitching. Connor crawled back and laid a hand on the guy's shoulder.

"Hey buddy, it's over. They're gone now. You can get up."

Although Connor stayed with him in the water-saturated crater for half-an-hour, the man couldn't move. His frantic yelling and crying set Connor's teeth on edge.

"Shut him up," said someone passing the crater. "Just shut him up."

He called for a corpsman, and the medics hauled the man away.

Connor joined the chow line as the attackers screamed off into the distance—to get more bombs, he assumed. He didn't know what the medics could do for the guy in the crater. Drugs, he guessed. Uncle Harry came to mind, but he shoved the thought away as he held out his tray.

They sustained three air attacks that day, but at least they got their foxholes dug.

Connor turned to a nearby cavalryman as he and Jakes draped thatch over the rest of their new home. "How far out there are they?"

The soldier maneuvered a matchstick into the corner of his mouth. "You mean the Japs?"

"Yeah, I mean the Japs."

"'Bout four-five hundred yards."

"What?"

"Yeah. They got trenches, an' foxholes, an' weapons emplacements. We draw a bead on one of them clusters, an' they just move on to another'n." He paused and took the matchstick out of his mouth. "Guess you could call it a cluster fuck."

Connor stared at the man. He thought the set-up sounded like a prairie dog village with front doors and back doors and rattlesnakes hiding in between. He knew they'd find out for himself soon enough.

December 22, 1943

Connor walked through dense jungle, water dropping from the edges of his helmet down his neck and past his eyes. His wet fatigues clung to his skin, heavy and clammy. The squad formed a line, weaving through the jungle like the snake that gave them their name. Hayes, their forward scout, would suddenly slow, crouch and wait.

Hayes cocked his right ear, the best one, he'd told Connor. His eyes scanned almost 270 degrees and his nostrils flared. The whole squad would bunch up then, waiting for the go-ahead.

During one of those pauses, Connor looked at the canopy half a football field above. Hardly any sun leaked through the ceiling of leaves. He knew the sun shone that day because he'd seen it before they stepped into the overgrowth. They dropped to a knee when a kookaburra interrupted the silence with a raucous laugh. Connor swallowed a rock in his throat and began walking again as the bird flapped off into the canopy. If he weren't so damned miserable, he guessed he'd laugh, too, at this string of nervous men, fidgeting and fingering their weapons, stalking through the rain forest in dripping clothes they'd been wearing now for three days.

Fifteen minutes later, Hayes dropped to a knee. The squad stopped, looking for traps. They knew the Jap foxholes lay just a few yards ahead. If they could get close enough—without getting killed or captured themselves—they could drop grenades in those trenches and foxholes, cutting off enemy escape routes. Hayes motioned to the right, machete flashing as he cut through the undergrowth. The hacking made noise the Japs wouldn't fail to notice. Connor crept up to his forward scout.

"What you got?"

"Looks like abandoned emplacement."

"Let's just drop some grenades and get out."

"Make sure nobody's there."

Connor understood. He didn't want to get shot either.

The men crawled, slid, and sweated through the undergrowth behind their scout. As he cut and whacked, Connor focused on the fact his trigger finger held a machete. With his rifle in his left hand, he felt naked. He'd tried slashing the undergrowth with his left hand, but it didn't work very well.

They slashed a semi-circle around a cluster of foxholes and interlocking trenches. Satisfied they were empty Connor gave the order to blow them up. He couldn't decide whether he hoped the destruction would bring the wasps out to fight or not. They hadn't seen a Jap all day—only signs they'd been around.

By the time they'd pitched their grenades into the enemy facilities, the men looked ready to collapse and sunset approached. Connor gave the order to return to their perimeter.

After the noisy grenade concussions, silence surrounded them—not a bird call, not a bandicoot shuffling in the underbrush, not a breeze stirring in the canopy. He noticed Green, crouched over his weapon, fiddling with the trigger mechanism and Martinez flipping his safety on and off, on and off. When they finally flopped in their wet foxholes, they had not seen a single Japanese soldier. He knew the enemy had not been far away.

No one moved—until they noticed the leeches. A flurry of stripping and picking the blood-filled bodies from wet, withered flesh followed. When they arrived in the mess tent, along with other similarly soaked and exhausted troops, they breathed a little easier.

That night, Connor and Jakes piled more thatch on their roof, and they crawled into their foxhole. Connor woke to rain dripping through thatch onto his forehead. He squirmed out of the way and dozed off again. He woke a second time to a flurry of thatch and snapping claws. He jumped out of his cot muttering.

"God damned land crabs."

He grabbed the animal behind the claws, chucked it to the floor and smashed it with his rifle butt. "Fuck," he muttered, lying back on the cot in a puddle, water pouring onto his belly.

"That any way to treat your pets?" Jakes muttered. They lapsed into silence.

"Fuckin' rain."

The two men dozed again, waiting for dawn—or at least a lapse in the rain.

At about 12:30 hours, they heard scattered rifle fire. Peering over the edge of the foxhole, Connor spotted movement outside the perimeter. He moved his squad up next to the sentry, watching for enemy while Green and Moore set up the machine-gun. He spotted a shuffling of leaves and pointed, just as Green opened fire.

"Damn," whispered Mendez, motioning toward the rear. Connor nodded and Mendez moved in silence toward one of the attackers, just as a Japanese soldier headed for the American ammo dump. Quick as a cobra, Mendez struck, slitting the enemy's throat and dropping him to pursue another. A sound from behind crates of ammunition startled the enemy soldier and he dropped, changed direction, and headed for the jungle with Mendez close on his heels.

As the Japanese outside the perimeter withdrew, Connor spotted Mendez still following the Jap along the flank and into the jungle. "Mendez!" he yelled as Green fired another blast, but the man kept moving.

About an hour later, with the Japanese troops turned back and silence restored, Connor heard an exchange of passwords and a, "Psst! It's me, Mendez."

"Good, Get back to your foxhole."

December 23, 1943

Next morning, standing in the chow line, Connor spotted Mendez. "So, what happened out there?"

"You saw me followin' that Jap headed for the ammo dump. Well, I got him, but then I saw another'n. I thought I was gonna get me another Jap."

"Yeah?"

"Anyway, he stepped into the jungle—seemed like I was always just a step behind him. Then he took a hard left 'n I almost caught up." Mendez studied the toes of his boots, kicking a little rock around. "Then I looked up an' I was on the wrong side of the Japs 'n they was comin' my way."

Connor and Mendez picked up trays at the edge of the mess tent.

"And?"

"I never been so scared in my life, Sarge. Didn't have time to run." he gulped. "You know how those roots—I don' know what kind of tree—they split an' spread out like walls?"

"Yeah?"

"Well, I tripped over the edge of one of them damn things and went sprawlin.' I just knew I was a goner. But I crawled clear back next to the trunk and rolled up in a ball, an' they ran right over me."

Connor held out his tray and waited for the food to plop onto his plate.

"Mendez," he said, "do you have any idea how lucky you are to be here for this good Army chow?"

Mendez inspected his tray. "Yes, sir," he mumbled.

"Just don't be running off on your own like that. Understood?"

"Yes, sir."

Connor started to walk off then turned around. "Any idea how many of them were out there?"

"Only about ten or fifteen that I saw, but I heard a little noise up the line."

Connor nodded and walked on. Before he got out of earshot, he heard Mendez talking about him as he sat down with Hidalgo and Martinez.

"He's got about ten years on us." "So what?" asked Martinez.

"He's kind of a mother hen. Thinks he's gonna bring us all home, safe an' sound."

"I'm okay with that."

"Not much chance of it," Hidalgo interjected. "Odds against it."

"We know, Hidalgo," Martinez said, "but he's gonna try. I can follow a man like that."

SEE WILLY SEE

Connor grinned and found a place next to Peters.

Patrolling later in the day, Connor's squad fell into the rhythm they'd established in Panama, ignoring the downpour sliding off their helmets, down their necks and inside their ponchos. They lifted water-soaked boots along with the mud dragging at their feet. Once off the trail, creeping among coconut palms on swampy grass, the men scanned treetops for Japanese snipers, rifles ready to fire before fired upon, straining to hear through the roar of rain. A few feet into the jungle edge, the roar turned to a whisper of drops trickling from leaf to leaf down the canopy. Single file, they moved off the trail and hacked their way through vines and underbrush. They took turns walking point, giving each man a turn. They'd marched that way for about an hour when Connor realized he hadn't seen Menardo for a while.

"Hey," he said, touching Hayes' sleeve. "You seen Menardo?"

Hayes looked around. "No, Sarge."

Connor made his way up the column, looking for the missing soldier. "All right," he said. "Take it easy. Hayes, I need you to go find Menardo."

Hayes melted into the jungle. The rest of the squad found their places among buttress roots, breaking out cigarettes. Forty-five minutes later, Hayes and Menardo seemed to materialize.

"Where the hell you been, Menardo?"

"Spotted a faint trail and thought I'd follow it a little ways."

"You crazy? Don't be goin' off on your own like that."

"No, Sarge."

"All right. What did you find?"

"There's this deserted bunker out there. Nobody around. I watched it for a while, but nobody showed up. I don't think they're using it."

"Let's go take a look—see if we can find anything of value to intelligence. Where's Peters' squad?"

"When we fanned out, they went off to the right."

"Okay. Keep your eyes open."

The men followed Menardo to an opening in the understory. Connor peered into semi-darkness. He looked for a trip wire. Finding none, he opened a wooden chest set beside a makeshift table. He reached inside for a stack of papers. "Might be some intelligence in here."

He lifted out a sheaf of pictures, family photos—a man holding a small child's hand and a woman holding a baby. He held them looking into them as though he could see the life of the man who put them there. He took a long moment to put them back. He closed the box.

"We'll haul this back to base." He tapped the lid. "Make sure there's nothing in here they can use—ammo, weapons, grenades, radio. Then torch it. Let's get back 'fore dark. This is way too close for comfort."

The rain had stopped while they inspected the bunker, although leaves continued to drip. When Connor turned back toward base camp, he spotted Beacon.

"Damn it. Get that helmet back on your head."

"My brain's broiling."

"I know, but I can see you a mile off—in the dark."

"Yeah, Beacon," said Green, slapping him on the back. "You wouldn't look good with a hole in that gorgeous blond noggin."

Grumbling, Beacon slapped the offending helmet back on his head.

December 24, 1943

Sunlight seeped into the jungle. Connor awoke to somebody in Stan Peter's area yelling. "God damn it, Cormac. Them fuckin' yellow bastards! God damn it!"

Connor and Jakes watched in silence, along with Peter's squad, as a couple of stretcher bearers hauled Giles Cormac over the side of his foxhole. Smack in the middle of the encampment, the trench should have been safe, but the man's throat had been cut. Connor glanced at Jakes who shrugged his shoulders.

"Guess we won't be talkin' no longhorns anymore."

No one spoke when Tom Chisum flopped on his butt in the sand. "I shoulda heard something," he moaned. "I slept right beside him—not two feet away. I shoulda heard them sneaky little bastards."

Connor remembered standing in the chow line next to the two men a couple of nights before, joking with Chisum, an amiable giant of a man, and Cormac, eyes sparkling through glasses he always polished with a white handkerchief and big, meaty hands. Connor couldn't remember what they'd joked about.

The remainder of Christmas Eve passed in camp with the 112th taking their turn on patrol and Bushmasters holding the defensive line against small-scale attacks. Throughout the day, artillery and mortar fire pounded known enemy positions. Even when the Japs retreated, American artillery continued to seek them out wherever they tried to take cover.

At night, the enemy kept trying to infiltrate American lines and the Americans kept pushing them out. While the noise of those attacks strung Connor's nerves tight, the silence in between kept him awake. That's when he felt his body tense like stretching fence wire against a solid corner post. Again and again, he'd consciously released his muscles, one by one, starting with his toes. Each time he released his scowl, his legs twitched. He would hear a leaf rustle in a light breeze and wonder, "Is that a step?" Jakes would shift in his sleep and Connor would have his rifle in hand, bayonet fixed.

By morning, his anger began to bubble over. Give the bastards credit—slipping in and slitting one throat. It's a masterful psychological tactic. Too angry to admire it, Connor ground his teeth.

December 25, 1943

Connor spent a mostly uneventful Christmas Day at base camp. Cavalry units withdrew, under attack, from their forward observation post near Umtingalu, a village to the northeast along the coast. They dug in next to George Company amid rumors that the attackers constituted an advance guard of a much larger Japanese force. The Americans had pecked away at small numbers of enemy soldiers that they couldn't pin down. Like shadows, the Japs disappeared as soon as the U.S. Army found them. Reinforcements on the Jap side would make the job harder.

In the afternoon Connor found a log and wrote a long overdue letter to his parents. It appeared that Arawe would soon become more active, so he wanted to take advantage of the relative quiet. He'd send it the next day with wounded going back to Finschafen.

SEE WILLY SEE

Dear Mom and Pop,

Quiet day here on Christmas Day. Some of the officers crawled out of their foxholes this morning and serenaded us with Christmas carols. What a bunch of caterwauling! The Army fed us some little pieces of Christmas turkey, then a couple of platoons headed out for a forward observation post.

I don't know which are worse, the Japs or the land crabs. Had one fall through the roof a couple of nights ago snapping his claws like castanets. Made a big hole in the roof and the rain just poured in on me, of course. So, land crabs are on my list. God, Pop, they're bigger around than a disc blade! And the mosquitoes they got here are big as anything in Panama. We all have yellow skin from the Atabrine.

It's getting close to sunset around here. Honestly, it's like the sun just crashes into the ocean and sizzles out. One minute it's daytime and the next it's night.

Don't worry about me. I'm gonna be fine. See ya when this is over.

Connor

The suspense didn't last long. All night the planes came in waves. Just as the Americans began to assess the damages, another shrieking phalanx of Zeros followed by the roar of bombers would scream overhead. Some of the men crawled out of their collapsing foxholes and shot at the planes. A few of them connected and, once or twice, the screaming engines changed tempo in a downward spiral that ended somewhere out to sea. Next morning, they hauled casualties, dead and wounded, picked out of craters. When Connor counted his squad, all were present and accounted for, but Peters had lost another couple of guys.

Connor didn't know Joel Wagoner very well, but he couldn't help remembering how devastated Tom Chisum had been when he lost his friend. He thought Chisum would go back to the states where his shattered arm could heal. He hoped his mind would heal too.

December 26, 1943

Reconnaissance patrols searched for more than a few, isolated enemy. This time, they sought a large, noisy column marching from the north. Reinforced Jap units could overrun their line at the neck of the peninsula.

Since Cormac's death, the Americans had moved more slowly, crouching on the jungle floor. A broken twig, a whiff of breeze fluttering the canopy, a bird chirp, even a particularly loud drop of water flattened the whole squad. Connor saw eyes narrowed, scanning the leaves, endless, gigantic leaves. His heart pounded in his throat and the others swallowed hard as well. He couldn't decide which he hated more, moving around the jungle searching for the sneaky little bastards or taking a turn on the main line of resistance, waiting for them to come find him.

That night, the Japs attempted to infiltrate. Fifteen soldiers attempted to sneak in along the coast from the east. They killed a couple of men before the cavalry's light mortars sent them back. Connor heard the ruckus and spent the night listening to rats scurrying among the coconuts and Jakes' heavy breathing. He wondered how the man managed to sleep.

In silence and blood, the men settled into days of nerve-wracking inaction broken by occasional attempts to infiltrate the lines. In daylight, U.S. reconnaissance patrols looked for a new column of enemy. After less than two weeks on the lines, George Company troops' nerves were strung tighter than a barbed wire fence singing in a prairie wind. Bleary-eyed and tired, Connor anticipated the real battle that had not yet begun, crawling out of his foxhole and making reconnaissance patrols. Day after day, he and his compatriots looked for the Japanese reinforcements. All they found were a few hit-and-run soldiers that would set up a machine-gun on the U.S. perimeter. kill as many as possible, then disappear into the swamp.

Night melted into morning. Connor lost track of days. He remembered back in Panama how he'd counted the days until his hitch ended. Then he'd counted again. He'd only been on the front line for a couple of weeks, but the lack of end time depressed him. He had no days to count.

December 27 passed almost exactly like the 26th, giving Connor an even stronger sense of endlessness.

December 28, 1943

He woke to another day of monsoon rain. Lost a boot in the mud on his way to the mess tent. Stood one-footed to fish the offending boot out of the sludge and slip it back on his wet sock. The Cavalry's B Troop set out to retake Umtingala, but sniper and light mortar fire sent them back to the American lines. C troop set out in the opposite direction. They lost six men to machine-gun and rifle fire. Connor heard the commotion as George Company and the remainder of the cavalry held the line against a force of twenty to thirty of infantry. The Japs tried to sneak in through the swamp and take out American mortars. Caught in the act, they retreated before the cavalrymen, a platoon from George Company, and the mortars they'd tried to capture. The Japs lost seventeen men in the process. Connor felt too exhausted to cheer.

In the mess tent, Connor stood next to Peters. They eyed each other. Their blank stares said it all. Nothing else to say. Waiting for that anticipated enemy force stalled conversation.

As the year neared its end, American soldiers on Arawe had sustained more than a week of small raids—just enough to keep them awake. And, just to be sure, Washing-machine Charlie, the Japanese fighter pilot with his out-of-synch engine, had continued his nightly strafing runs. Every night, the Americans hauled ass out of their foxholes to turn back a few enemy soldiers. The threat of a single silent soldier sneaking into camp just to slit one throat never left Connor's mind. He could see his fear echoed in every rigid face he glimpsed.

December 29, 1943

Mid-morning, the daily recon patrol scrambled back into camp, its leader heading directly for General Cunningham's tent. "Japanese reinforcements hauling ass in our direction," said a cavalryman as he flopped on the ground next to Conroy and Peters. "I'd count on a big raid tonight."

Within minutes, Connor's platoon had grabbed rifles and grenades, shouldered their packs and snatched up ammo. Connor checked with the radioman and got a thumbs-up. The men barely spoke.

There were only shuffles and clicks of equipment. They set out to patrol the swamp. Only a gentle swish of water marked their progress. They followed along the coastline to root out any straggling enemy soldiers hiding there. When they waded onto dry land, one man at a time on a scattered front, they dropped to the jungle floor for a brief rest. Connor scanned the tired men, all soaked to the skin, picking off leaches.

"Beacon," he said, "get that damned helmet on your head."

The rest of the squad turned to look at Beacon's glowing mop.

"Hey," said Green, "I got an idea. Maybe next time we're in Australia, you can dye that cotton top."

"Nah," said Wilson. He stood and scooped up a handful of mud from the swamp they"d just crossed. "You can rub a handful of this stuff onto your shining tresses."

Eiseler plopped his helmet on his head. "If my brain cooks, it's all on you guys."

They moved on with Hayes and Mendez ahead scouting. Their progress slowed to a near halt. Each step meant a brief stop to look, to listen, and to sniff the air.

Connor turned to the new guy. "Smell anything?"

"Rotten plants."

"The Japs have their own smell."

"Wha'da'ya mean?" He sniffed.

"You'll know it when you smell it. Kind of musty, salty, fishy. Different from American stink."

They slipped north from the swamp—around what Connor hoped marked the west edge of Japanese emplacements. They hadn't probed far when he heard what he'd looked for—Japanese soldiers moving toward the American front line. They observed enemy activity for what seemed like hours. They crept back to the swamp for a long wade and a report to Captain Cochran. While they were gone, the rest of the Arawe contingent further fortified their position. Sandbags built up the foxholes, mortar and machine-gun positions along the front lines. Their front curved across the swamp to their left and the limestone bluffs to the right. New interconnecting slit trenches allowed them to move along the line as needed. That night they crawled into their foxholes, rifles ready and grenades within reach. The big attack didn't materialize—just the same small, probing attempts to infiltrate.

SEE WILLY SEE

December 30-31, 1943

George Company's rotation kept them on the front lines for a couple of days while cavalrymen patrolled. Connor knew Japanese reinforcements had dug in, but the big attack didn't come and didn't come. The Americans went out on daily patrols to pin down the new positions.

Artillery and mortar fire seemed completely ineffective. Connor could hear their mortars coming from one place then they would come in from an entirely different direction. He figured the constant shelling in such a concentrated area would eventually clear out enemy cover and they'd be hanging out there in full view. Given the amount of firepower poured into the few hundred yards ahead of the American lines, he couldn't believe the shelling hadn't completely denuded it yet. It seemed the little rats could crawl around in fallen trees and tangled vines without ever poking a head up to look around.

Cormac and Chism never left his mind for long. Damnably effective war of nerves. *Six days since Cormac and every night a few Japs try to infiltrate the lines. Every man startles awake at the tiniest sound. A dozen Japs can wake us all up while their Jap buddies sleep peacefully in their foxholes.*

He fingered the safety, listening to the satisfying snick when it released. He could order his men to watch for any motion—anything that might mean the expected attack. They probably waited on full alert like he did anyway. He scanned the sky. Aside from Washing Machine Charlie, they hadn't had an air raid in days. With the carriers out of the area and the air base on the little island off the coast incomplete, it seemed like an opportune time for the Japs.

Sure enough, Japanese fighters and bombers conducted waves of air raids New Year's Eve and into the early morning of New Year's Day. Connor heard bomb bay doors opening and bombs whistling into the dense encampment followed by the roar of explosions, one after another, as the bombs "walked" down the peninsula. The ground shook. Sand from the walls of his foxhole sifted down the sides. He felt like he was being buried alive.

January 1, 1944

Happy New Year! Cavalrymen swooped into camp yelling, "We got 'em. We got 'em! We found the little bastards." B Troop grabbed packs and weapons and moved out before the enemy could move again. Connor heard intense firing. Stretcher bearers struggled toward the evac hospital. By the end of the day, the cavalrymen had to withdraw with three dead and seventeen wounded. For the next couple of days, the action fell back into constant probing on both sides—like a badger poking a rattlesnake.

At sunup January 4, the 112th G Troop slipped into packs and checked weapons. Metal snapped and clicked as soldiers readied equipment for action. The men moved out of camp in what Connor hoped would be a surprise attack. Throughout the day, Jeeps laden with stretchers, front and back, came at intervals. Three dead, twenty-one wounded.

One of the jeeps passed, carrying a wounded man, a stitching of blood across his chest, blood bubbling at his mouth. Connor looked into the man's eyes and saw a kind of unexpected acceptance—as though the man had known all along. The waiting had ended for him and he'd either survive or he wouldn't. Connor felt the wounded man had entered another country, somewhere separate from the rest of the soldiers still striving to remain whole.

Further attacks on January 6 and 7 made no headway. They may have disturbed the Japanese units like they'd been disturbing him. He wondered if George Company shouldn't try some night maneuvers now that they knew where to find the little bastards— they'd trained for it—tick up the tension on their side a little bit.

He smiled at the thought.

January 10, 1944

Ships arrived, sending out landing craft with Easy Company and a Marine tank company. Connor helped unload supplies and carry dead and wounded to the boats for evacuation to Finschafen. Next day's foot patrols yielded nothing, but Connor knew for sure that, once the tanks got into action, things would change.

On the 12th, Fox Company landed. The new troops moved out the following morning, along with tanks, to probe Japanese positions a mere quarter of a mile away. They continued pushing and retreating for three days before the main attack began. For those three days, George Company helped hold the line, keeping the enemy from breaking through the swamp to the left or their flank to the right.

While the tanks and infantry prepared for a full, frontal assault. Army engineers scrambled to build an emergency air strip on one of the little islands off the peninsula. On the morning of the 16th a squadron of American B-24 Liberator bombers dropped their loads on the Japanese, as B-25s strafed them. While the bombs fell, American soldiers huddled in their foxholes, only a few hundred yards from the action.

"That's more like it," Connor mumbled as he ducked before a particularly close explosion that blew in the edge of his foxhole, spraying mud everywhere. Jakes yelled something he barely heard. The blast had nearly deafened him. An artillery and mortar barrage added to the noise and confusion as Easy and Fox companies moved into his line of sight through the slit between sandbags and logs holding the roof.

SEE WILLY SEE

At 0800 hours, the bombardment stopped, and tanks growled forward, each followed by a platoon from Easy or Fox. Connor's squad held the rightmost position on the American line—the position closest to the limestone cliffs and the trail that followed them. As the day wore on, an occasional Japanese squad would attempt to break through, but mostly the tanks and forward companies kept them too busy for sneak attacks.

At 1300 hours a particularly bold enemy squad slipped along the bluffs and headed for the ammo dump. Reece reported them to Connor, who sent Hayes, Eiseler, and the machine-gun crew after them. Intermittent machine-gun bursts and an occasional crack of rifle fire followed their movements. When the party returned at 1630, Green reported Eiseler missing. They'd killed or wounded several Japs, but Eiseler had disappeared from their right flank.

"I think he followed the Japs toward the caves," Hayes said.

"Maybe he caught up with the tanks," Green said. "We were pretty close behind them when we lost the Japs and turned around."

That night, Connor found out where Eiseler had gone. His tortured voice spread through the jungle and echoed off the rock cliffs. In only a few moments, the squad had gathered with several of Peters' men, crouching next to his foxhole.

"Let us go get him, Sarge."

He climbed out and listened, a chill running down his back. "I don't want to risk any more of you."

"We're trained for this. Why'd we spend a year in Panama?"

"I know." Connor shuddered, crouching in the circle of angry men, as the screams gathered intensity "But they've been training for years, too, and they're dug in out there—and it's dark."

"We ain't afraid of the dark."

Just then, Captain Cochran arrived. They all stood and saluted. "I hear you've got a man missing."

"Not anymore," Connor said, "I've got a squad—a couple of squads—itching to go get him."

Cochran paused and listened for a moment. He took a deep breath. "Your orders are to remain right here and hold this line."

"But Captain," Wilson interrupted, "I don't know how long he can last. Listen to him."

"I know, soldier. My hearing's just fine. But I can't risk any more of you." He remained silent, looking from one frustrated, angry soldier to another. "Not a move out of this camp. You got it?"

They all saluted. "Yes sir," they growled.

Cochran turned to Connor. "I want all the squad leaders in the mess tent. On the double."

The 158th officers and non-coms gathered to figure out how to keep the men of Second Battalion from mounting a rescue. The 158th was a well-trained jungle-fighting regiment, Cunningham admitted, but a foolish attack in the middle of the night could be a disaster. We don't have intelligence about the enemy numbers and positions. Just can't do it. He agreed to send a recon unit in the morning.

"Can we do it, sir," Connor asked. "He's in my squad."

Cunningham stared at him, considering. "You wait for orders."

Jaw clenched, Connor crawled back into his foxhole, eyes wide, staring into the dark thatch covering him. The howling went on intermittently all night. Maybe Eiseler had mercifully passed

out in between. Or worse. The intervals of silence set his nerves on edge. He tried not to imagine what they were doing to his soldier Not the biggest, toughest man in the unit, Eiseler had earned Connor's respect. He was as tough as any of them.
He imagined grinning Jap faces surrounding Beacon's golden mop of hair, like a circle of evil moths around a flame. Only the moths did the burning. That's their plan. Keep us all awake, strung tighter than fence wire an' pretty soon we'll all scream in terror.

Eiseler fell silent abruptly about an hour before daylight. Connor hoped it didn't mean the Japs had killed him.

January 17, 1944

At the crack of dawn, Connor scrambled out of his foxhole and headed to HQ where he got the go ahead to find Beacon. After a hurried breakfast Connor's and Peters' squads headed into the jungle in the direction where they'd last heard Eiseler's voice. They didn't have far to go. As they neared the edge of the cliffs, they began to hear a low buzzing sound.

Connor raised a hand to halt the column. The men gathered around.

"I don't know what we're hearing," Connor said, but it could be some kind of trap. "What do you think, Peters? Hayes and Mendez in the lead? Let's go through the jungle where there's at least some cover."

Jungle backed up to the cliffs. Every muscle in Connor's body filled with adrenaline. The Japs could be anywhere—hiding in the caves with machine-guns ready, at the edge of the trees—anywhere.

They crept forward, stopping every few feet to listen as the buzzing intensified. After ten minutes, a light shone through the edge of the jungle. A clearing. Mendez stepped into the space first, freezing and peering ahead with Connor right behind him. The two squads came forward one-by-one.

A man-shaped thing hung by his wrists along the trunk of a tree, his head on his chest. He didn't look like Eiseler. They'd so thoroughly pulverized him it was hard to recognize him. Connor breathed through his mouth, overwhelmed by the smell of burnt flesh, hair, and blood.

"Why is he all black?"

They moved forward, heads up, eyes and ears alert for an ambush. The buzzing became angry, and mounds of flies began to disperse from the soldier's body.

Connor swatted at insects that bounced off him as they abandoned their feast.

"Cut him down!" Connor snapped, his voice strangled.

Eiseler's burnt and bloody hand moved as they eased him onto the ground.

"Christ! He's alive." Connor squatted next to the soldier's head.

Eiseler's eyes popped open, and he gagged on something bloody stuffed into his mouth.

Retching, Wilson rushed to clear it. "Christ! It's his balls. Get the stretcher!"

Eiseler moved his head almost imperceptibly left and right.

Wilson sat, cradling Eiseler's head, looking into expressionless eyes.

Connor assessed the man's injuries. The fingertips he held lacked fingernails and looked burned. Dried blood saturated what remained of his shredded uniform.

"Beacon," he said

The man tried to speak, and Connor leaned closer. "Dropped. Helmet. Sarge."

Connor remembered the white-blond shock of hair he'd repeatedly yelled at Eiseler to cover.

"It's all right, Eiseler," he said, tears welling in his eyes, "it's all right."

Wilson held his friend, looking into hopeless eyes—until Eiseler's muscles relaxed. Wilson hung his head a moment then looked up at Connor, nodding. He swallowed hard.

"At least," he swallowed, "at least he died among friends."

The two squads remained silent, shuffling their feet, and clearing their throats. Connor reached over and closed the man's eyes. Among the squad, some lips moved, and a couple made signs of the cross.

"Let's get him out of here," Connor said, motioning for the stretcher.

No one said a word as they trudged back to base camp, waving off a horde of flies bent on consuming their friend one molecule at a time. Back at base, the stretcher bearers continued to the field hospital behind the lines, where Beacon would be bagged, tagged, and returned to his family in a flag-draped box. Connor hoped the chaplain would say a few kind words over him.

January 18-March 15, 1944

Although the main attack on the 16th had driven most of the Japanese Army out of the area, "mopping up" operations continued for another two months. The Americans did everything they could to make sure they cut off any possible Japanese supply lines.

Sometimes the Bushmasters or cavalrymen dragged Japs in stolen American fatigues out of the chow lines and often at night the enemy would raid the supply dumps grabbing a random crate and running with American soldiers on their heels.

On patrol, the platoons bunched closer than before. One afternoon, Connor's and Peters' squads followed a trail. Mendez brought up the rear until he caught up with Connor.

"Spotted a Jap just wanderin' around," he said. "Followed him a few steps into the brush."

"What'd you find?"

"Don't know. Dead Jap. Looks like he just up and died."

"Wha'da'ya mean?"

"No wounds. Malaria maybe? Starved?"

"Starved?"

"Skinny. Sick."

"Let's go take a look."

The squads doubled back to the dead soldier, lying shirtless and saturated along the trail. Hordes of flies rose from the body only when the soldiers waved them away. Some of them collided with the men and bounced off, speeding into the canopy. As Mendez waved them out of his face, he pointed out the Jap's emaciated condition. The men stood silent for several minutes looking—rain dripping off their helmets onto the dead man.

"He just laid down and died?"

"Stumbled around some and leaned on a tree for a while, then just slid down dead."

"That's too fuckin' easy," Wilson grumbled. "After what they did to Beacon, they ought to suffer."

Connor noted a lot of heads nodding and voices grumbling as the men stared at the corpse.

"Let's take him apart like they did Eiseler."

Before Connor could respond, Wilson produced a knife and sliced off an ear.

"Wilson, what the fuck you doin'?"

"Back in Arizona, when we get too many coyotes, we get a bounty for the ears. We got too many Japs here. This is for Eiseler."

"For Christ's sake."

"Let's get out of here," Peters said.

"Yeah," said Wilson, "maybe we'll find some live ones."

Mendez and Tayo Reese from Peters' squad probed the area in concentric circles around the corpse, finding another dead enemy a few yards down the trail—and another about a quarter of a mile further. They also found numerous dumps where raging dysentery had overcome the Japs. From the second dead man, they followed a trail of emaciated corpses to the apparent location of the Japanese Army's previous front lines then returned to base where Wilson made a stringer for the ears.

Although the Japanese ground forces had little effect after the main battle on the 16th, Japanese airmen managed to light the nights with bombing and strafing runs through the American position. Finally, on February 1, anti-aircraft guns arrived, and the air raids came to a halt—none too soon for Connor.

Day after day, the Americans probed the jungles of New Britain, looking for Japanese resistance. The remainder of the Japanese troops continued to put up fierce resistance, but on their patrols, the Americans found enemy troops too scattered and sick to mount much defense.

March 15, 1944 — Finschafen, Papua, New Guinea

Second Battalion pulled out, headed for rest and relaxation back at Finschafen where they were re-outfitted with new weapons to replace anything broken or lost. New recruits joined them, to replace lost men. Connor's quad got Joe Johnson, a volunteer from Hastings, Nebraska, Peters got his Johnson's brother, Sam, and a couple of other guys.

From Finschafen, Connor wrote home to reassure his parents.

> Dear Mom and Pop,
>
> Just wanted to send a quick note to let you know I'm okay camping out over here in the Southwest Pacific. The good news is that we don't have any sand fleas. Our pets here are a little larger. I told you about the land crabs. They crawl around at night and sometimes they drop in through the thatch in the roofs of our foxholes. Then we get to wrestle them out of our beds. Pretty nasty fighting with them.
>
> How're the cattle wintering? Did you have enough rain last fall to graze them on the winter wheat? It's hard to imagine you're doing winter chores while I stew in my own juice here in the southern hemisphere.

Gosh, I don't have much to say, and the sun's about to set here.

Hope we get this over soon so I can come home.

Connor

As usual, he told Nora more, but he had no idea at that point where she might be.

Dear Nora,

I'm writing to let you know I'm okay and hope you're the same. I saw my first newspaper in a while yesterday and I see that you've been traded for some German prisoners, so I guess you're on your way home. Halleluiah! Mom as usual, had it right. She said you'd get home before me, but I'm hoping I won't be far behind. Have you heard anything from or about Daniel? I hope he's okay too.

A new guy joined my squad a couple of days ago. His name's Joe Johnson and he came from just southeast of Hastings. His brother Sam's in Peters' squad.

Their family got a raw deal. Apparently, the Navy or the Marines or somebody decided the middle of the U.S. would be a good place to make ammunition, so they took a bunch of farms to build a depot for making and storing ammo. Gave those families ten days to pack up and move out. Can you imagine trying to pack up a farm and move it with no place to go?

They didn't get enough for their farms to buy new land—especially on such short notice. Had to take their livestock to the sale barn and take what they could get, lined up the equipment on a neighbor's farm (one that the government didn't take) and auctioned it off—decades of work and surviving the dust storms just gone.

Joe and his brothers joined the Army because they didn't have anywhere else to go. Joe's pretty down-in-the-mouth. He's tall, thin, and slump shouldered. His uniform fits him like a sack. He just droops around here, bent over, eyes on the ground, chin thrust forward. He rarely speaks unless spoken to and then answers in monosyllables, practically whispering.

Seems like there's no end to what this war's doing to people.

Connor

After a couple of months rest and re-outfitting, Connor received a quick note from Nora that wound him tighter than a two-dollar watch.

Dear Connor

We've been exchanged. The Embassy staff boarded a ship for the states from Portugal, but I decided to stay in Spain and wait for Daniel. He brings refugees and downed Allied pilots over the Pyrenees to the embassies in Barcelona and Madrid. I left a message in Barcelona and I'm hanging around the British Embassy in Madrid. Mostly I'll be moving around so I'm not sending an address.

Wish me luck and try to reassure Mom and Pop, would ya?

Nora

"Aw Jesus H. John Henry Christ!" Connor exploded.

"What's the matter with you?" Lopez asked.

"My lunatic sister."

"The one in the Foreign Service?"

"Yeah. They got 'em out of Germany and I'm damned if she didn't turn around and get herself into Spain to look for her boyfriend."

"Don't sound real safe."

"Hell no." Connor stomped off to sulk in his tent. He didn't even have an address where he could write to her. She said she'd be moving around so he shouldn't even try. That's what worried him. If she'd just stay put in an embassy, she might be safe.

By mid-May the Bushmasters reassembled, along with a field artillery battalion and a couple of companies of medical personnel to make up the 158th Regimental Combat Team. Leaving the relative safety of Finschafen, the new team boarded a troop ship that would take it 600 miles along the north coast to Arare in Dutch New Guinea.

Maps at their final briefing revealed their objective: Maffin Airfield. They were to relieve the 163rd team. The battle had already begun. They would fight for a road that stretched twelve miles along the coast. Herndon pointed out land features they would pass—the Tor River, the Snaky River, and Lone Tree Hill. "This map shows a single tree," said Herndon, "but that tree represents dense jungle on both sides of the defile." He tapped the map with his pointer. "You'll have to get through that pass to take the airfield. The 163rd has been struggling to get through, but they've been strangled there."

He lowered the pointer, holding it in both hands. "You've had the training and we're giving you the equipment to get this job done. I have every confidence in you." He took another look around, making eye contact here and there. "Dismissed," he said.

SEE WILLY SEE

May 21, 1944 - Arare, Dutch New Guinea

When the Bushmasters landed, they milled around waiting for instructions like a herd of cattle in a catch pen. The brass soon realized they'd landed on the wrong beach so the soldiers reboarded landing craft to move a mile west to Arare. It took a while to unload three thousand men with all their gear, reload them onto landing craft, and unload them on another beach. It would have taken much longer to wade through a mile of swamp. Soldiers of the 163rd continued to hold the current front line at the Tor River. Others waited for the Bushmasters, who would replace them.

"How bad is it?" Connor asked.

"Not so bad until you get to Lone Tree Hill."

"What's goin' on out there now?" They trying to take the hill?"

"Nah. They're just holding the Tor River bridge, so you guys don't have to start over."

Connor kept working. "Intel said there are only a couple thousand Japs in the area."

"Bad intel far as I'm concerned."

"So, you guys didn't get to Lone Tree Hill?"

"Got there. Couldn't get through. Wish you luck."

A sniper firing from the jungle about a hundred yards inland interrupted them. Someone in Bravo Company knocked him out of his tree, and First Battalion, having never seen combat, stood and started moving again.

SEE WILLY SEE

The battle-hardened members of Second Battalion hugged the ground, waiting. When a machine-gun sprayed the landing area, they chased the Japs back into the jungle. As Connor strung concertina wire, another sniper took pot shots at his crew. He grabbed his rifle and turned his gaze to the jungle's edge. Damn smokeless powder. Can't see where it's coming from. He spotted a movement and fired. Damn bird. He continued to stare while the others worked. A rustle of leaves. He fired again. A muffled cry. Got him. Now for the kill. He moved closer, keeping to the brush, waiting for another tell-tale rustle of leaves, flash of sun on metal, or a shot. In moments a falling body rustled down from the canopy. The sound stopped about thirty feet up.

Crap.'Spose I'll have to drag 'im down to find out 'f he's dead.

First and Third Battalions scratched out shallow holes where they spread ponchos and settled down for the night. They'd lost half the day loading and unloading, but, in the dark, battle-hardened Second Battalion troops found themselves, or dug themselves, substantial shelter. They covered their deep foxholes with thatch and timbers broken by earlier fighting. They stuffed the bottoms with anything they could find to keep them out of the inevitable puddles. Night passed without an enemy attack. For two quiet days, the 158th set up tents, including HQ, mess tent, and a field hospital. They waited for orders, knowing they would soon advance into ground the enemy had held for more than a decade.

May 23-24, 1944 -- Arare, Dutch New Guinea

With HQ in place, Third Battalion moved to relieve their counterparts in the 163rd at the Tor River. In a faint glow of sunrise, Love Company moved west, the tread and splash of their feet on the wet beach echoed by the clicks and clanks of full packs. Muted voices followed their progress. From his perch next to the tent he shared with Jakes, Peters, and Lopez, Connor watched soldiers form up along Army-straight rows of tents and head west. Perfectly happy to remain in camp, he wrote to his parents.

Dear Mom and Pop,

Well, they've moved us again. That last place was pretty rough, but intelligence tells us there aren't many Japs here, so this should be a cakewalk.

I got a strange letter from Nora just before we loaded the troop ships. She says instead of going home, she's going back into Spain to look for David. I assume she's written you about him. Anyway, I suppose she'll be all right in the British Embassy in Madrid or Barcelona. That's where she said she'd go. Do you have any addresses for those embassies so I can keep in touch with her?

Third Battalion's moving out right now. Apparently, they're going to take the lead on this one. I'm basking in the sun next to our ritzy accommodations. Guys walking by on the way to the front are telling me I can just hang around here and write all the letters I want. They say they'll take care of this.

Believe me, that's okay with me.

I don't have much to say, just wanted to get in touch and let you know I'm still in one piece and intend to stay that way. How are you? It hasn't been long since my last letter, but have you heard anything from Nora?

                                          Connor

The ak-ak of machine-gun fire to the west interrupted Connor's letter writing. He raised his head and swallowed his dry throat. The distant sounds intensified, and he could distinguish the cracks of rifle fire and the deadly snap of machine-guns like a cog ripped from its sprocket. He hoped the screaming whistles and explosions came from Mike Company mortars.

He retired to the mess tent where muted voices, ladles clanking on metal pots, and eating utensils on plates drowned battle sounds.

He'd just walked back out into the sun when he learned that First Battalion had orders to move up, along with the 603rd Tank Company. Apparently, Jap resistance was worse than expected.

He watched the tanks clank their way to the front, turrets pointing straight ahead, grim-faced gunner's heads poking out. A few soldiers hitched rides on the clumsy Trojan steeds, jumping on and hanging on to the armor. Motors growled and treads clanked on wheel sprockets, gripping the sand like skeleton fingers. The sight of flamethrowers turned his stomach.
After First Battalion marched out, Connor tried to write more but he found himself wordless. He couldn't describe his immediate surroundings—not only because of the government censors, but also because he didn't want to frighten his parents. So, he signed the letter and stuffed it into his pocket to send along with any casualties evacuated later. Maybe he'd think of something else to say.

Jeeps bearing the first wounded arrived in the afternoon. The casualties came balanced between the backs of seats and the tops of spare tires, and sometimes on the hoods. Their wounds had been field-dressed. Many of them oozed blood through the bandages.

The man sitting on the front passenger seat of a jeep got his attention, yelling and pointing.

"Look out! Over there." He turned abruptly. "Over there. There's another one." His head jerked in another direction. "Look out." He ducked under the dashboard screaming. "They're gonna get us."

Connor shivered as the jeep passed. Maybe he could move to a tent somewhere far from the main line to the hospital. By the end of the day, he'd counted twelve wounded and eight dead. One of the jeep drivers told him Love Company had a man missing. When he stepped into the tent, Peters looked up from cleaning his handgun. Lopez stopped sweeping his knife across the whetstone. Jakes' snoring stopped.

"You look like hell. What happened?"

"Third's missing a man."

They all stared at Connor, their eyes narrowed. Nobody moved.

"Hope they find him," Peters remarked.

They nodded. Peters' pistol slide clicked. Lopez spit on the stone and the knife slid with a swish.

Connor flopped on the cot next to Jakes. He fidgeted. He got up and went outside. He found a craps game and got into it.

At the end of the day, a jeep driver told him First Battalion had crossed the Tor and dug in for the night. King and Love companies made it within 400 yards of the day's objective—a little village called Maffin I. No one had word about the missing soldier. Connor spent the night, ears pricked, thinking he heard faint, far away screams.

He awoke to rain pounding on the tent. At 0700, Mike Company mortar rounds whistled and boomed in the distance. A few moments later, he heard the shouts of artillery men loading up in their position to the east of camp. Seconds later, the deep-throated explosions of artillery blew the camp awake. The howitzers fired continuously their roar bouncing off jungle to the south. After fifteen minutes, the last of the howitzers barked and the echoes died away. Connor heard distant machine-gun fire.

He started for the mess tent as the rain stopped and the temperature rose. He listened to shuffling and grumbling of men scattered in their various shelters. Throughout the day, they played cards, read, wrote letters, cleaned weapons, sharpened knives, and stayed alert—waiting. Connor figured Third Battalion's brave words would probably prove premature. He knew he would soon join the fray.

For him, something fundamental had changed on the Arawe peninsula. He still felt confident that he'd survive, but he'd realized that survival wouldn't be enough.

Used to spending time by himself, he studied things—a beetle crawling over leaf litter or a snake undulating over a tree branch. He needed active occupations—things to do, something to keep his mind busy. He lit cigarette after cigarette and threw them away after a drag or two. He hated the waiting.

He still thought about the missing soldier. He realized he might lose his life, but worse would be losing the soldier next to him—one he sent into battle.

Later that afternoon, his apprehension proved well founded. Easy Company marched west. Connor expected to move out in the morning. While he waited for orders, he swore that he heard every jeep that came into the compound. He counted seventy-five wounded and twenty-eight dead. Three tanks also clanked back for repairs. Orders came as the sun disappeared. The rest of Second Battalion would move out in the morning.

May 25, 1944 – Tirfoam River, Dutch New Guinea

With artillery shells screaming over their heads, George and Fox Companies marched to the Tor River. Exhausted soldiers of the Third, going back into reserve, met them along the way. A little banter broke out between the two units, but mostly they moved in silence.

About mid-morning, forward units fired mortars and machine-guns. Connor couldn't see what they were firing at, but he could hear the rattle of a shell going into a barrel and the sneeze of mortar fire. Shells whistled and exploded. The sharp dusty smell of cordite filled the air. At noon, Second Battalion crossed the Tirfoam and fell out to eat their C-Rations, while the First rested 500 yards ahead.

Connor and Jakes perched on a fallen log. "No peaches." Jakes remarked.

"Peaches! What about peaches?"

"Nothing better than a fresh peach."

"Really? Peaches?"

"Might be my last meal." Jakes' eyes twinkled.

Connor eyed him. "Christ Jakes, that's not funny."

Jakes shrugged and levered open his ration can.

As they'd marched west, Lone Tree Hill loomed larger. The airfield lay just beyond. Supposedly, the enemy couldn't put up a fight. Connor remained unconvinced. He'd seen too many dead and wounded.

Lone Tree Hill, a 175-foot coral promontory covered with dense jungle, guarded the north side of the pass. Mt. Saskin and Hill 225 guarded the south. The Americans were to slip between those promontories. Enemy soldiers dug into coral caves and armed with every modern weapon imaginable held both. Only 1,000 yards through that pass to the airfield but the Bushmasters had to fight their way through about 2,500 yards of trail between the beach and the jungle to get there.

Spread out across a hundred yards, Fox and George companies brought up the rear, keeping the Japs from slipping in behind. George Company, on the left flank, patrolled the edge of the jungle, probing deep into the swamp. As they had done in Panama, the scouts spotted snipers first. Connor sent them to bring down enemy riflemen in silence with their throwing knives. By 1500 hours, G Company had wandered deep into the jungle.

Intermittent fire on the front line near the foot of Lone Tree Hill, turned into a barrage of machine-gun and artillery fire. Hayes returned to report and Connor held up his hand. He waited for the rest of the squad to catch up. He turned to Jakes.

"Where's Peters?"

"Back on the trail."

Connor listened to the roar up ahead. "Sounds like somebody's in trouble up there."

"Yeah."

"Hayes, what'd you see?"

"Men headed east."

"East? Deserters?"

"Japs."

"How many?"

"Many."

"Company?"

"More."

"Battalion?"

"Sounded like the whole army. Makin' lots of noise."

"Christ. How far out?"

"Coupla miles."

"Radio man's with Peters?"

"Yup."

"Fuck. They're flankin' us."

The men slipped back through dense undergrowth to meet up with the rest of George Company. Connor found Captain Cochran. Gave a quick salute.

"Captain, my scout found Japs flanking us to the south."

"Probably just a patrol checking our perimeter."

"He thinks it's a battalion or more."

"A battalion? That's absurd. Intel says there are only a few thousand of the bastards in the whole area."

"My guys never let me down, Captain."

"They're wrong this time. General Patrick's pulling back the forward lines, Conroy. Our orders are to . . ."

"Patrick?" Cochran glared at Connor.

"Sorry Sir."

"Krueger's been replaced. Our orders are to establish company perimeters along the road."

SEE WILLY SEE

"The Japs could surround us and push us right into the ocean."

"There aren't enough Japs left in the area."

"Let me take out a patrol. Find out what they're up to."

"Too late in the day. Go set up your perimeter."

"We're bottled up on the beach here, while the Japs move around at will. Why the hell did the Army keep us in Panama, training us to fight in the jungle? We're useless here."

"Just dig in and repulse any attacks on your position."

"Damn it, Captain."

"Dismissed."

Connor threw a salute and stormed out, stomping sand all the way back to George Company. Jakes looked up from cleaning his rifle, "How'd it go?"

"Just like you'd expect." Connor plopped down on a log, elbows on knees, head down. The rest of the squad watched him.

Connor sat thinking as the sun sank behind the jungle. The men drifted off to their foxholes.

It's the waiting'll get you. Even in daytime, looking for the movement of a leaf. Not much to think about except how the guy next to you's gonna get it.

He couldn't stop thinking about the Japs moving south of them. He trusted his men entirely. If they saw Japs, he had no doubt the Japs were there.

But where are they now, and what are they doing? We'll sit here until they surround us, and we're overrun. Orders!! Sit. Hold this piece of white sand. The Japs move like ocelots. They've had years to dig themselves in. They won't expect us to dig 'em out, prowling through the jungle like panthers—like Bushmasters.

He raised his head and looked around. In the fast-growing dark, he made a final check on his squad.

"Jakes, is everybody here?"

Jakes counted. "Yup. Twelve plus you and me."

"Remember that speech we got back in Panama about how we'd have to use our initiative and act independently?"

"Yeah."

"All right, here's what I propose. You can go along if you wish—or not. If we get caught, we'll be court-martialed, maybe shot for desertion."

"What you got in mind?"

"Move out of here right now. Peters' squad has this perimeter covered. Circle over to the right." He gestured a wide circumference. "We'll make sure we don't run into the Japs. We know how to be quiet. We'll hit and run. They won't know what hit 'em. Give 'em a taste of their own medicine."

"I'm in," Jakes said.

"Me too," said Hayes.

"Anybody else?"

"Boring hanging around here."

"Yup."

"We'll travel light. Back by morning or not coming back. No rations, just water. Grab as many grenades as you can lay your hands on. All the ammunition you can carry. Jakes, Hayes, and Mendez, you're almost as lethal with knives as with guns. Make 'em count. We'll move in and out silent as snakes. Let's get out of here without getting caught."

One by one, they gathered at the edge of the jungle and disappeared into overhanging foliage. They hacked their way, single file trading off the lead. After about an hour of sweating, hacking, and stopping to listen, they found a broad trail.

Satisfied that they were on the right track, Connor stopped the squad.

"There'll probably be more coming up behind, so Mendez, I want you bringing up the rear—and stay sharp."

They moved forward, hugging the jungle on both sides of the trail, slinking through shadows. Connor heard a "thunk" and a murmured "son of a bitch," as one of the men tripped on a root. Moisture dripped from the canopy. The wet straps of his pack cut into his neck and shoulders, making it hard to catch a breath.

Jakes slipped out ahead of him. A quiet gurgle and the swish of a body sliding down the front of Jakes' fatigues.

"One down," Jakes murmured, "Fifty million to go."

"Let's not stumble into the middle of them."

"I got 'em spotted. Fifty yards at two o'clock."

"How many?"

"Dunno. Maybe a company. Kinda scattered out."

"They know we're here?"

"Prob'ly not."

"Close enough to lay a grenade in among 'em?"

"Might be easier to pick off some stragglers first."

Connor located Hayes and Mendez, sending them to the front to help reduce the odds. With six or seven enemy laid quietly along the trail, Connor called up Martinez.

"Let's make your baseball career count."

"What?"

"I need somebody to slip up on those Japs and lob a grenade in the middle of 'em."

"It's dark. I can't see where I'm pitching."

"You can hear 'em. Grenades don't have to be accurate. I'll bet you can get close enough by sound."

"Maybe, but that'll be like smacking a wasp nest with a stick."

"That's why Green and Moore are going with you—to spray the wasps."

"Jesus, Sarge." Martinez grinned, pulled a grenade out of his pocket and started to move forward through the shadows.

"Wait a minute," Connor whispered. "Let Green catch up."

Connor's hands sweat as the men moved closer. He heard his own heart thump. Then he saw Martinez step out in the open.

There's the wind up, and the pitch.

The jungle erupted with Japanese scrambling and yelling. Connor's men rolled off the trail, rifles clutched to their chests. The machine-gun muzzle flashed.

Japanese soldiers ran right into the gunfire in confusion. As singles separated themselves from the mass, American riflemen picked them off.

"Now!"

Moore and Green swept up the machine-gun and tripod. The rest leapt to their feet and sprinted a hundred yards up the trail, where they melted into the jungle. They caught their breath and regrouped. Nobody followed them.

"They probably think we're a whole battalion," Connor said.

"Maybe." Jakes rolled his shoulders.

"We can't use that trail. They know we're here," Connor said.

"We're close," Jakes said, "but it's slow goin' in the dark."

"Any ideas?"

"We can do like they do. Get clothes off the dead ones and get in among 'em."

"Then what?"

"Pick off the stragglers until we can get another bunch of them."

"Shit, Jakes, you're one fucking crazy Indian."

"Hey," said Jakes as he tried to fit into a Japanese uniform, "these are some big Japs. This thing almost fits me."

Green and Moore had slipped into uniforms, too. "Yeah, these duds fit."

Wilson tugged at the arm of a Jap uniform. "Can't get this damn thing off. Look at these things. Just like ours. How would they tell in the dark?"

"Cut's a little different."

"How?"

Connor took a good look at the clothes he'd begun to don. "I'm not sure. Don't matter in the dark. We need to smell like Japs."

"But they're still too big for Japs."

Connor stood motionless. *Dammit. It's the Tiger Division. I heard they have a lot of six footers. Our intel's a joke. Tiger Division's tough. In it since China. Crap.*

They finished dressing and rushed to catch up with the enemy.

They infiltrated the rough Japanese line, keeping their heads down and faces obscured. A soldier strayed off the trail to relieve himself. Jakes left him in the jungle. Another got behind. Hayes grabbed him, slit his throat, and dragged him into the understory.

Connor worked his way into the center of a platoon. He casually dropped a grenade and fast-walked to the edge of the jungle as though he had diarrhea. He barely made it into the trees before the blast sent him sprawling.

Throughout the night, they crept in and out of enemy lines, gathering information as well as eliminating enemies. Japanese yelling provided cover for their movements. When light began to filter through the canopy, they returned to their starting point, changed back to their own fatigues, gathered their weapons, and slunk to their position on the George Company perimeter.

"What's our story?"

SEE WILLY SEE

"We chased a bunch of Japs back into the trees. Got lost in the dark."

"Anybody gonna believe that?"

"Don't have to. We're all here. Some Japs are gone. Nobody can prove different."

Connor walked out first, hands high, yelling, "Don't shoot! Connor Conroy, Sergeant, George Company, serial number 37035232."

Soldiers just crawling out of foxholes stared as the rest of the squad followed him, shouting their own names, ranks, and serial numbers.

When Connor reported to him, Carpenter looked skeptical. "How many Japs did you get out there, Conroy?"

"Don't know, sir. It was dark. Maybe a company."

"A company? You're full of shit."

"Martinez pitched a grenade in the middle of a whole bunch of Japs and Green had the machine-gun ready to shoot the stragglers. Jakes and Hayes are really good with a knife. Sir."

Carpenter narrowed his eyes. "Nah. There's not a company out there."

"Sir . . ."

Carpenter had made up his mind. "Don't you pull a stunt like that ever again."

"Like what, sir?"

"Don't you get cute with me, Conroy. I'll bust you lower than a snake's belly."

"No sir," Connor said, throwing an insolent salute and starting to leave.

"Sir?"

"What now?"

"We took some Jap uniforms so we could blend in with them."

"So?"

"They fit us, sir."

"They fit you?"

"And Green and Moore, and Tats, uh, Wilson. Even Jakes— almost."

Carpenter stared eyes narrowed. "Six footers, you think?"

"Quite a bunch of them. Don't I remember something about a Tiger Division?"

"Yeah, but they're not supposed to be anywhere near here."

"Somebody forgot to tell them."

"Yeah." Carpenter leaned back. "Dismissed."

May 26, 1944 - East of Snaky River, Dutch New Guinea

At 0700, fire spouted from U.S. destroyers offshore in the Bismarck Sea. The ground shook. Explosions only a few yards away spread fire. Lone Tree Hill, backed up to the ocean, blossomed with flames. Howitzers behind the lines lit up Mt. Saskin and Hill 225. Two battalions of infantry, concentrated in just a few square yards between the Snaky River and the bombardment, were helpless. Connor ducked into his foxhole, arms protecting his head from flying debris. He hoped the gunners knew what they were doing.

Once the noise died away, First Battalion, out in front, probed the hills. Assigned to the rear, Second Battalion, George and Hotel companies, moved forward as needed, clearing jungle along the trail. Under Carpenter's command, the platoon spread out and patrolled short distances into the rain forest.

Slopping through swamp, Connor reviewed the previous night's action. *What happened to those bastards we tangled with? Tiger Division? Did they double back to see what hit 'em? How many? Did Carpenter talk to the brass? Would anybody pay attention before it was too late?*

Always listening for the tiniest sound, sniffing the air for the scent of enemy, he started at the blast of Dog Company's heavy machine-guns, visualizing the thick tubes, bucking and jerking on the tripod and sending out a spray of death. He'd crouched behind those guns himself, firing his rifle at anything that moved while the gunner laid out whole swaths of men.

At 1030, the platoon had probed deep into the jungle southeast of their original perimeter. They'd encountered no resistance—not even a lone sniper. Artillery blasted ahead to the northwest. It appeared to come from Lone Tree Hill. The Japs must have pulled back to their defensive positions. First Battalion must be getting hammered.

He heard a snap, like a broken twig. He dropped to the ground. The rest of the squad dove for the dirt, too.

He scuttled forward on his belly.

"What we got up there, Jakes?"

"Dunno."

As Connor ordered his advance scouts to investigate, a ghoul-like creature separated itself from the underbrush. A strange-looking man squat-walked toward him. Connor pushed himself up on hands and knees and stared, mouth open.

Must be a villager from Maffin I.

After trying to talk to the little man, Connor tried "talking" with his fingers.

"How many?" Connor held up one finger then two, then three.

"Japs?" At least the man knew that word.

"No," Connor shook his head and pointed at the man. "You."

The native held up four fingers.

"Where?" Connor brushed his hand in a circle around the area and shrugged.

He gestured behind him.

As the squad cautiously got to their feet, Connor gestured "come."

The man disappeared back into the undergrowth, returning with a woman and two children in tow. The adults limped.

Connor pointed at each twisted left foot.

The Dani man bowed repeatedly. Connor raised his shoulders and pointed again.

The man's face showed understanding. "Japs."

"What the hell are we going to do with them?" Green demanded.

"We're sure as hell not going to leave them out here for the Japs. Send 'em back to HQ. Let the brass figure it out. These people probably have a good idea what we're up against. Maybe the brass will believe them."

Just as he turned back to the Dani, the zing of a rifle round buzzed by his shoulder. From his position on his belly, he checked for the natives. They'd dropped, too.

"Everybody okay?"

Green glanced around. "Yeah."

"Hayes," Connor whispered. The man scuttled up to his shoulder.

"See who's up there. We'll keep him distracted."

Hayes moved back a few yards and disappeared. Connor raised his helmet on a stick a couple of times to draw fire, but the third time got no response. After a long half hour, Hayes returned.

Connor touched the villager's shoulder, turning the man to face him. He pointed at his own chest.

"Connor." He touched a finger to Hayes' chest. "Hayes."

He repeated the performance with each of the men. Then he touched the native man, cocked his head and raised his shoulders.

The man nodded. "Mutengke Ronuka." He touched his wife's shoulder. "Idesah." The girl was Siphera and the boy Ruggithorn.

"Mutengke Ronuka," said Connor. "Japs. How many?" Connor gestured a broad arc around their position. "Japs?" he asked, raising his shoulders.

All four of their "captives" nodded furiously.

Again, Connor held up fingers. The native man responded by holding up ten fingers, then flashing his hands open and closed over and over. He only stopped when Connor grabbed his hands and nodded.

"All right. Gordon, Menardo, take these people back to Carpenter and see what he wants to do with them. We'll keep working our way south and west."

The little group disappeared back along the route they'd just crossed. He turned to the rest of the squad.

"We're out of position. Sounds like all the action's up ahead. Keep your heads down."

By the end of the day, they'd caught up with the platoon. On the way, they'd encountered enemy snipers and a small recon patrol. That night, the battalion received orders to clear Hill 225 where the Intelligence and Reconnaissance Platoon had barely escaped an ambush during the day. First would secure Lone Tree and push through the defile.

Friggin' idiots. We nearly lost a Recon platoon today. Their report confirms ours. The brass thinks this is a cakewalk. Six men dead, ten wounded just today. For what? Not even half a damn mile.

From his bivouac near the Snaky River, Connor stared at the hills. Chewing a matchstick, he assessed them. Lone Tree loomed to the right, shrouded in dense rain forest and butting against the South Pacific. To the left, he scanned Hill 225 and the foothills between him and the objective. Mt. Saskin towered over 225, affording a perfect position for firing down on the smaller hill. He now knew that those hills swarmed with Japs.

SEE WILLY SEE

May 27, 1944 - West of Snaky River, Dutch New Guinea

During the morning barrage of fire from off-shore destroyers and land-based artillery, Connor wished he could curl up in his foxhole and hold his hands tightly over his ears. When the shelling stopped, the Americans tried again to break through to the airfield. While Fox Company pushed up Hill 225, George held a position in the rear, with battle lines a scant 1,000 yards ahead.

Connor reached for the side of his face to wipe off phantom blood at the ak-ak of a machine-gun burst. He flinched when a mortar blast crunched into a line of trees far ahead. He had to get used to the noise every day all over again. He barely heard Carpenter's orders over the din.

Moving southeast of the front, George Company intercepted Japanese patrols coming in from behind. With Hayes in the lead and Mendez bringing up the rear, the squad hacked their way to the ravine between 225 and the foothills. Connor pulled on his collar.

"You sure we haven't died 'n went to hell?" Wilson panted.

"Pretty sure we have."

"Fuckin' mud. Can't lift my feet."

"It'll fall off when we get back into jungle."

Crack! A tree next to Wilson's head sent splinters flying. Both men dropped into the mud.

"God damned mud."

SEE WILLY SEE

Connor glanced around at men just raising heads. "Sonsabitches." Johnson raised his rifle. A rustling and a thud followed the crack. "Got him." Johnson started to stand.

"Stay down," Connor yelled.

When no more firing followed, the men raised themselves from the ground, one by one, walking to a cluster of broken palm trees. They inspected Johnson's kill. Wilson kicked the Jap's rifle away and checked for a pulse. He stood, grinning.

"You got him sport. Welcome to the club."

He reached down and severed an ear, skewered it with his pocket-knife and strung it on his stringer.

They engaged in firefights with small Japanese patrols throughout the day and returned to their bivouac on the Snaky at 1800 hours. A small part of Connor's mind registered gratitude that he'd lost no one on the sweltering, swampy, stinking, muddy piece of ground they'd patrolled. As they entered the American perimeter, they faced a line of ponchos wrapping dead soldiers waiting for busy jeeps to evacuate them. Next to the dead lay a line of wounded. Connor recognized some of the faces, although he couldn't name anyone. He figured they came from the First. Those guys had been up on the Hill and in the pass. The firing had been intense all day.

One of the wounded moaned in his morphine-induced sleep. Connor was glad he couldn't see the wounds under the bloody bandages wrapped around the soldier's head. Next to him lay a man with two shattered legs. Connor hoped the guy would survive the amputations. He shuddered. He couldn't imagine the rest of his life without legs.

He turned away and lit a cigarette.

Connor heard general grumbling around camp that night. The soldiers found plenty to complain about—artillery that hit the wrong target, intelligence that underestimated enemy forces, maps so inaccurate that Easy and Fox Companies ended up on the wrong hill, the withering heat, and knee-deep mud. Alpha Company had succeeded in occupying the crest of Lone Tree Hill and remained there to hold it overnight. Tank support would arrive the next day. Landing craft would deliver the machines on the beach west of the Snaky—since the bridge would not support them. Tanks would lead the charge through the defile. That left George, Fox, and Easy companies on their own.

May 28, 1944 -- Hill 225, Dutch New Guinea

"Look here!" Connor exploded when he got his orders.

"I know Sergeant." Carpenter sighed. "We've just gotta be smart and do our best. We've got some great warriors in this platoon . . ." He let his voice trail off and Connor saw his eyes lose focus.

Connor saluted. "Yes sir."

Carpenter's platoon had been separated from George Company. The bulk of the company would join Easy and Fox following the nose of Hill 225. Carpenter would advance the left flank and work to the summit, taking out the any Japanese fortifications on the way.

The platoon shrugged into their packs and gathered their weapons. "Hey Sarge, where's the water?" Wilson held out his canteen.

Connor sighed. "Didn't come."

Wilson shook his tin flask. "What do you mean didn't come?"

"Some dumb ass forgot to load it when they brought the tanks."

"This is all I got." He shook the canteen next to his ear. "Almost gone."

"I know." He turned. "Hey you guys." The squad gathered around. "We're out of water. Save what you've got."

"What the fuck? We supposed to drink our sweat?'

Connor sighed. "I don't know. We just do what we can with what we've got."

"Crap."

"Fuckin' Army."

They took the far-left flank at the very outside edge of the American line. Fox and Carpenter's platoon began the day at the eastern edge of an unnamed hill east of their objective. From their bivouac bordering the road, they penetrated the jungle single file at about five-yard intervals. With Hayes leading, the squad crossed the ravine where Fox had barely escaped an ambush the previous day.

By 1100, Connor stood in the ravine between 225 and the foothills. A week of bombardment had left the hillside pocked with craters and clearings surrounded by denuded tree skeletons. He could see one large cave entrance with the mouths of Japanese artillery pieces in the opening. In an area that had once been a clearing, Kunai grass stood in a broken field—six to ten feet in clumps and flat in others. Most of the hill remained covered with dense jungle. Connor assumed it crawled with enemy soldiers.

Although the entire regimental front line stretched barely 1,000 yards north to south, only sound provided clues to locations of the various companies. Machine-gun, rifle fire, and the growl of tanks to the right testified to the presence of Bravo and Easy along the road. According to the morning briefing, Alpha, Charlie, and most of George tried to clear the enemy from caves on Lone Tree Hill on the other side of the road. Fox remained on Hill 225, off to the right of Carpenter.

SEE WILLY SEE

Raindrops pattered from leaf to leaf adding to the shuffle and squish of boots in the leaf litter and mud. No one spoke. Even a whisper seemed like an explosion of sound. Connor looked around at his men. They licked dry lips and cleared raspy throats. Even in Panama, Connor had entered the jungle with a constant feeling of watching eyes. Now, it felt like a hand squeezing his lungs.

As they moved, they watched the Japanese cave and the muzzles of enemy mortars and heavy machine-guns. Infantry patrols ambushed Americans whenever they could. Connor walked, scanning with eyes and ears, sniffing the air like his old farm dog, careful to avoid tripping on exposed roots and vines. A bird fluttering from limb to limb brought his rifle to his shoulder and his body into a crouch. Embarrassed, he looked around. Jakes nestled in the blades of a buttress root. Several other men, rifles to shoulders, peered into the dusky light.

The platoon approached the nose of Hill 225. With the ravine behind them, they began climbing. As they moved higher and farther west, jungle dusk began to thin. They popped out into the cratered clearing Connor had studied with field glasses. A plainsman who had spent his life in open spaces, he shrank back into trees and underbrush. He'd adapted and now those open spaces meant death.

Carpenter halted the column. As they waited, the radio squawked with orders from Captain Cochran farther down the hill. Hayes murmured something incomprehensible in Pima/Maricopa.

Carpenter said Kikimi Price from Peters' squad had relayed orders. Connor assumed they would have to take the cave. He reached for a cigarette and lit up, staring at the hilltop while he waited. No reason to be subtle. The Japs knew they were coming.

"How far you figure it is up there?" Mendez chewed on the inside of his cheek.

"Don't know," Connor said. "Too fuckin' far. Wish they hadn't bombarded the place. We could've sneaked up on 'em through the jungle."

"Maybe we should."

"Too late for that, I guess."

When the orders came, he shrugged on his pack and looked at the cave. Fox would cross to their left, farther up the hill through the jungle. They would clear out any enemy positions along the edge of the trees. The platoon would only have the fortifications at the top of the hill to take out as they charged.

"Cannon to the left of them, cannon to the right of them, volleyed and thundered," Connor murmured.

"Huh?"

"Nothin'."

Connor struggled for breath. He tried not to think of how he would breathe, running uphill, carrying his rifle with eighty pounds of equipment on his back, dodging machine-gun fire and mortar rounds. He shifted the straps on his pack, glancing at the lip of the cave on top.

A light clank. Jakes stood off to his left, sweat dripping off the end of his nose, shifting his pack. Green and Moore squatted behind him, Green with the machine-gun balanced over his shoulder. He'd learned to shoot it from the hip. Moore carried the tripod. He could handle the gun if needed.

Connor looked back at Wilson bandoliers of ammo slung across his broad chest. With his scarred eyebrow and the fighting cock tattoos facing each other on his upper arms, he looked rough as a boxcar. Connor scanned the rest of the squad. They looked ready, faces rigid, unyielding, carbines clutched across their chests. He nodded. They were the kind of men you want at your side when someone's trying to kill you.

But that was the problem, wasn't it? You want them at your side, not dead on a hillside. He considered all the men on top of that hill, crawling around like a bunch of ants, ready to eat your insides out one tiny bite at a time. He glanced around at his men one more time. He knew all those guys. He'd hauled their asses back to their tents when they'd been too drunk to walk. He'd ignored their threats to scalp him. He'd stood in the chow line with them. He'd watched them sort out enemy infiltrators in American fatigues.

When Jakes told him the Japs smelled different, he'd learned to tell their scent.

Except for Johnson, he'd been with those guys since Pearl Harbor—more than two-and-a-half years, marching, soaking wet, up the same hills, and hauling ass up the same beaches. He didn't mind at all trusting them with his life. It made him crazy knowing he might give the order that got them all killed—even though he would just be following his own orders.

He licked his lips and gazed at the top of that hill, wondering how many were up there. He looked for a path up the hill, a series of rocks or hummocks, shredded trees or mortar craters—any land features that would provide cover. If they could run from one to the next, maybe they could make the crest.

He saw a flash from the top of the ridge. God damned, mother fucking Japs just sittin' up there waiting for fresh meat. How long did Eisler stay awake while they stabbed bamboo sticks under his fingernails and toenails and lit them? How many hours before they hung him up and ripped him open like a side of pork?

He tried to forget the starving Jap soldiers on Arawe and their bivouac with its photos and letters. He didn't have to struggle too hard to shut out his mother's advice. "Remember, as much as you can, that the man trying to kill you is a human being." Not as far as he could see. If he had to kill the bastards, he damn well better remember they're bastards. You can't sort out the torturers from the family men when they're shooting at you.

Connor gathered his squad, pointing out craters and rocks, humps in the hillside, and broken trees where they could take cover on the way up the hill.

"If we have to charge up the face of this fuckin' hill, let's do it smart. Plan your route from one bit of cover to the next. I know it ain't much, a little rock here, broken tree there. It might save your lives."

Even as he said it, the idea seemed futile. Squatting in the tree line, concealed by brush, he dripped sweat off his beak. It burned in his eyes. He looked at each of his men, one at a time, then closed his eyes and waited for the order he knew would come in moments.

Carpenter gestured up the hill. They rose to their feet. They started walking, slowly at first, but when the mortar fire began, they ran, ducking and dodging. They all made it to the first line of mortar craters. Jakes stood to wave the squad forward, shadowing Connor against the afternoon sun. In a stitching of machine-gun fire, he toppled back into the crater. Connor screamed for a medic, reflexively wiping the splatter off the side of his face. He took a few seconds to press his hand over Jakes' wounded calf to slow the bleeding. The corpsmen arrived with a stretcher and started running with their load, groaning under the weight.

A mortar round landed just a few feet away. Connor started running again, zig-zagging uphill with Green, Moore, and Wilson on his heels. He ducked behind a large rock on the second bench with the machine-gun crew and looked back for the rest of the squad. Hidalgo had gone down, and Mendez was dragging him to shelter in another crater, yelling for a medic. Connor hoped the Japs hadn't sighted on that one yet, but in the instant he thought it, a mortar round sighed overhead, and ripped into the occupied crater. Again, he screamed for medics and gestured toward the crater.

He looked around for Reese, Gordon, and Trigg, eyes bouncing in his head like they were still running up that hill. They were lying flat on their bellies on the hillside below him, protected by a hump in the hill's back. Menardo and Martinez sprinted past him, heading left for some Kunai grass along the margin of the hill.

Menardo took an awkward leap and fell. Martinez dragged him along until he, too, stumbled, clutching his right leg. He crawled to the protection of the tall grass pulling Menardo by the arm.

Connor looked back at Reese, Gordon, and Trigg where they'd been pinned. Mortar rounds came in around his rock. The machine-gun crew squeezed in tighter.

Gordon raised his head a few inches and it exploded in a spray of blood.

Reese and Trigg leapt to their feet and sprinted for the grass. Trigg tripped and rolled up in a ball, partially protected by his pack. He squirmed around until he could get to his feet and run, this time making it into the grass. Japanese machine-gun fire raked the area, cutting a pattern in the vegetation. Connor couldn't see if anyone had been hit or killed. Reese had made it to the grass and Trigg had tucked in there too. Alive or dead? Who knew?

Connor maneuvered himself to the edge of the rock. He took off, running in a crouch. Green had the machine-gun cradled in front of his hip, firing a steady stream at the Japanese cave. Moore and Wilson ran right behind him. Connor zig-zagged, crouching as low as he could get. Hayes came up beside him. *Where'd he come from?* Two steps later, Hayes went down, and Connor stopped beside him, screaming, "Medic!"

Gasping, blood running from his mouth, Hayes grabbed a pouch he had slung on a rawhide string around his neck. "Jakes," he gasped, blood bubbling.

"Jakes?"

"Give. To Eagle."

Connor grabbed the pouch and ran. Firing kicked up dirt all around him. Crouched like a turtle under eighty pounds of load, he pumped his legs until he reached the top of the hill where he careened into a cluster of GIs from Peters' squad. They were now behind the Jap machine-gun and mortar emplacements. Connor looked around for Green.

"Hey, did Green make it up the hill?"

One of the men, bent over like him, panting, pointed a few yards down at a crumpled soldier, lying on his side.

"Where's his gun?"

"Moore picked it up. Ran right into the mouth of that emplacement, firing from the hip. Ammo carrier followed him. Don't know what happened to 'em."

Connor struggled for breath—unable to move, unable to think—looking down the hill for any sign of his squad.

"How 'bout the guys in the grass?" he wheezed.

"Don't know man. We gotta get outa here. Radio man says we're ordered to retreat."

"Retreat!" he panted. "What fuckin' dumbass orders a retreat when we're standin' on top of this fuckin' hill." He panted. "Half my guys dead on the fuckin' side of it." He paused. "How the hell're we supposed to get back down without losing the other half? Where the fuck's the radio man?"

Connor stood silent. Finally able to stand upright, he looked down the hill. The cave with the mortars and machine-guns lay amid a jumble of rocks.

"I ain't leavin' here 'til that cave's shut."

"Can't get to the fuckin' thing."

"Like hell I can't. How many God damn grenades you got?"

He gathered four grenades, stormed over to the rocks, and started crawling. When Connor loosened some rocks, a Jap poked his head out. The soldiers standing by took pot shots at him. Perched at the top rim of the cave, Connor pulled the pin on the first grenade.

Tottering on the edge, he held the grenade until the fuse was almost spent and thrust it as far inside the cave as he could throw. *Damn. Wish Martinez was here.*

Alone he held his position and kept pulling pins and tossing grenades even as the edge he clung to shook with the impacts. Out of ammunition, he crawled back.

"Where's Peters?"

Lopez shook his head. "Carpenter?"

"Don't know. Think he went down way at the bottom of the hill. You're the highest-ranking officer on this fucking hill."

"Alexander, Means, Andreas?"

They all stepped forward, Alexander balancing a machine-gun.

"Whadaya say we finish what my crew started?"

"No ammo."

"Fuck."

Connor looked at Moore's and Wilson's bodies, crumpled in the dirt.

"Cover me."

He scuttled over to his men, crouching next to Wilson and feeling for a pulse. No one fired at him. He checked Moore too.

"Sorry Tats," he whispered as he turned the body over to remove the ammo bandoliers.

Once he had the crew armed, he went back to the ledge. The enemy had leveled it to haul equipment into the cave. He gestured Alexander to follow. One by one they took their places on either side of the cave's mouth.

"Okay, we go in blazing. If anything's alive in there, they won't be for long."

He gestured. The four men stepped inside spraying the cave with lethal fire. Connor held up a hand. With ringing ears, he started checking bodies for remaining life. The others joined him, looking for Jap canteens as they searched.

The silence broke as a roar echoed. The men turned. A Jap stormed from the depths. All personnel scrambled with their weapons. Connor tightened the grip on his rifle but couldn't raise it to his shoulder fast enough. In the second or two of wild movement among the machine-gun crew, the Jap stopped and stared. He made eye contact with each in turn.

Nobody moved.

During that suspended instant, the Jap drew a knife from a sheath on his hip and thrust it upward beneath his solar plexus into his chest cavity. He fell in slow motion as Connor and the machine-gun crew watched open-mouthed. They remained

SEE WILLY SEE

standing, motionless. A puddle of blood spread from under the soldier.

Connor gazed with blank eyes at the other men. They all stood frozen. They turned their heads and stared at him. He knew he needed to say something.

"Keep checking for live ones," he said. "Look for water." He laid his rifle on the ground and unholstered his handgun. "I'm gonna see if there are any more of the bastards in there."

He penetrated to the back of the cave, left shoulder brushing the wall as he held the pistol ready to fire. When he found nothing of interest, he returned to the mouth of the cave.

"Let's get the hell out of here."

They gathered up their weapons and a couple of canteens and left the cave.

Connor stood alone, mind churning.

"He come out of the pitch black in the back of that cave an' he must have been seven foot at least."

"Yeah, an' then I saw this flash an' he poked that blade right in his middle like stickin' a pig."

The cluster of men stood in silence.

"What'd make a man do somethin' like that?"

Connor waved them forward. "Let's get the fuck out of here."

Two men each picked up Moore and Tats, hauling them under the arms and by the ankles. Connor found Reese and Trigg tangled up in the grass, dead. Menardo and Martinez lay just a few feet away, riddled with bullets.

SEE WILLY SEE

Connor took Martinez under the arms, trying to cradle the lolling head. One of Peters' guys took his feet. The hill dragged Connor down. He stumbled to his knees—still holding the dead soldier in his arms. He struggled to his feet. He kept licking cracked lips and wiping sweat off the side of his face with a shoulder. Though the hill remained relatively dry, his feet seemed to stick.

Halfway down, they met medics coming up with stretchers. Connor stood at the end of a stretcher, holding Martinez. The medic touched him on the shoulder.

"We'll take it from here."

Connor bent to maneuver the dead soldier onto the exact center of the stretcher. He stepped back without a word.

"You hit?" asked another of the medics. Connor stared.

"You've got blood all over you."

He continued staring. "Must be Hayes' blood."

"Ain't no deer around here. You're hallucinating, man." He shook his head. "There's no deer here."

Connor frowned. "One of my men."

"Whatever you say. Sure you're not hurt?"

Connor stood, arms hanging loose at his sides. "Nah."

Another man had hauled a couple extra rifles. Wordlessly, he returned Connor's, who took it and resumed walking.

That's Martinez and Menardo, Green, Moore, and Wilson. Hayes, Reese, Trigg, Gordon. His brain shut down. He kept walking.

"Jakes," he whispered to himself. "I don't know about Jakes."

SEE WILLY SEE

He kept walking down the ravaged hill he'd started to climb up with thirteen other men just a few minutes ago, or hours ago, or weeks ago. Who knew?

Hidalgo and Mendez. I didn't see them go down. Johnson either.

As he shuffled down the hill, his thoughts kept cadence. *Martinez, Menardo, Hayes, Green, Moore, Wilson, Reese, Trigg, Gordon. Hayes, Martinez, Green, Moore, Wilson, Menardo . . .*

May 29, 1944 -- Snaky River, Dutch New Guinea

First Battalion got orders to relieve the last battalion of the 163rd Infantry back at the Tor River. That left Second and Third to hold the line at the Snaky. George, the remaining men together again, had bivouacked at the Regiment's outside edge. Hidalgo, Mendez, and Johnson still hadn't appeared. Connor hoped they'd been wounded and carried back to the field hospital. Or that they might have gotten separated from the platoon. Hidalgo and Mendez could stay alive in the jungle until they found their way back. If they were all together, they could help Johnson. Connor refused to consider the possibility they'd all died on Hill 225.

Fox Company had followed the platoon down but spent the night on the nose of Mt. Saskin. In the morning, Connor heard the firefight as Fox fought their way to George's perimeter. The company covered them as they made their final push into new Snaky River positions.

All day, Japs sniped at them from the edge of the jungle. If someone drew a bead on a sniper's position, the enemy would retreat into the heart of darkness. Occasionally, the enemy set up a machine-gun to spray the encampment until the two battalions' furious response drove them back.

SEE WILLY SEE

The Americans maintained their positions on the river, until three that afternoon. Colonel Herndon then ordered the two battalion commanders to move their units behind the Tirfoam River, more than a mile east. George Company would set up about halfway between the Tirfoam and Tor. They would hold their positions until relieved.

Connor slogged through the ordeal of packing up equipment, including the company command post. He barely flinched when the snipers kicked up sand around him. Once he'd located the source of firing, he would grab his rifle and fast fire into the trees in the general vicinity of the enemy position. Then he'd turn back to loading bundles of materiel onto the jeeps. His pack seemed to have doubled in weight and he staggered a few times during the two-mile march back along the trail. Dry sand dragged at feet he could barely lift. Intermittent sniping continued throughout the march. His throat felt like sandpaper. Still no water. He shuffled along the edge of the jungle, avoiding as best he could. the sucking mud on the trail.

We're spread out here like a bunch of grazing cows. Twelve miles of coastline and twenty-one positions to defend. Tiger Division out there just waiting to pick us off. We saw 'em, heard 'em. Thousands of the bastards. Wonder how many of us are left.

For a moment, he watched Peter's guys digging their foxholes. He got to work. With Cochran's command post backed up against the Pacific, George Company's three platoons spread in a semi-circle to the south facing the jungle. By the time the company set up camp, the sun had reached the tops of the canopy on Lone Tree Hill.

Connor crawled into his foxhole and stretched out on his poncho. Waves, surging ahead and sizzling back, lulled him into a near doze. The setting sun poured onto the beach. He drifted off, shivering.

Damn. Atabrine not working. I'm getting it now. How many of them big Tiger Division Japs out there waiting to slit my throat while I shiver?

He never stirred. The company lost a couple of men during the next twenty-four hours—no one in Carpenter's platoon. Mostly the Japs kept anybody from resting—except Connor. He spent that twenty-four hours tightly wrapped in his wool Army blanket.

May 30, 1944 — West of Tor River, Dutch New Guinea

Next morning minor attacks continued. They dropped off some time in the afternoon. Lack of action seemed to Connor, awake by then, more ominous than the constant sniping.

He'd become adept during the five months since landing on Arawe at identifying the sounds of armaments—American and Japanese. Although he guessed regimental headquarters at more than five miles away, he identified the explosions he heard late that afternoon as enemy grenades.

Here it comes, he thought, but the silence returned. He sat in front of his foxhole and watched the jungle with his rifle across his knees. He noticed others pacing with rifles ready, or sitting as he did, alert and waiting. He chewed the side of his tongue—something he'd also learned at Arawe as a substitute for grinding his teeth—which gave him a headache.

Silence continued as the company waited for an attack they knew would come. Just before the sun plunged behind Lone Tree Hill, Connor heard distant shouts. He frowned at a dim-far-off sound like a radio or phonograph played at full blast. He and Lopez exchanged a glance.

"What the hell?"

"Sounds like a record player."

"Or a radio."

"Is that *The Rose of San Antone*?"

The music stopped just as the sun plunged behind the hill—without even a farewell bird call. At 0630, Japanese mortars and machine-guns replaced it. He imagined he heard yelling and screaming.

I can't really hear voices, can I? It's five miles down there.

He sat peering into black jungle and swamp just a few yards away. Would they over run the Second Battalion perimeter, too?

Connor heard a quiet voice. "I wish they'd just do it an' get it over."

Battle sounds intensified. Connor heard explosions he couldn't identify, along with mortar blasts. He saw flashes, like dry lightning, far down the beach. He followed the fighting by listening to the blasts.

That's First Battalion. They've been chewed up as bad as I have.

"Where the hell are they?" a voice muttered as the battle sounds continued. It had been hours with no attack on their perimeter.

"Maybe they're not coming."

"Maybe not." The glow of a cigarette lit up a haggard face. And so it was.

May 31, 1944 – Arare, Dutch New Guinea

The Army moved again, all the way back to the Tor River. Second Battalion remained on the west side to hold the crossing. That evening the regiment's perimeter had shrunk. Instead of twelve miles, the soldiers dug in over four miles. George Company secured its position with deep foxholes, machine-gun emplacements, mortar support, and surrounded itself with concertina wire.

Connor sat next to his foxhole smoking a government-issue cigarette. Eyes narrowed he scanned the swamp just a few yards south.

A voice murmured in the darkness. "Where do you think they are?"

Connor shrugged. "I don't know. Out there somewhere. All around us."

"I heard your guys spotted Japs moving east a few days ago."

Connor felt a stab of loss. He remembered Hayes coming back from a scouting sweep. "Yeah."

"How many are out there?"

Connor took a deep drag. "Who knows?"

The men smoked and talked in little spurts. They traded off watching and dozing until morning.

With the first touch of daylight, Connor reported to Col. Cochran, "I'm going to the evac hospital to check on my men."

Cochran nodded.

Connor slung his rifle over his shoulder and headed for the bridge. The four miles to the evac hospital were lined with American soldiers, all ready for an attack. He felt many eyes on him, but nobody spoke.

Damp smells of blood and alcohol permeated the hospital tent. The subtle, sweet aroma of spoiled meat and the ubiquitous New

Guinea scent of rotten bananas stopped him. He hesitated then dropped the tent flap. He surveyed cots on both sides of a center aisle. Cot by cot, he looked for Hidalgo, Hayes, Mendez, Johnson, and Jakes. A young kid with bandaged eyes lay at the head of the line. A soldier Connor recognized from the mess tent had a bandaged stump lying across his chest where his hand should have been. He had that same look of resignation Connor had seen before. He looked toward the other side of the aisle, grateful that he couldn't see under the blanket covering the first man. The second looked back at him with dead eyes.

Connor paced down the row recognizing no one from his squad. A medic bent over a soldier changing a blood-soaked bandage around his upper arm. The man thrashed in a morphine haze.

The medic looked at Connor. "Give me a hand here. Hold him still."

Connor grabbed the arm and retched when the bandage came off. "Did you work on a man named Hidalgo?"

The medic kept working. "Don't know names," he said, "I know wounds."

Connor continued to hold the man's arm. "How about a big guy with a leg wound?"

"Last cot on the left. You can check the casualty list over there."

He gestured with his head.

Jakes' eyes popped open when Connor stopped to look at his washed-out face. He sighed in relief. At least someone survived.

Jakes stared back with blurry eyes. He glanced around the tent as if to get his bearings. "Hayes," he mumbled, "Mendez, Green?"

"Can't find 'em. Hayes got it right next to me. Didn't look good. Green didn't make it. We carried him off the hill."

SEE WILLY SEE

Connor stepped over to the tent wall and checked the list. His throat hurt as he swallowed, over and over, to clear the lump. He found no order in the list. Maybe they listed them in the order they carried them in, dead and wounded mixed together. He found Hayes near the top. Dead. Connor had not had much hope for him. Green, Moore and Wilson were listed together.

Hidalgo—dead. Mendez—dead. Johnson—dead. Menardo and Martinez made the list side by side with Reese and Trigg. He'd been sure about Gordon and the list confirmed it. By the time he'd got to the end of the names, his chin rested on his chest.

Jakes' eyes demanded answers when Connor got back to his cot.

"Seems like we're the only ones made it—from the squad."

Jakes closed his eyes.

"Peters got it too." Connor wanted to run. "Anythin' I can get you?"

"Water."

Connor asked the medic and held Jakes' head so he could drink.

"Thanks." His eyes remained closed, breathing shallow.

"S'okay."

"Think I'm goin' home."

Connor's eyes traced Jakes' shape beneath the blanket, cringing at the absence of shape on his left side.

"How bad?"

"Lopped below the knee."
Connor stood beside Jakes unable to move. He clutched Hayes' pouch in a white-knuckled hand. He looked down the long line of

wounded men. Some of them would go back to the fight. Most of them would go home in a few weeks. He still hadn't looked Jakes in the eye.

He looked down at his hand. He laid the pouch on Jakes' chest. "Hayes gave this to me. Said give it to you."

"How'd he get it?"

"He . . ." Connor stood eyes closed, his memory flashed. Hayes climbing a cocopalm like a spider, the silent arc of his throwing arm and the flash of the knife settling between the enemy's ribs. Martinez winding up and pitching hand grenades into clusters of Japs, pretty as you please. Green storming right into the teeth of the machine-gun nest, firing from the hip, muzzle flaring. Wilson right behind ready to feed him ammunition and Moore covering with his rifle. In the instant he recollected his location in a field hospital, he wondered if that movie would ever stop playing in his head.

"He got it on that third bench, running for the top."

"Didn't even get to use it."

"What?"

"His knife."

"No." Connor hung his head, remembering Hayes sprawled on the slope between the bits of cover they'd noted before they started the run. "Looks like you're all taken care of."

He turned to go, but Jakes grabbed his sleeve. Connor turned back.

"I hear you spent a summer in the Grand Canyon."

"Yeah?"

"Tell me about it."

Connor shrugged. "You grew up there, Jakes. What can I tell you?"

"I'm tired, Conroy. I need to remember my country. How did it look when you first came up to the canyon rim?"

Just as Connor started to respond, the medic came by pushing a cart of equipment.

"What's your blood type, soldier?"

"Mine?"

"Well, I'm not gonna take blood from these wounded—if I can help it."

"O negative."

"Good. Universal donor. I need to take your blood."

"I think I've got malaria."

The medic sighed. "So does everybody else here. Some of 'em will die without blood and I ain't got any more. I'll get you a cot. You can rest next to the big guy." He laid the empty blood bags and hoses on Jakes' belly. "I'll be right back."

Jakes watched while the medic started Connor's blood draw. He also gave Jakes another shot of morphine.

"Okay Conroy. You got nothin' better to do. Humor me. Before or after you broke your leg?"

"After. I spent the winter in Montana healing up with my Uncle."

"Go on."

SEE WILLY SEE

Connor laid back, taking in a gulp of air, and letting it out in a long sigh. It was the first time he'd rested since Hill 225. Maybe he wouldn't call it resting so much as inertia—like the long, unconscious night up the line, shivering.

"With my leg healed and warm weather blowing in, I started with a hike to the mailbox, and a ride into Glendive. I jumped an empty boxcar headed west toward the mountains. At the rail yard in Billings, I hopped out and found a friendly-looking brakeman to see what I could find out about lines running south. I found an empty boxcar on a train headed for Denver and settled in for the long ride.

"I spent two bone-jarring days as the car registered every seam in the rails with a bang. Twenty whistle stops to load and unload cargo and passengers."

The medic checked on his blood draw. "You're okay, keep pumping that hand."

Jakes raised his head and turned to Connor. "Hey, d'jou go to sleep?"

"No. Just thinkin' how I'd like to be on that train right now."

"Yeah. Me too. Tell me more."

"From the rail yards, I hiked to U.S. 34 west and headed for Rocky Mountain National Park. I travelled some of the prettiest country in the West, whistling and walking. I hitched an occasional ride 'n spent a week wandering around the park. Then I got on Colorado 119 where I walked and hitchhiked until I could get on 285, wandering around a few days in Pike National Forest and climbing Pike's Peak to see what kind of panorama I could snap from there. Hitched my way over the pass at Pagosa Springs on my way to the four corners."

"Damn, you like to talk, white man," Jakes interrupted, "Get to the canyon. When d'you get there?"

"Mid-May sometime. Spring anyway."

"What did it look like? Were the locoweeds in bloom?"

"Angelfire? Yeah. Up on that campground."

"We call it toloatizn. We use it in our ceremonies."

"But it's poison."

"That's why the old ones make the tea."

Connor glanced at his friend who peered at the canvas roof above his head.

"You got there in the mornin'?"

"Early. Sun just comin' up."

"Long shadows on the right."

"I could hear the river muttering to itself just before I reached the rim. Until then, it just looked like a ravine. We had a couple of rough cuts on the farm. It looked like that until I got to the edge. How would you ever suspect the magnificent, towering architecture of those walls?"

"Makes your heart stop, don't it?"

Connor glanced at Jakes. "Yeah. It really does."

"I remember first time my father took me down there. I musta been four or five. He had my hand and he always laughed about how I almost squeezed his fingers off when I looked over the edge."
"Kinda makes you dizzy, don'' it?"

"What else you remember?"

Connor thought for a moment, trying to think of something to take Jakes away from his injuries—his future.

"I'd heard about the Grand Canyon from the beaches of California to the glaciers in Montana. I stood looking out over miles of water-tortured rock and the green-flowing river that cut it. A mile deep, I'd heard. He paused, thinking about what to say. "Speaking of dizzy, I got some great pictures."

"Yeah. You white guys think you can take stuff home in them things."

"I looked over that sheer edge of pink and gold rock. I saw this great view, but a tiny pedestal of stone partially blocked it. I stood there looking down at the river. The moving water made me dizzy, but when my head cleared, I jumped."

"You did what?"

"I jumped. I wobbled a little then took my shots. I got dizzy again, so I turned around with tiny baby steps and jumped back. Loosened a shower of rocks that bounced and clattered down the pedestal. I shivered."

Jakes' voice rumbled out of Connor's reverie. "You're supposed to soothe me, Sergeant, not scare me to death."

Connor had started to get into Jakes' way of thinking. "The river," he said at last, "that green, shining, rolling presence. It murmured along no matter what we were doing. You could hear it from any place on the ranch. After work we'd go down and splash around.

"Didn't need no bathtub."

"That first day, after fooling around with the camera, I found the trail. In Jacob's Lake they told me a fourteen-mile walk with the campground about halfway. It seemed much longer than seven miles, toes crowding the ends of my boots. I stopped at the campground for a bologna sandwich and trekked on to the bottom. If I hadn't climbed around in the Rockies, I'd have frozen half-way down."

The medic came over and checked the tubing. "Looks like we're gonna get a couple of units out of you. Just relax and I'll disconnect you soon."

"At the bottom, I located a clump of bushes, secluded from the rim and the trail, stripped off and washed out my clothes. I spread them on the bushes and dove into a cool eddy that cut underneath.

"I thought I'd had a heart attack. I knew mountain water was cold, but I didn't expect that desert river to freeze my kahones."

A couple of medics came in with a stretcher. Connor glanced at the new man. Didn't recognize him. Seemed okay. Probably shell-shocked. Some of the brass didn't believe men like that. Thought they were cowards.

"How are your kahones now?"

"Fine." Connor watched as the medics started an IV. "I settled into a little, smooth depression next to the bushes and spent the night, listening to the gurgle of water."

"Nothin' like that sound." Jakes gazed at the tent roof. "And seeing stars in the slice of sky." He yawned.

Connor glanced at the sleepy soldier. "You ready for a nap?"

"Nah. Go on."

"I listened to the river while I packed up. Plopped my hat on my head and followed the trail to the Ranch. I spotted a tall, long-legged woman hanging sheets to the left of a stone-and-beam building that looked like a headquarters. Flashed her a smile and yelled, 'Hello,' from about a hundred yards away, so I wouldn't startle her.

"She looked up and smiled. 'Hi.' She took a clothespin out of her mouth. Pretty in a mourning dove kind of way. You know what I mean?"

"Yeah. Not flashy like your white women."

"Well, Jakes, white an' not flashy. Anyway, you wanna hear this or not?"

"Go ahead. Did ya get a job?"

"Yep. She said they wanted to build more cabins since their guests were starting to come back. I told her about building trails and cabins and stuff in the CCC. We introduced ourselves. Her name is Gracie. She sent me inside to meet her husband, Marvin."

"That's too bad."

"What's too bad?"

"Pretty woman. Married."

"Oh yeah. More too bad than you think."

"That sounds like another story."

"Which one you wanna hear?"

"Tell me about the river."

SEE WILLY SEE

The medic wandered by, checked on Connor's blood draw. "You okay there?"

"Yeah. Getting pretty thirsty."

"I'll get you some water."

"You know," Connor continued, "Gracie and the river kind of go together. I remember one afternoon we'd knocked off for the day and I headed to the river to swim and relax. There she was all by herself, fly fishing. She didn't hear me come up, so I just stood watching. She was so graceful—her back perfectly straight, her face at rest, eyes intent on that line. I could have watched her arm working that line all day."

"I never saw no fly fishin'."

"Aw, it's so graceful. She stood on the riverbank concentratin'"on that shining line arcing up over the water, dripping and dropping into a hole under the bank. Her eyes followed a little bit of a fly as she dropped it on the still surface of a deep pool. I watched her fishing all alone and wondered about her. Why by herself? I wondered why Marvin never joined her. I realized I hardly ever saw them together."

"That sounds like trouble."

"Yeah. Sometimes I noticed her standing with her arms across her chest, watching the crew. She never came close enough to talk and she didn't stay long, but it seemed a little spooky. Once in a while, the crew stayed at the bunkhouse while I swam. Those times, Gracie stayed a lot longer and one of those evenings, she came down and sat on a rock.

"She said hello, and I squinted up at her. Against the sun, you know. 'You must really love this river,' she said. 'I believe you're here every night.'

"I got out and grabbed my towel. We talked about rivers in Nebraska and what I would do after my job there. Started to walk away and she followed. That made me nervous. I asked her about Marvin.

"As we walked back toward the buildings, she moved closer so that our hands bumped together as we walked. I'd move away to give her enough room on the trail, but she seemed to follow me. 'Well,' I said, 'I think the boys have a hot game of cards going.'

"She laid her hand on my arm and looked up into my eyes, and I thought, 'Oh, man I'm in trouble,' but she dropped her hand and turned to walk to her house."

The medic came back to unhook Connor's line. "That's good," he said, "we got a couple of pints here. You'll want to take it easy when you get moving. Maybe dig into one of those C rations." Connor glanced at Jakes, wondering how long he'd been snoring.

"Yeah, I'm starving. Skipped mess."

Jerry got him a tin and opened it for him. "Thanks for the blood."

Connor sat. "Hope it does some good."

The medic lingered, so Connor asked about the attack he'd heard a couple of nights earlier.

"Yeah. It got pretty hairy. One of 'em even got in here."

Connor gave him a sharp look. "He do any damage?"

"Nah. We'd sent most of our casualties out with the 163rd and were just pickin' up the new ones. Lieutenant somebody still had his sidearm an' when the Jap busted in, he drew and fired. Guy just dropped."

"The lieutenant wounded?"

"Yeah. Right hand mangled."

"Seems like he did okay with his left."

"Close range, ya know?" He sat on the cot next to Connor. "Name was Carpenter, I think."

"When daylight came, we found American soldiers all tangled up in their foxholes with Japanese soldiers—some of them alive, some of them not. The Americans, that is."

"Hand to hand?"

"Yeah. They got our artillery and some of our machine-guns—turned 'em on us. The men who survived were out in the open and the Japs attacked them. They jumped in foxholes and blew themselves up. I heard we had guys fighting with trenching tools, knives, fists, rocks, anything they could find."

They fell into silence. "Why is Jakes still here? You said you sent your earlier casualties with the 163rd."

"Oh. They ran out of room, and he was stable."

"But you're short on blood."

"Weren't then." The medic gathered the used tubing and supplies, taking them to the disposal area.

Connor stood, checking once more on his sleeping friend, and headed back to George Company. A little lightheaded, he climbed into his foxhole and fell onto his cot.

"Where you been?" Lopez asked.

"Field hospital."

"Anybody we know?"

"Jakes' the only one."

"Everybody else shipped off?"

"Everybody else dead. My squad. Peters bought it too."

"The whole squad?"

"Yeah. Carpenter's wounded too. Right hand."

"That makes you platoon sergeant."

Connor studied a wrinkle in the canvas overhead. "Fuck that."

June 1, 1944 – Tor to Tirfoam River, Dutch New Guinea

During daytime quiet, Connor made one more trip to the field hospital. It seemed like he and Jakes had made a connection he couldn't define. He knew he needed to be sure they did everything they could for him.

With medical staff busy, he went directly to Jakes' cot. "You still here?"

Jakes opened his eyes. "Couldn't leave until I knew what happened between you that Gracie."

"Nothing happened."

"Pretty woman makin' herself available? Ha!"

"It didn't. Could have but didn't."

"Why not?"

"Boss's wife."

"There had to be plenty of opportunities for tipi creepin.' Her old man wasn't payin' attention."

"That's true, but . . ." he hesitated. "I told you about her flirting down at the river. Next time I went down there by myself, here she come in a bathing suit."

"Aha."

Connor grimaced. "Had a hell of a time getting away from her."

"Sure, you did."

"I did. I had to tell her I wasn't interested. Told her she's an attractive woman but I didn't want any misunderstandings. Told her she should get her husband to go fly-fishin' with her."

Jakes frowned.

"You white guys just go after our women?"

Connor's head jerked up. He stared at the other man, his friend he'd thought. He'd been sitting on a folding camp stool, elbows on his knees. He looked down at his hands. *Fuck. Where did that come from? How'd I get into this? Why am I talking about this? Son of a bitch.*

Connor held his tongue for a long moment. He sighed, looking back into his friend's eyes. "Jakes, I don't go after anybody's women." He picked at the ragged end of a fingernail. "I know white people have done unimaginable things to your people. I know they're still doing them."

Jakes made a grumbling sound in his throat and closed his eyes.

"Jakes, I don't know how to stop it all. I don't. The best I know how to do is treat people fair and stand with you when other people don't. I'm not a tin saint and I know I fuck up, but I'm doing the best I can."

Connor sat looking at his friend's closed face. He realized the connection he'd imagined earlier didn't really exist. *How could I think I knew this guy? I know almost nothing about him. What could I know?*

Connor picked up his rifle and stood, still looking at Jakes' face. Then he turned and left the hospital tent without a glance either to the left or the right. Shoulders sagging, he returned to the Tor River Bridge, crossing to the battalion's encampment. He slipped his rifle strap and set the weapon on a log by his foxhole.

Lopez sat on the log sharpening his knife. "How's Jakes?"

Connor shrugged. "Well as can be expected."

"Think they'll ship him out?"

"Soon's they have a transport."

Connor dropped onto the log, hands hanging between his knees. Lopez's knife resumed its swish across the stone.

Should write home. Three-and-a-half years since I been there. Hard to remember. Don't seem real. Seems like . . .

A scream came from the edge of the jungle, a hundred yards away. Without thinking, he brought his rifle off the log and into his shoulder, firing into the cluster of Japs. He barely registered the fixed bayonets and light machine-gun. He aimed and fired because that's what he was supposed to do. The report of Lopez's rifle cracked in his left ear.

The Japs withdrew.

Lopez picked up his knife and whetstone. "They been doin' that all mornin'."

"Checkin' for weak spots. They get this bridgehead they'll have us in a pincers."

Connor didn't return to the hospital tent, even when Third Battalion relieved the remains of Second at the bridgehead. He was too busy patrolling the jungle with his platoon. What was the point anyway? They'd taken good care of Jakes over there.

Connor didn't mind patrolling so much. The jungle felt closed compared to the open fields where he grew up, but he'd become accustomed to it. He'd learned it could be lethal—like when you stepped on one of the many venomous snakes, but the tension in the back of his neck felt familiar. He couldn't remember any more when it hadn't been tight as a piano wire. After that open space on Hill 225, though, the rainforest felt like a warm blanket. You just had to watch for the stickers.

He didn't know the rest of the platoon as well as he'd known his own squad, but he knew enough to trust them. He'd been through enough with them to know they were tough, aggressive fighters and they wouldn't let him down. He wouldn't let them down, either.

Jungle didn't get my guys anyway. They knew jungle. It was that fuckin' blasted hillside. We can patrol the jungle 'til the cows come home and stay alive. All I've got to do now is keep these men alive. Fuck the Army's objectives. Fuck the recon and intel. Brass never pays any attention to the grunts anyway.

As he crept along, scanning vegetation for enemy, he listened to little sounds, squelching boots, men's whispers, tiny clanks of equipment, the click of a rifle strap. When a large parrot flapped squawking out of the understory, he flinched, but kept walking. He took a deep breath, inhaling a moist tea of wet mud, rotting vegetation, and steam.

Each day the platoon reported on a rainforest honeycombed with enemy. In briefings Connor learned what he'd known for days—

there were thousands of Japs out there. The U.S. brass had even begun to believe what he and his men had said. From just a few enemy troops, the Army had raised its estimate to nearly 11,000— almost three times the number of American troops when they'd landed at full strength.

Don't do a fuckin' thing for Green, Wilson. Moore, and all the other guys stretched out on Hill 225. The Generals—it's like they just shrug and say, 'Oops. Sorry. Maybe we should have listened.' Fuckers. Since we've almost got our asses whipped several times, at least they'll probably wait for reinforcements now.

He was wrong.

When he got the order to again move on Lone Tree Hill, he didn't even flinch. He made no response except a little tic he noticed in the corner of his eye. A flush that crept up his neck. When he reached for a cigarette, his hands trembled. He pitched the fag on the ground as his rigid body began to move. He knew where those hare-brained orders had originated. Leaping to his feet, he stormed to Colonel Sandlin's tent. Before he' even stepped through the flap, he started yelling.

"What the fuck ya think yore doin'? Ya wanna get *all* my men killed? I'm not taking anybody back up that hill. Whatsa matter'th you people anyway? Haven't ya got enough men killed?"

Sandlin leaned over a table where he'd been working on a map of the area. "Shut up soldier before you get busted."

"Busted? You think I give a damn if I get busted! Bust me so I don't have to get any more guys killed." He reached for the stripes on his arm, trying to pull them off. "You can have these goddamn stripes right now!"

"Shut up, Conroy. We've got orders and we're gonna follow 'em."

Connor started to speak.

"Shut the fuck up, soldier."

Connor stood, glaring. He opened his mouth, but Sandlin held up a hand.

"You're in the Army. You follow orders."

As Connor stood, nose to nose with the Colonel, his brain shut down. *Aw what the fuck. Ain't nothin' I can do about it.* The fire left his eyes.

"That's better," Sandlin said. "We know there's a lot of Japs out there."

Connor considered the officer's face. "Not much you can do about it either, is there, sir?" Did he see the same helplessness he felt in the other man's face, or just Sandlin trying to decide whether or not to bust him.

"Dismissed," Sandlin said after a long moment. Connor gave a stiff salute, a precision turn, and left.

When Second Battalion received orders to push cross-country, maneuvering into the rainforest far to the south, Connor breathed a little more freely. *This is what we trained for. We know how to do this.* He felt for First Battalion. They would stay in the open, pushing west along the coast road. At 1600 hours everybody had orders to stop and organize night defenses. That part gave him pause. Night defenses always seemed porous. The Japs could silently slip among the hammocks and slit a throat. He'd seen the slick of congealed blood spreading among the trees.

At 0830, after a concentration of artillery fire, supported by a platoon of tanks, the two battalions advanced—that is, the First had tank support. No heavy equipment could penetrate the trees and swamp where the Second would patrol. Connor's platoon formed a snake probing new territory. The morning began with barely a glimpse of enemy. Scouts probed south and east of the platoon as it moved, step by careful step deeper into the rain forest. Preoccupied by oppressive silence, Connor reached for a thick vine and gripped a smooth, undulating body. *God damned snakes.* He let go and moved on, hoping his pulse would settle.

Like a dismembered snake the platoon wound through Japanese-held territory. Connor could see only two or three others at a time. As he moved in an erratic line, he realized the other men often disappeared completely and he had to have faith that they would reappear beyond the next tree trunk. He knew how to live off the country, but he'd be up against the Japs all alone if he lost his platoon. Could he evade the whole Japanese 36th Division?

Captured, he'd end up like Beacon. He checked Rivera ahead of him and turned to locate Wagoner behind. At least there would be three of them. No safety in numbers, but at least he had company, whatever happened.

Machine-gun and rifle fire ripped the silence ahead of them and the three hit the ground. Connor belly-crawled forward toward the rest of the platoon. He found Price first, standing among some buttress roots. Price gestured forward to the machine-gunner and the ammo carrier crouched behind with ammunition draped over his palms.

"Where's the radio?"

Price gestured left at the same time Connor spotted movement on the ground in that direction. He noticed Lopez scaling a nearby palm with his knife in his teeth. Price raised his helmet on a stick to draw fire so Connor could see the target.

In minutes, the rest of the platoon had joined the men on the ground. As they lay scanning the trees for a flash of sun on metal or the snick of a shell going into a chamber, they watched Lopez. Connor couldn't quite see the sniper, but assumed he hung in the top of the canopy. In the silence, they heard a thunk, a groan, and then the noisy fall of a body through layers of leaves and branches.

About an hour later, Connor thanked his Irish luck when Price dropped to the ground, just as machine-gun fire raked across the squad leaders, splintering trees. In seconds, Peters' crack rifleman had spotted the gun and killed the gunman, along with a second Jap soldier who stepped up to take over. The Japs melted back into the brush.

Over and over that morning, the battalion had to retreat before intense enemy fire and superior numbers. By late morning enemy riflemen and machine-guns had pushed the battalion back toward the main road. By noon, Connor could hear rifle and machine-gun firing and the tank company growling forward and firing on whatever they'd found ahead of them. They'd made little progress against the Japs in the jungle and returned to the road for the night.

For three more weeks, the Bushmasters continued to pressure the Japs wherever they could. On June 22 the Sixth Division relieved them. They loaded up and headed to Finschafen for R&R. They'd lost seventy killed, two hundred fifty-seven wounded, and four missing. Connor wondered if he would ever see Jakes again.

June 22, 1944, Finschafen, Papua, New Guinea

Back in Finschafen, Connor tossed his worn pack under a cot, in a tent, and lay on top. Rain pounded the canvas, but Connor felt not a drop. He sat up and pulled off his boots, removing the rotten laces. His socks weren't in much better shape. A trip to the quartermaster's would fix that. He'd tried to keep his feet dry, using the Army-issued foot powder, but they looked raw. He'd have to visit the infirmary, but not until he'd had a nap.

SEE WILLY SEE

A hot evening meal, served in a dry tent, seemed too good for Army food. Besides the food, he got free entertainment from Tokyo Rose. Apparently, she liked country music, because she still played a scratchy rendition of *The Rose of San Antone*. In a distorted broadcast, she warned the Americans they couldn't survive an attack on the Japanese.

He spent a couple of days and nights in his tent, tightly wrapped in a woolen Army blanket waiting out his fevers. He'd decided they weren't bad enough to report. What were they gonna do anyway?

They had no cure to give him. The Army had made that abundantly clear in their indoctrinations about VD—as if they'd ever seen a woman—about jungle rot, and malaria along with all the other jungle fevers. Almost everybody had malaria. He'd seen guys much worse than he in the field hospital. Others walked around the bivouac in 90-to-100-degree heat wrapped in wool blankets.

Between episodes of the shakes, he checked his equipment and made sure the platoon had everything they needed. When he felt normal, he spent time with the native laborers. The Aussies called them Fuzzy Wuzzies, an all-inclusive term for the many tribes of natives. He found them next to the docks, smoking American cigarettes and waiting for the next ship. They'd sustained a couple of casualties unloading ships, but the men he'd worked with before welcomed him with smiles and back slaps. He located the two English speakers and asked about local foods and medicines, working to learn a few words he could use with any natives he met on the next island.

He wrote home to reassure his parents of his continued good health. He didn't think of it as lying. He was still alive after all. Anything else would have to come later, if it came.

>Dear Mom and Pop,
>
>We're here on rest and relaxation, so I've got some time to write.

SEE WILLY SEE

I got a note from Nora. She sent it sometime in March, so I guess you got one too. Have you heard anything more? Did she find Daniel? Do you have an address—or maybe she's on her way home now.

I'd sure like to know if she's okay. I guess she is if she's at the British Consulate, but I'd sure like to hear she's on a ship to the states—or better yet, that she's landed on good old American soil.

We got some more new guys, but I don't know much about them as they just got here. I got a field promotion a while back. I'm a platoon sergeant now. Pay's the same, so I guess it don't matter much.

Must be getting about wheat harvest time back there. How does it look? You got enough help with all us guys gone? You wrote that Jack O'Neill got through Pearl Harbor. Did he get out yet? Never seen a guy scoop so much grain as Jack. He could probably make up for three of us regular guys.

I've just been over to check on the Fuzzy Wussies I worked with a few months ago. They seem to be well-fed and well-rested—except of course for man-handling the materials off those ships.

It's raining here, surprise, surprise. This is the dry season, so it only drizzles about half of the time; then it cuts loose the rest. It's cutting loose right now. I guess we've got a couple of weeks before we get back in it, so I'll be laying around and resting. Just remember if you don't hear from me for a while, no Jap's got a bullet with my name on it.

Tell Sis I'm okay next time you write.

Connor

It seemed like the Japanese Air Force had given up on Finschafen. In the ten days there, not a single bomber dropped its load on the Army's Headquarters. It might have something to do with the anti-aircraft guns. He would miss those handy weapons when he moved on to his next assignment. As a final treat, Tokyo Rose sang to them during the evening meal on July 1. She told them 'the butchers of the 158th are preparing to land on Noemfoor.' Connor had just learned that fact himself and wondered where she got her intel. She promised they would face a 'wall of steel' on the island.

July 2, 1944 - Noemfoor Island, Dutch New Guinea

The Bushmasters waited on transports anchored at the west end of New Guinea, while the Navy and Air Corps bombed Kamiri Airfield on Noemfoor Island, a speck of land fifteen miles by twelve-and-a-half miles. The Japs had three airfields there, in various stages of completion. The U.S. coveted those fields to provide air support for upcoming campaigns.

Bombardment complete, soldiers bailed over the sides of the ship and down the netting to the metallic clank of their own equipment, their own curses, and an occasional hollow bong when a landing craft drifted against the hull of the ship.

When the boat dropped its ramp, Connor walked up a shredded beach onto the Japanese Kamiri Airfield, under clear blue skies. The only resistance the 158th faced consisted of about forty Japanese soldiers who greeted them, milling about with their hands in the air. Connor raised a hand to halt the column.

"Watch out for those bastards. Make damn sure they don't have grenades."

The opposing sides stared at each other across a chasm of race and culture, anger and hate, as the rest of George Company joined the platoon. The enemy uniforms hung loosely on their thin frames.

The Japs smiled and bobbed their heads at him, filling his ears with incomprehensible chattering. Connor lowered his rifle and squinted at the cluster of nervous men surrounding him.

"What the hell, Sarge?"

"What happened to the walls of steel?"

"Probably some kind of trap."

"Maybe they'll take a look at us, and they'll all just surrender."

A replacement, Sundermeier, waved his rifle at the little men.

"What're we gonna do with 'em?"

"Go find Cochran. Tell him we got a bunch a' prisoners. See what he wants us to do with 'em."

Connor waved his rifle at a spot out of the way of incoming landing craft. He gestured at the Japs to sit.

"Watson and Vargas, cover these men. If they make a move, shoot 'em. The rest of you guys let's go find out where we're s'posed to be."

All along the beach, landing craft were pulling into the shallows, dropping ramps, and disgorging men and materiel. Connor scanned the sky. Not an enemy aircraft in sight. Had they abandoned their airfields? Not a single shot had been fired—no snipers, no machine-guns, just a bunch of eager prisoners. What a strange landing.

Cochran paced the beach, rounding up George Company. "Turn the prisoners over to Intel and Recon." He pointed to a busy area west of the beachhead. "Get your platoon formed up. We're going to the Kornasoren Airfield. ASAP."

"Just us, sir?"

"Second Battalion."

Connor threaded his way through rough lines of shirtless men handing off supplies. For once the brass hadn't selected his unit for unloading the ship. With the prisoners off his hands, he gathered his platoon, checking equipment. He made sure his ammo carrier had plenty of bullets, and that the radio man had a working unit. Within an hour, Colonel Sandlin led the battalion out of a chaos of shouts, roars, and clanks.

A new recruit caught up with Connor. "Where are they, Sarge? I thought they'd be shooting at us."

"Out there somewhere." Connor swept a hand toward the rain forest. "We got a break, private, but keep your eyes open."

Connor raised a hand to halt the platoon. He lit up a fag while a couple of guys from Easy Company probed a Japanese dugout, sneaking far around to the right and coming in behind the nest.

They found no Japs and the column moved ahead. Over and over through the morning, one unit or another sent men out to surround and probe Japanese defenses. They met no enemy.

Once Third Battalion caught up, the Second spread out and turned south toward the Kamiri River. They pressed over ridges and valleys, as they crawled deeper into the jungle in dimming light.

The flutter of a jungle bird turned the men's focus on that spot in the canopy. The whisper of branches rubbing together sent one of the new men to the ground. Connor noticed the man's red ears when he got back to his feet. Walls of dark, dripping green made the new men skittish. Connor noticed them fidgeting with their rifles and looking around wide-eyed. They stumbled frequently on vines snaking through the understory.

A sudden crack! Ping! sent everyone to ground. "He's hit," Vargas whispered.

"Who?"

"Lopez."

Connor crawled forward. His second in command lay crumpled in a heap, helmet ripped off in his fall. "Where's he hurt?"

"Damned 'f I know," said Vargas. "Don't see no blood."

Lopez groaned. He reached for his head, feeling his scalp.

"You're not bleeding." Connor fished the damaged helmet out of the undergrowth. "Looks like it saved your skinny brown ass." He pointed out a dent in the crown.

"I'd just glanced down looking for trip wires." Lopez took his helmet from Connor and examined it.

"You're gonna have a big headache for a while. Where'd it come from?" Connor scanned the canopy.

"Right. About three o'clock."

"How far?"

Lopez looked at Vargas, "Fifty yards?"

Connor sent Lopez and Oneida, to slip around behind the sniper. They nodded and disappeared into the undergrowth. Connor moved around balancing his helmet on a stick and poking it up here and there to draw fire. The recruit at his elbow flinched visibly at every rifle pop. When one of the shots connected with a clank, making a large dent in his headgear the recruit ducked.

Connor fingered the dent, then stuck it up again in a new location. After about thirty minutes, Connor heard a thud and a groan. Soon Lopez came back up the trail.

"Where's Oneida?"

"Makin' sure he's dead."

Just then, Oneida appeared, striding along the trail, grinning, a bloody ear hanging from his belt. "We got 'em Sarge."

"Okay, let's get going."

For the next three hours, the platoon moved in jerks and starts up the steep trail, piling up whenever Oneida or Price dropped to a crouch. Price reached the jungle's edge, dropping abruptly as he faced an open outcrop. The ridge curved away to the left with visible signs of recent human activity.

Connor crept forward. "Looks deserted."

"Maybe," said Price.

"You and Oneida get in there. Hug the rock face. Check it out."

Connor watched, marveling at how silently the men moved to the edge of the outcrop. They huddled for a moment against the rock before moving across, backs against the ridge. They returned in moments. "Cave in the middle," Price reported, "sounds like something moving inside."

"Alexander and Means, follow the edge of the jungle behind that outcrop and come in from the other side. We'll wait till you get in position. Price, you're with me. We'll slip up on the edge of that cave and step in firing when I give the signal. The rest of you guys stay here until you see me call you up."

For the next half-hour, the only sounds were an occasional click of metal loops on the soldiers' rifle straps, a branch slapping back on a helmet or a face, the thud of a boot hitting an exposed root, or the crunch of gravel. Even the birds stayed silent.

When the men reached the cave mouth, they paused. Connor raised his hand then dropped it, grabbing his rifle and turning into the interior and stepping aside so Price could come in beside him. Both men opened fire as they stepped in. So did Alexander and Means. By the time they realized what they were shooting, it was too late. Three Japanese nurses lay on the floor, hands still tangled in the skirts they were pulling up to reveal their sex.

"Stop!" Connor screamed. He stepped in and looked down at the three bodies, pools of blood spreading under them. He noticed one girl's tiny hand lying palm up as if beseeching him to help. But he had no help left to give. He squatted beside her, touching the still-warm hand.

"What the hell are you doing here?" He stared at her delicate features.

The other men shuffled their feet, watching Connor and the three women—the spreading blood stain on the cave floor.

Connor reached out and pulled their skirts down over their thighs, laid their hands across their chests and closed their eyes. He stood.

"Nothing we can do for 'em. Gather up any supplies you find in here. No sense leaving anything the Japs can use." He stepped to the cave entrance and waved the rest of the squad in.

"Hey, Sarge," Oneida called from the back of the cave. "Take a look at this."

"Yeah?" Connor walked back to join Oneida. Ten cots, all holding Japanese men in extreme states of starvation, stood in a line. Most of them lay tightly wrapped in blankets, shivering.

"Holy shit." He stood speechless for a few moments. "We can't take these guys anywhere. Too weak."

"We should shoot 'em. Put 'em out of their misery."

Connor looked from one starving enemy to another, catching the gaze of a man on the far cot. The eyes, large in a shrunken face, stared back. The man slowly reached for his breast pocket and fumbled for something, never averting his gaze. Connor stepped up to the cot looking for a grenade or a pistol. Instead, he helped the soldier take a photograph from his pocket. A young woman and a child. Not beautiful, but not ugly. The man's eyes never left Connor's face as Connor laid the photo on his chest and placed the enemy hand over it. The eyes changed to a kind of peaceful acceptance.

"What do we do with 'em?"

Connor scraped filthy fingers through his hair. "They may have some intelligence value," he said. "If they live long enough."

Enemy soldiers had suddenly transformed into men with wives and sweethearts—hearts still beating. His mother's voice tugged at his memory. 'Try to remember, as much as you can, that you're a human being.'"

"Is there any food in here?"

"Don't see any."

"If we leave 'em here, the Japs may come back for 'em." Connor moved back to the cluster of men.

"They couldn't carry 'em out either."

"Intel might want to talk to them."

"You think they'll come out here?"

"Hell. It's only a couple of miles. It's cleared."

"Yeah. But it's jungle."

"Oh fuck." Connor drew his pistol from his belt and stepped back to the dying soldier who smiled. He dropped the pistol to his side, staring back at the man, and stripped off his pack. He fished around for C-rations, then glanced around at the men on the cots.

"I don't know if these men have the strength to feed themselves."

"You're gonna feed them bastards?"

"Leave 'em some C-rations. Keep 'em alive so the intel boys can come back and question 'em—if they want to."

"N'if they don't?"

"Then it's their problem."

Connor pried the lid off the tin and laid it on the soldier's chest.

"Give 'em each a tin an' open it for 'em."

He stepped out to the cave entrance, where the rest of the squad milled around. "Musta been some kind of hosital. Gimme your C-rations."

"What?"

"C-rations. Buncha starvin' soldiers in there."

"GIs?"

"Nah. Japs. Keep 'em alive for interrogation." Grumbling, the men dug out ration tins.

"Three nurses," said Price.

SEE WILLY SEE

"Whada they look look like?"

"Dead."

"Too bad."

"Yeah," Price said, dropping his pack.

By radio, they notified Intel back at the Kamiri Airfield. Connor took the lead, moving on toward the Kamiri River. As he crept through underbrush that entangled his feet, listening and looking for movement, he didn't wipe away the tears that ran off his chin.

"Do you think intel'll come back and get 'em?" someone whispered from behind him.

"Don't know."

Fuckin' war. Connor stumbled along, reckless with rage. He tried to ignore a malarial chill that ran up his back. *What would happen if they held a fuckin' war and nobody came?* He tripped on a root. *We did that. We cut off their supply lines. It's not enough to shoot 'em and bomb 'em, we're starvin' them to death.*

Get a grip on yourself, Connor. We didn't ask for this. They started it. He plodded along. *Doesn't that just sound like a kid on the playground.* He moved a little faster as the jungle began settling down for the night. *They killed a lot of good men at Pearl Harbor and Wake and Guam . . .*

He stumbled, bruising a wrist as he caught himself on a woody vine. "Oh fuck, I'm tired . . ." Lopez gave him a hand up.

On the north bank of the Kamiri River, they waded into water thick with mud. One by one they crossed, spreading out to divert the attack that didn't come. By dark they'd picked off the leeches and hung their hammocks. One by one and in small groups, the rest of the battalion crossed the river and set up a perimeter.

SEE WILLY SEE

August 10, 1944 — Noemfoor Island, New Guinea

Connor had seen his fill of Noemfoor. Plodding through dripping jungle, not even sure anymore what he looked for, he had plenty of time to think.

As he scanned the trees for snipers, he remembered the first slaves he'd encountered—naked or nearly-naked people limping out of the jungle with their hands raised, smashed ankles dragging. Japs had used them to build their airfields. He still felt like retching when he thought about them. There'd been a lot more on Noemfoor— desperate, starving, crippled people.

God I'm tired. Can't keep focused on bad guys. Follow a man for miles by his bloody spoor—if you don't run your patrol into a machine-gun ambush or a sniper—then find him dead or near dead, eyes starin' out of a naked skull. Or he's lying curled up, shakin' an' teeth rattlin', while the canopy drips and drips and drips. Jungle probably cover him up in a week 'f his buddies don't find him and eat him.

Connor stared into masses of leaves, searching for a tiny bit of motion—the sniper who would leave him rotting on the jungle floor, making food for more of the monstrous leaves that surround his patrol. He plodded on without direction or purpose.

Just keep moving so the jungle don't eat me. Gotta keep these guys alive.

Surrounded by American G.I.s, he couldn't think of what to tell them, how to protect them. Pity for the enemy soldiers he'd been finding on the jungle floor overcame his reserve. He swiped the drip off his chin without realizing he wiped his own tears.

You gotta be sorry for the bastards, but then you see those little Javanese or Formosan men trying to walk on their wrecked feet.

SEE WILLY SEE

He felt another chill coming on, but he tried to keep moving, keep scanning. Lifting his feet became torture as a bone-cracking chill turned his stride into a jerk. His head felt like he'd been shot. He couldn't think. Random ideas popped into his head from nowhere.

What does it matter anyway? Nothin' matters. We'll just be out here walkin' around, lookin' for them walkin' dead men 'til we're dead ourselves. The jungle'll grow over us and won't make no difference we ever lived. Won't make no difference 'f it's us or them gettin' growed over. Birds 'n monkeys'll come back 'n chitter 'n howl over us. He grinned. *Good for the birds 'n monkeys.* His hands shook and he clenched his teeth. *Nope. No Jap bullet's got my name on it. Just endless walkin' and walkin' and walkin' an' seein' stuff I don' wanna see.*

He lost track of time. He stopped. He'd lost his squad. He couldn't see or hear even one of the others. What the hell. He'd blundered through the undergrowth by himself for hours—minutes? Who knew? He ran across a dead enemy with chunks sliced from the body—like roasts. He retched and stumbled on. His mother's words intruded on his thoughts. 'Try to remember that you're a human being.'

He'd found that harder the longer he spent fighting.

He penetrated deep into the jungle, listening and sniffing like a wolf. The dead man had overwhelmed his senses, making him stop and listen more often until he could smell again. He watched the canopy, looking for the sniper who would end him.

He almost missed another body lying along the trail.
To make sure the soldier was dead, he kicked it. The eyes opened. Connor flinched. He kicked again—savage blows to the ribs. The eyes never wavered, staring like they were staring into his soul.

'Remember, the man who's trying to kill you is a human being too.'

Even when his mom had said it, he'd thought she'd lost her mind.

Starving and sick, the enemy shivered. Connor sat and pulled the dying enemy's head into his lap. There in the jungle dusk, he held the soldier—a man as helpless as he. He held the soldier until his breathing stopped. Then he walked on, leaving the jungle to consume the remains.

He heard the clips on his rifle strap clattering. *God. Gotta stop that noise* That was his last thought before he collapsed, curling up and shivering. No effort of will could straighten him up to walk.

Through a haze, he vaguely heard Lopez and Sundermeier talking, like the flies buzzing over his face.

Must be losing my mind. Is this what it feels like to die?

He opened his eyes. The jungle appeared to swirl over him, and he pressed his eyes shut. He felt like he floated. He heard whispering.

Jakes? Hayes? His brain drifted. He couldn't remember the names. *Jakes. That's one. Something's wrong with him.* He drifted under the swirling trees. *Hayes. Is that a man?* He shivered teeth clenched. *Baseball. I love baseball. There's something I can't remember about baseball, about pitching.* He closed his eyes and drifted off.

August 15, 1944 - Noemfoor Island, New Guinea

Connor opened his eyes to a new reality. Flies buzzed in hot, tropical air. He stared at the tan ceiling of a hospital tent. *Where am I?* The heat and humidity felt like jungle. He turned his gaze to other soldiers on nearby cots. *I must have survived. How'd I get here?* He did a quick check of his limbs and their appendages. All there. He pushed off the blanket. He was sweating like a pig with the sun glaring through tent canvas. He pushed himself up, but his head spun, and he plopped back on the pillow.

An unknown face appeared above him. "I see you movin' around. Feelin' better?"

Connor rasped through cracked lips. "Than what?"

"I'll get you some water."

When the corpsman returned, Connor tried to sit—without success. The medic held his head so he could drink. "Just be still for a while. You're gonna be weak for a few days."

"Where am I?"

"Noemfoor."

He looked at the ceiling. "How long I been here?"

"Four days."

"Where's my platoon?"

"Prob'ly out lookin' for Japs."

"I need to get out there."

"Nah. You're goin' home."

"Home! What for?"

The corpsman stared at him. "Why, to get on with your life, I suppose."

He chewed on that with the corpsman standing over his cot.

Connor remembered Hayes, climbing the cocopalms, Martinez pitching that hand grenade into a cluster of Japs, Green storming right into the mouth of the machine-gun nest, with Wilson right behind him, and Moore covering with his rifle.

"Home," he murmured as he dropped back off to sleep.

When the Sundermeier brothers arrived to check on him, the sun had nearly set.

"Hey Sarge, you look like shit."

"I'm all right."

"Don't look it. Ya look like my coon hound when he actually caught a coon."

"I do feel like something caught me and shook me. What happened anyway?"

Sam found a camp stool and sat. "You collapsed. Laying all curled up in a ball like a baby, shakin' all over."

"How'd I get here?"

"How 'n hell dya think ya got here? We hauled your ass."

"No stretcher bearers?"

Joe folded his arms across his chest and moved to the foot of the cot. "We was all spread out. We ain't had any real opposition, so no corpsmen and no stretchers. Made a kinda stretcher outa our fatigue shirts 'n stuff. We got you to company 'n they had stretcher bearers there."

"Well . . . thanks for haulin' my sorry ass. Help me sit up, would ya? Corpsman thinks I oughta lay here 'n vegetate."

Sitting, he shook his head to clear it.

"When ya comin' back?" Sam asked.

"Corpsman says I'm not. Says I'm goin' home."

The three remained silent for a moment. "Congratulations." Joe said.

"I'll believe it when I see it. Maybe 'f I rest a day or two here."

The corpsman came down the line with water. "Day or two's not gonna do it."

Sam studied the corpsman for a few minutes. "He that bad?"

"It's gonna take months for him to get over the fevers—if he does. He's got the worst kind of malaria. You want him collapsin' when you're gettin' shot at?"

"Naw. I don' wanna haul his sorry ass outa the jungle again neither."

"We just came to see if you're all right. We got us some serious drinkin' to do."

"Drinkin'? Where the hell you gonna get booze?"

"Supply ship landed yesterday. Hey, find our folks 'n tell 'em we're okay when you get back."

Connor agreed. Worn out by their visit, he stretched out, pulling the blanket over him. Nightmares woke him later, reliving Hill 225, trying to get up and wash off the blood and muck. He tried to stay awake so he wouldn't go back there, but eventually he dozed, thrashing against the blankets.

We woke next morning with Dr. McCarthy standing over his cot, flipping through his chart.

"Will I live?"

SEE WILLY SEE

Doc clipped the steel chart back on the end of his steel framed bed, making a soft ding.

"I think so. You've got malaria, but I imagine you know that."

"Yup. When you sendin' me back to my unit?"

"I'm not. You have Blackwater Fever."

Connor frowned. "What's that?"

"A serious complication of malaria."

"When you sendin' me back?"

"Just a minute, Sport. I'm not done yet. You need rest. Lots of bed rest."

"That doesn't sound too bad. No ships to unload?"

"Nope."

"Coupla weeks and I'm back at the front?"

"No. You're outa here. Your heart sounds bad. You're not fit to fight."

"Hell, I've had that since I had Spanish Flu when I was a baby."

"You're done here. I'm worried about your kidneys, and you'll have to take care of yourself."

"Kidneys! What about my kidneys?"

"They're damaged. With treatment and rest, they should function pretty well."

"I'm a farmer, Doc."

SEE WILLY SEE

"You'll just have to wait and see how your body responds when you get out of the tropics."

Connor couldn't believe it. Useless in combat, so they were sending him home where he could be useless. "What good will I be at home if all I can do is lay around."

"It will take a while, but you'll heal. You can live a long, productive life, but no soldiering. There's that new G.I. Bill. Maybe you could learn to do something else."

"My pop wrote me about that," he took a deep breath, "but I'm too old. Got in a few months after my twenty-fifth birthday."

"That's a shame," said the doctor, "but I'm hopeful you'll recover." McCarthy patted him on the leg and moved on to the next patient.

As he lay, tightly wrapped in his wool Army blanket, Connor considered home. He thought he'd feel more exhilarated by the prospect of seeing his family and friends. His mother had been sending news about all the men signed up to fight. He wondered if any men still lived in Willow Grove. The Echternach boys and Jack O'Neill are gone. The Robinsons. Most of his graduating class, and Nora's. Cousin Keith—he was in Germany. Lee, Lawrence, Charlie.

Wonder how many'll get back.

He pictured his cows, tails swishing at flies, in the tall grass of the middle pasture. He grinned, remembering the quail that liked the fence line with its wild roses. They'd always answered his whistle call—in spring during breeding season. He envisioned the milking barn and his mom's cow. Carol she called it after one of her classmates.

Mom. She'll be ecstatic when I get back. Pop'll be real quiet. Maybe a pat on the shoulder. But his eyes—he'll be borin' into me, lookin' for the damage. I don't know if I can ever be any good for anything. Maybe I should build a cabin like Uncle Harry.

There's Pauline. Aw, she's married by now. Probably has a couple of kids. Be nice to have a couple a kids. He gritted his teeth. *Hayes won't never have any kids. Not one. Not one to pass on all that . . .* Connor tried to think of a word. *Savvy? Perceptiveness? Hell. Wisdom. That's the word. Hayes was a wise man. Jakes too. I wonder where he is now.*

He remembered all his good friends who went home in boxes. That's when the cadence started, very slowly at first—just Connor remembering each man's name and face in a kind of order. *Jakes. Hayes. Martinez. Green. Moore. Wilson . . . Mendez . . . Hidalgo . . . Gordon . . . Reese . . . Trigg . . . Menardo . . . Eisler.* He started it again, a little more quickly, *Jakes, Hayes, Martinez, Green, Moore, Wilson, Mendez, Hidalgo, Gordon, Reese, Trigg, Menardo, Eisler.* He fell asleep, shivering, whispering the names.

PART FIVE: THE ROAD HOME

August 16, 1944 – Noemfoor to Port Moresby, New Guinea

In the early morning, Connor stepped, shivering, and wrapped in a blanket, into an Army jeep for transport to the Kornasoren Airfield. By the time they loaded him onto a litter and into the cargo hold of a C-47 the aspirin they'd given him at the hospital had worn off and the corpsman gave him more. Barely aware of the aircraft's roar, Connor endured another bone-cracking bout of chills and fever as the craft lifted him over the spine of New Guinea. The transport soared in seconds over that one little defile on the way to Maffin Aerodrome that had taken the Army months and hundreds of dead soldiers to wrestle from the entrenched enemy.

By the time he landed in Port Moresby, Connor barely heard the engine's roar or felt the airplane lift over the spine of the island. Waiting for the next leg of his journey, he suffered less frequent bouts of fever. During his conscious hours, he saw his first woman. He lay back and closed his eyes. *The last woman I saw.* He stared out the window. *Australia. January or February 1943. Girls lined up along the docks waving handkerchiefs and yelling encouragement.* He tried to think. That had been almost two years. *Hell. These nurses are all business.* He looked back at the nurses tending to the other soldiers. *Guess I don't feel much like flirting anyhow.*

He looked back outside. The facility nestled at the foot of a bare knoll north of the peninsula with its deep-water harbor. He could see rainwater running down a muddy road off the hill. Several other buildings blocked his view of the port, but he got an occasional glimpse of sparkling water between rainstorms. In another direction, he peered through an obscuring curtain of rain at a black wall of trees—a living wall that swallowed men and refused to spit them back. He shouldn't have been in that hospital. He should have been in the jungle with those other men still bleeding and thirsting and dying out there. He was"t even wounded. Just sick. He never got sick, but there he lay on clean sheets, eating real food.

Medical staff wandered in and out, poking and prodding and feeding him endless doses and endless conversation about home. He just looked at them. He couldn't remember how home felt or how it looked. He figured out that he'd been away for three-and-a-half years—not as long as he wandered around looking for work and taking pictures during the dust storms. But the number had no meaning. It seemed like his whole life. He felt suspended in time—unable to go forward and torn away from what lay behind. His constant conversation with himself, and his family, especially Nora, that had started when he began learning language, had gone silent.

He tried to picture himself at home, but that felt like dreams he'd had as a kid in which he'd floated, suspended above his family—his imaginary self—looking at ancient history. How could he sit at the dinner table and eat his mother's lemon meringue pie? She would surely make it for him, since it's his favorite. But how could he enjoy something like that while all those other men were dead meat rotting in the jungle? He found himself repeating his name-cadence more and more frequently. "Jakes, Hayes, Martinez, Green, Moore, Wilson . . ."

SEE WILLY SEE

September 30, 1944 — Australia

How long had he been at Port Moresby? He boarded another C-47 for the hop to Townsville, Australia. After a day, maybe a couple of weeks, he climbed on a train for Brisbane. Other soldiers complained of the slow rate of speed, but it meant nothing to him. He could ride for a year—a decade. What did it matter?

Occasionally, one of the other men came by to ask if he'd like to join in a game of cards. One of the corpsmen tried to interest him. "You can get plenty of books in the car ahead. They've got all kinds." He just stared out the window, watching Australia stream past without really seeing anything. Sometimes he thought he should write to Nora or his folks, but he didn't know what to tell them. Besides, he didn't know where to find his sister.

His reputation for remembering useless trivia endured. Men came to him several times a day, staggering in the swaying cars, or stumping along on crutches swinging leg casts—to settle bets. Who won the World Series in 1928? Does the moon rotate as it revolves? What kind of bird makes that whirring, buzzing sound? How long does a parrot live? When they'd started betting on him back in Panama, he'd marveled at the questions they'd asked, but he'd lost his curiosity. He just gave them answers stuck in his head, or told them he didn't know, and turned away.

SEE WILLY SEE

October 15, 1944 — Aboard Ship, Southwest Pacific

After another unspecified length of time in a Brisbane hospital, Connor walked the gangplank into a gleaming white U.S. hospital ship with red crosses on the sides. He'd barely settled into his cabin with his supply of medicine when he heard a tap on the door.

"Go away."

"That any way to greet an old friend?"

Connor jumped up and opened the door. "Jakes?"

Jakes stumped in, guiding his crutches around the tight quarters. "You alone in here?"

"Nah. Bunch more comin. Havin' a party." Connor glanced at the leg—or the lack of it.

Jakes looked into his eyes. "Still gone."

Connor looked down at his own legs. "Nothin's real anymore."

"Hear you been sick."

Connor grimaced. "How you know so much?"

"Heard you was comin' into Port Moresby."

"You were still there?"

"Yeah."

"Why didn't you let me know?"

"By the time I left, you didn't know nothin'."

"Good to see you."

"Yeah." Jakes sat on a bunk.

They said nothing further, both staring out the porthole. Connor finally roused himself. "What're they doin' for you? Are they doin' everything they can?"

"Sendin' me someplace when we get back, so I can get a fake leg 'n learn to walk with it."

"How can I help?"

"Can't. Everything's fixed up. They did a good job at the evac hospital. No more operations."

"That's good," Connor lapsed back into silence. He'd have liked to say something, but his mind had emptied. He didn't want to remind Jakes of their last conversation.

"Nightmares?" he finally blurted.

"Dreams! I see Martinez pitchin' that grenade into them Japs."

Connor smiled. "And Hayes, crawlin' up that cocopalm 'n thowin' that knife."

"Green 'n Wilson 'n Moore. See them, too."

Connor frowned. "You do?"

"You told me all about it. I can see 'em doin' it."

Connor gritted his teeth. "I got 'em all killed."

"You're the damnedest man for taking responsibility for what ain't your fault. You didn't do that. You ain't that almighty. Even for a white boy."

"I led 'em up that fuckin' hill."

Jakes fingered Hayes' little pouch without speaking. He looked at Connor. "Coyote playin' tricks."

After a few more moments of silence, Jakes stood, filling the little cabin with his bulk. He stepped out and closed the door.

What the hell? Bad Spirits? What tricks?

Connor thought about what Jakes'd said a couple of days later, remembering how, when they finally reached the top of that Godforsaken hill, the brass ordered them to retreat and how they'd cleaned out that cave. His head filled with noise as he remembered. Nobody tells you about the roar—small arms fire and machine-guns and mortars and grenades exploding, men yelling and screaming and crying. Just the noise's enough to scare you to death. Then he remembered. Harry had told him. His stomach felt painfully hollow—hungry in one way, but bilious in the other. Nobody had told him yet how to shut off the endless film loop. He remembered how the broken film strip flopped when they got their VD movie. If only he could snap the brittle cellulose acetate in his head. Connor clenched and unclenched his fists, wishing he had something to hit, wishing he could get his hands on the higher-ups. Alone in the cabin, he allowed his rage full rein.

Mostly, the other guys avoided him. He spent a lot of time alone.

When he finally left the cabin, he paced the third deck. An unknown G.I. stepped up accompanied by a buddy stumping along on crutches, swinging a plaster cast that started at his hip.

"You Connor Conroy?"

Connor nodded.

"Buddy here says you know stuff."

Connor shrugged, hoping he could just answer their question and get rid of them.

"We want to know who won the Rose Bowl in 1940."

"Stanford, 21 to 13."

"You didn't even think about it!" the guy growled.
"How the hell do you know?"

"They played Nebraska 'n I'm from Nebraska."

"Time to pay up," said the guy on crutches with a grin.

"Hell no!! This is a put-up job. I'm not payin' anybody."

Connor heard "put up job" and wheeled on the soldier.

"What?"

"You heard me. This is a scam."

Connor stood nose to nose with the soldier, while the guy on crutches tugged on his arm.

"What's the matter with you?" Connor demanded.

"You superior son of a bitch."

Connor towered over the guy, but disease had left him diminished—thin and gaunt.

"You superior son of a bitch—you'll probably marry a WAC."

Just as the guy finished the sentence, Connor's fist connected with his temple, knocking him flat. Before he could get his arms up to defend himself, Connor dropped to his knees, straddling the shorter man's body, landing savage punches to his head and chest. By the time the orderlies could break it up, Connor had bloodied the guy's face and torn his own knuckles. Orderlies carried the soldier away.

Connor fished a pack of cigarettes out of his pocket with trembling hands and struggled to light one in a little breeze. He could hear the other man's crutches pounding along behind. As he stood smoking, he looked toward the horizon and wondered what had got into him. He'd never taken kindly to charges of cheating, but fist fights had never been his style. And he couldn't stop. He wouldn't have stopped if they hadn't dragged him off the guy—he'd have killed him. What for? For saying he'd marry a WAC? Hell! Maybe he would. He had no opinion about the WACs. Heard Josie Robinson had joined up and she was okay. Not his type, but okay. As for scamming somebody—well, the knucklehead could just go screw himself.

He consciously slowed his breathing, taking in a lungful of air and then calming his breath. He looked at his bloody hands and decided to go below and wash them. He flung his cigarette overboard and scrambled below decks to the head where he scrubbed and scrubbed. He found himself scrubbing away at mud and blood and bits of flesh. When he finally dragged himself back to reality, he stood embarrassed, looking at a short line of soldiers, waiting and watching him through the open hatch. He turned off the water, wiped his hands on his bathrobe, and ducked out past the waiting men.

The next time he saw Jakes, Connor stood at the rail again, smoking a cigarette and watching the water go by—his mind blank.

Transferring his crutches to one hand, Jakes leaned his side into the rail. "How you doin'?"

"All right. No fever today."

Jakes looked down the side of the ship, watching the water curl around the hull. "How'd Hayes get it?"

Stomach churning, Connor took a drag and dropped the remains of his cigarette over the side, following the sparks. "I told you back in the field hospital."

"I can't remember much about the field hospital."

"On that third bench. He was runnin' right beside me. I don't even know where he came from—just there all of a sudden."

"He was pretty fast."

Connor looked up at Jakes. "Fast? He'da set records for the 100-yard dash."

"Fast even with a hundred pounds on his back."

Connor snorted and looked back over the side of the ship, tearing up as he remembered.

"We were runnin' along and then they cut him down. Machine-gun burst across the chest." He shook his head. "Don't know how they missed me. I was right beside him."

He stopped, staring at the black water on the dark side of the ship. "No," he said, frowning, tears running off his chin, "he got ahead of me. He outran me—took the one meant for me."
Jakes watched Connor's face contort.

"He just dropped. Blood everywhere. Conscious long enough to say your name and pull at that pouch. 'Jakes?' I say. 'Give to Jakes.' Then he was gone."

Jakes pulled the blood-stained pouch from where it nestled around his neck. "Know what's in here?"

"No idea."

"Sand."

"Sand?"

"Sand from his pueblo." The two men studied the pouch. "An' sun, an' cactus, an' wind . . ."

"He carried that all this time? Why?"

Jakes put the pouch back around his neck. "The stories."

"What stories?"

"His stories. How he was born. What the sky looked like when he shot his first deer. How the air smelled when he got to Panama. The sound of the rain dripping through the jungle the day he found that dying Jap and noticed the dead man looked just like his cousin."

Connor's head jerked up with a sharp look into Jakes' quiet eyes. He said nothing as he fished the cigarettes out of his pocket, offered one to Jakes. He turned back to the rail, leaning on his elbows, and stared at the far horizon, his mind churning. He felt the warmth of Jakes' bulk as the Indian stood smoking beside him.

"So . . . he felt like he was killing his relatives?"

"You felt it too."

Connor looked at the other man's profile, recognizing the truth in his quiet remark. He turned back out to sea. "On Noemfoor," he murmured, "we found this cave . . ."

"It's the hands," Connor said as he finished his tale, "the nurses' hands, lying there, palms up like they're begging. And so tiny."

He flipped his cigarette over the side, watching the sparks falling and falling. "I wake up screaming at the men to stop firing—but it's always too late."

Jakes turned and leaned on his elbows, looking out. "Too late when Hitler started it."

The two men stood leaning over the rail, watching the ocean rolling along as the boat plowed through it. They felt the ship vibrate with the roar of the engine beneath them. After the antiseptic air below decks, Connor enjoyed the fresh salt smell.

"You ever have nightmares, Jakes?"

Jakes took a drag on his cigarette and pitched it overboard. "Yeah. I see Eisler. Only I'm torturing one of them poor, starving Japs whose face changes into Eiseler's."

"God! Think they'll ever go away?"

"Maybe. When we get back to our people. Tell our stories."

A few days later, Connor stood at the rail watching a pod of dolphins pacing the ship. One surprised him with a tail walk. The water was a long way below, but Connor felt sure that dolphin looked right at him.

"What're ya tryin' to tell me, little fella?" The dolphin dropped back into the water. He continues to watch the spot where the animal had disappeared. It reappeared, with a sharp series of clicks.

Connor grinned.

The dolphin dropped back. Connor continued to stare at the undulating bodies. Something about their graceful forms and the sunlight glinting on green water reminded him of a poem he'd once read.

"You are a child of the universe. No less than the trees and the stars, you have a right to be here."

Could that be true? It had been a long time since he'd felt he had a right to be anywhere. The dolphin and the words remained in the back of his thoughts for the rest of the day.

October 30, 1944 – San Francisco Bay, California

Connor and Jakes again stood at the rail when somebody yelled, "Landfall!"

The two men glanced at each other, then back out to sea. "I'll believe it when I'm standing on U.S. soil," Connor said.

"You gonna go up and watch for it?"

"Nah. You?"

"Nah."

The two smoked as men streamed past, many on crutches, swinging casts, pushing wheelchairs, and peering through bandages—all heading for the bow. It was a slow, stumbling, silent promenade.

Jakes turned his back to the sea. "Get them all up there and the boat'll flip over." He turned to Connor. "What're ya gonna do?"

"Go home, I guess. Raise cattle . . . You?"

"Not sure. See how the leg works."

In Connor's years away, home had come to seem like an hallucination, a dream he'd used to take the edge off the nightmares. He no longer believed in the real place. His intellect recognized its existence, but his gut felt the surge of waves like endless reality. Sometimes it seemed he'd sailed on a ghost ship that would continue to drift until it simply faded away.

The ship steamed on. He saw a faint outline on the horizon. As it continued, the form became more distinct. Soon the ship surged under the great orange bridge into San Francisco Harbor.

Connor and Jakes watched the other men head below, returning with their packs and belongings. Connor stared up at the span as it materialized from the fog. He looked at the old fort on its right side.

"Believe it now?"

Connor glanced at Jakes. "Just looks like a mirage."

He looked at the men who had gathered around them—thin, yellow men colored by the Atabrine they'd dosed with for months—years. They all peered through the fog at America, whatever that meant to each man. He noticed that some cried, some laughed, but the look in their eyes—sheer terror.

Just like me. I have no right to be here while all those others remain behind struggling, fighting, bleeding, dying.

His eyes swept over yards and yards of bandages, plaster casts, crutches, and wheelchairs and he shuddered.

How the hell will these men ever make it—and they're the lucky ones. They don't have to go back.

He remembered Uncle Harry, sitting alone in his little house, spitting on his little stove, saying his names over and over.

Maybe I'll pull up a chair beside him. I'm sure following his lead.

Jakes broke into his thoughts. "You come."

"Come?"

"To the reservation—when you get out."

"How will I find you?"

"You'll find me."

The orderlies herded them to their quarters.

"Come on you guys, let's get organized. Get you fixed up so you can go home."

Connor gave Jakes a quick handshake and walked off, unsure what to expect for the rest of his life.

"Maybe I will go to the reservation," he muttered as he headed for the hatch. "Maybe Jakes and me, we'll just crawl down into a canyon and disappear."

He turned back to Jakes, stumping along behind. "Hey Jakes," he said, "Hold on a minute."

THE END

Reader's Guide

See Willy See takes Connor Conroy (C. Willy C.) through his years bumming around during the 1930s as well as training and fighting World War II in the Southwest Pacific. Does that large time span still allow you as a reader to get a sense of the era(s)?

The author intentionally chose an actual Army regiment for her story—a unit that included Native American and Hispanic men. Does she portray those men and their treatment accurately and fairly?

Aside from fighting a war, what struggles do Colburn's diverse characters face? How do they deal with those struggles?

How does Connor share in them?

Even though he can receive no answers during his hobo years, Connor keeps writing and mailing letters. Does his letter-writing throughout give you a strong sense of the importance of his family?

Do the flashbacks to Connor's hobo days provide enough backstory to give you a sense of the man pre-war? Do they help you to understand his sense of adventure as he wanders the country's gems, the National Parks, his attitude toward his country, and is reactions to the events of the story?

Do you get enough of Nora's story to understand Connor's concerns for her?

What do you find most surprising, intriguing, or difficult to understand? Why? What specific scenes or passages captured your attention? Were they interesting, profound, disturbing, sad?

What made them memorable? What did they reveal about the characters?

What have you learned from reading this book? Did you gain any new perspectives?

If you would like to have the author participate in a club meeting either in person or by phone link or Skype, you can contact Ms. Colburn at faithanncolburn@gmail.com.

Author Bio

As the daughter of a combat veteran, Faith A. Colburn grew up knowing that war leaves the men who fight them with holes in their lives that they just can't share. Colburn has attempted in this novel to reveal some of the reasons why.

She started out wondering how a Nebraska farm boy might respond to the two decades of displacement and hardship and what might make people more or less resilient. Her three related novels, *The Reluctant Canary Sings, See Willy See*, and her work in progress entitled *Gravy* provided her a way to explore those questions.

An award-winning journalist and author, Colburn has worked most of her adult life as a writer. With her decades of living on the Great Plains, she's intimately familiar with the land and its people. Her work has appeared in numerous newspapers and magazines. She has published two memoirs and a collection of essays describing her home on the prairie. This novel is a bit of a departure, as it is set partly in Panama and New Guinea, but almost all of the character are plainsmen and women.

Colburn earned Master of Arts degrees in creative writing and journalism from the University of Nebraska, as well as a Bachelor of Arts in Journalism and Political Science.

Other Works by this Author

The Reluctant Canary Sings: The only way to save her family was to sing, but her singing career never provided the safety or security she craved. Bobbi Bowen's story begins in Cleveland, 1937, the second dip of a double-dip depression. When she leaves the apartment she shares with her parents, she passes the Holy Rosary Soup Kitchen with its straggle of shuffling men and women in their bedraggled coats. At home she ducks her parents' fights— sometimes ducking a flying plate or saucer. The mob has a big presence in Cleveland, even post-prohibition, and there's a serial killer leaving dismembered bodies all over town. How will Bobbi navigate the hazards?

Threshold: A little boy stolen, a plainswoman married to the homeliest man she ever saw, a Canadian homesteader who takes in his hired man and the whole, growing family, a husband in a hotel with a turtle in the bathtub, desperate to save a marriage— either one of them. This is a family like a prairie, woven of many strands.

From Picas to Bytes: When Joseph Claggett Seacrest arrived in Lincoln, Nebraska, on April 1, 1887, the April Fool joke was on him—the newspaper job he'd come to take did not exist. This book chronicles 100 years and four generations of Seacrest journalism— from fights to establish and defend first amendment rights, to support their communities through donating money committees, to adoption of new technologies that kept the newspaper's doors open when most mid-sized dailies had died.

Prairie Landscapes: The ramblings of one mind prowling the Great Plains, this book brings you face to face with the prairie and its creatures—a black cocker spaniel with a white necktie who befriended a runt pig—and an almost-immortal banty rooster. The landscapes stretch from the tall-grass prairies of eastern Nebraska to the grass-frozen sand sea called the Sandhills, to the Pine Ridge in the northwest corner.

SEE WILLY SEE

Sample Chapter: Gravy

March 31, 1945 — Colorado Springs, Colorado

Bobbi Bowen gave up a few short weeks too soon or she'd never have been in Colorado—clear out in the boonies.

She'd been singing with the Jimmy Jones orchestra on December 7, 1941, when the Japanese attacked Pearl Harbor. The next thing she knew, she sat on a bench in the bed of a cattle truck, jostling over her first gravel road. She wondered what she'd got herself into as she bounced against a bunch of other new recruits, on the way to basic training at Fort Des Moines, Iowa.

After a cattle truck, how much worse could it get?

She found that out during the first couple of days in the Women's Auxiliary Army Corps, waking up in the dark to a screaming whistle and marching, marching, marching all over the base. She only had time late at night to regret the radio show she'd missed because of her previous engagement with Uncle Sam.

On the other hand, she couldn't regret the three square meals and the warm roof over her head after four years of scrapping to keep her family alive. That's why she'd signed up in the first place. The Army hadn't let her down, and it did get better once she had her specialty training and a duty post building and installing radios for B-24, Liberators.

In Colorado Springs, right at the east face of the mountains, she got a part time gig singing at a nightclub when off duty. She guessed it could have been worse and maybe she'd still be able to take that radio job after the war.

~~~~~~~~

SEE WILLY SEE

With his partner, Connor walked into a nightclub, blue with cigarette smoke. A combat veteran from the Pacific Theater, converted to military police until his enlistment was up, He'd struggled for months with disabling bouts of malarial fever, in New Guinea and Australia, on the way home on the hospital ship, and back in the states. Finally, he felt better, so the Army sent him to look for AWOL, drunk, and disorderly soldiers. He did not look very hard. He figured if the others had been through what he'd been through, the Army ought to give them a chance to get away from the base and at least try to act like normal people.

Give them a chance while they're among friends who understand, to adjust to the so-called normal world. Some of them might get sent back. Europe's about done, he hoped, but the Japs would kill themselves killing us before they gave up. He swept the room looking for anybody about to start a fight. The worst of it was that the guys just wanted to fight. They'd lost friends. They'd seen and done things nobody ought to see and do. And they were mad about it.

It's a kind of insanity. We're all plumb stark-raving mad. I sure don't feel very sane. Wonder if it'll ever get better.

Just as he started to leave for the next bar, the drummer started up with a steady tom-tom. A new song. Blues in the Night. A 1941 tune the band leader said. New to Connor anyway. A woman stepped up to the mic and began singing.

He blinked. *Wow! What a voice! Pretty good for this little burg. I'll just listen to the end of the song.*

He leaned in the door frame, wishing he were off duty. "Hold on a sec, Sam."

Wonder where that sweetheart came from and why I haven't noticed her before. I'd like to be sweet talking in her ear. His partner, Sam, had been standing outside the open door.

"Come on, Connor. We got a fight across the street."

Damn!

Connor turned and high-tailed it. He caught up to Sam on the far side. They stood for a second in the doorway, listening to grunts and yells and crashing furniture.

"What've we got?"

"Looks like a buncha flyboys and a buncha grunts."

"Crap."

Connor waded in, grabbing men by the shirts and hauling them out of the bar as two more MPs, Air Force, arrived from up the street. By the time they had the fight under control, Connor's shirt had buttons missing and he'd ripped his pants.

Offenders loaded in a paddy wagon, he and Sam tramped down the other side of the strip, catching their breath.

"Hey, d'you see that canary they got in the Peterson Club?"

"Yeah. She's a looker, ain't she?"

"And, man, can she sing!"

"Bobbi Bowen. Says so on the poster."

"Don't suppose she'd have anything to do with the likes of us. That's a class act."

"Probly not."

Connor kept thinking about her, though.

That voice. It's just like she's singing to me. Sam's right. She's stacked.

SEE WILLY SEE

He finished his shift with his head in the Peterson Club, thinking for once, about something other than the Army or New Guinea or his rage and grief. For once, he didn't spend the night counting cadence—*Eagle, Mendez, Green, Moore, Wilson, Hidalgo, Hayes, Gordon, Reese, Trigg, Menardo, Martinez, Eisler—Eagle, Mendez, Green . . .*

~~~~~~~~

Singing in the Petersen Club that night, Bobbi had spotted a tall military policeman at the back of the club, scanning the clientele. She thought she knew all the MPs, but that guy was new. He came in with another MP, Sam something. Maybe she could get him to introduce them.

I hope he's not one of those shell-shocked combat veterans who come in here and break things up. He's an MP, so probably not. He's supposed to protect us from those scary guys. Maybe he never left the country. I wonder if he's got money.

Standing stage left after her number, still moving with the music, she imagined the stranger. He'd left before she finished her number.

Maybe he didn't like me. Maybe he considers entertainers sluts. Maybe, like the other GIs, he believes women are cheap. Maybe next time, he'll be out of uniform and have his hands all over me. Maybe . . .

SEE WILLY SEE

SEE WILLY SEE

SEE WILLY SEE

SEE WILLY SEE

SEE WILLY SEE

www.ingramcontent.com/pod-product-compliance
Lightning Source LLC
Chambersburg PA
CBHW070419010526
44118CB00014B/1817